THE REVELATION
OF JOHN

OTHER BOOKS BY GEORGE E. LADD

Crucial Questions About the Kingdom of God
The Blessed Hope
The Gospel of the Kingdom
Jesus and the Kingdom
The New Testament and Criticism
The Pattern of New Testament Truth

A COMMENTARY ON THE REVELATION OF JOHN

by
GEORGE ELDON LADD
Professor of New Testament Theology and Exegesis
Fuller Theological Seminary

WILLIAM B. EERDMANS PUBLISHING COMPANY
Grand Rapids, Michigan

CONTENTS

5

INTRODUCTION

I. *Authorship.* The author of the book designated himself simply as "John" (1:1; 1:4; 21:2; 22:8). He was well known by the churches of Asia, calling himself their brother, who shared with them the tribulation and the kingdom and the patient endurance (1:9). The question arises: Who was this John? It is clear from the style of the book that he was a Hebrew Christian, saturated in the Old Testament. The early church generally accepted him as the apostle of Jesus Christ, the author of the Fourth Gospel. This was clearly attested as early as A.D. 150 by Justin Martyr and around A.D. 200 by Irenaeus, who had lived at one time in Asia. This apostolic authorship was widely accepted by the ancient fathers. Such authorship is entirely possible, for there is a solid historical tradition that John lived to a ripe old age in the city of Ephesus.

We must note, however, that John did not designate himself as an apostle, and in 21:14 he mentioned the apostles as a group but gave no hint that he was to be included in this circle. He did, however, claim to be a prophet (22:9) and called his book a prophecy (1:3; 22:7, 10, 18, 19). If the author was not the apostle, he was a well-known prophet in the churches of Asia who is otherwise entirely unknown to us.

There are, admittedly, serious difficulties in recognizing the Revelation and the Fourth Gospel as coming from the same pen. While there are numerous similarities between the two books (e.g., only in the Fourth Gospel and Revelation is Jesus called the Logos), the style of the Greek is strikingly different. The language of the Gospel is smooth and fluent and couched in accurate and simple Greek; the idiom of the Revelation is rough and harsh, with many grammatical and syntactical irregularities. We know from many references (see Rom. 16:22)

7

that the use of an amanuensis or a secretary was common in the ancient world; and the differences in the style of the Gospel and the Revelation may be accounted for by the difference in subject matter and by the use of secretaries. Possibly a disciple of John actually penned the Gospel, while the Revelation reflects his own rough Hebraic Greek.

II. *Date.* Tradition has ascribed the Revelation to the last decade of the first century when Domitian was emperor in Rome (A.D. 81-96).[1] Some scholars have argued for an earlier date, but this is unlikely.

III. *Setting.* Many scholars consider apocalyptic literature almost by definition to be "tracts for hard times" and to have been produced by persecution. This may well be true of the Jewish apocalypses. The problem they faced was, Why were God's people suffering such persecutions? Where was God's salvation? The Old Testament prophets saw God active both in history and in the eschatological consummation, but the apocalyptists despaired of history and found hope only in the eschatological intervention of God. The world and the age were hopelessly evil, having fallen under the power of demonic angelic powers. God was far away in the heavens, but soon he would arise from his throne, destroy the demonic powers, and deliver his people.

Following this theory, many scholars have reconstructed the setting of the Revelation in terms of an imminent worldwide persecution of the church by Rome. The church was about to face practical annihilation; to steel God's people in the face of their trials, John wrote to assure them that though they must expect to suffer, the coming of the Lord was at hand to overthrow Rome and to deliver his church.

The problem with this theory is that there is no evidence that during the last decade of the first century there occurred any open and systematic persecution of the church. In popular Christian thought the idea has prevailed that there were ten

---

[1] Irenaeus, bishop of Lyons in Gaul in the second century, wrote, "It (The Revelation) was seen not very long ago, almost in our generation, at the close of the reign of Domitian" (*Against Heresies* V.xxx.iii). Victorinus (third century A.D.) wrote, "When John said these things, he was in the island of Patmos, condemned to the mines by Caesar Domitian" (*Commentary on The Revelation* 10:11).

great persecutions of the church that were practically universal in scope:[2] by Nero (A.D. 64), Domitian (A.D. 95), Trajan (A.D. 112), Marcus Aurelius (A.D. 177), Septimus Severus (late second century), Maximinus (A.D. 235), Decius (A.D. 250), Valerian (A.D. 257), Aurelian, and Diocletian (A.D. 303). It is true that widespread persecution was promoted by Decius, Valerian, and Diocletian, but earlier persecutions were local in character or relatively mild in execution. Nero did indeed instigate a vigorous if brief persecution of Christians, but only in Rome and on a single occasion.[3] The alleged persecution by Domitian was by no means empire-wide but was directed against a few families in Rome.[4]

It is clear, however, that Christians were experiencing local troubles in Ephesus, even though we cannot reconstruct from independent sources the extent of the opposition. John's exile establishes the fact of persecution in Ephesus, and this may as well have been due to local consular action in Ephesus as to an imperial decree in Rome. In Pergamum a Christian named Antipas had been killed, presumably some time previous to the writing of the letter to that church (2:13). There is, however, no hint of any general persecution. The church at Smyrna was warned of imminent imprisonments (2:10) and apparently faced the threat of the death penalty, for Christians were urged to be faithful to death. Other Christians had already suffered martyrdom, for John saw the souls of the martyrs under the altar calling out for vindication (6:9). But the reference is general in character and could include Old Testament as well as New Testament martyrs.

We must conclude that it is impossible to establish from extrabiblical historical sources a situation of worldwide persecution of the church which is reflected in the Revelation. The prophecy of the Revelation goes far beyond any known historical situation in the first century. While the Rome of John's day embodied antichristian tendencies, the portrait of Antichrist in Revelation 13 is far larger than historical Rome.

[2]This idea was popularized by one Paulus Orosius, a fifth-century historian.
[3]See Tacitus, *Annals* XV.xliv.3.
[4]See Ethelbert Stauffer, *Christ and the Caesars* (Philadelphia: Westminster, 1955), pp. 163ff.

Concrete references to persecutions in the Revelation are all illustrations of the hostility the world bears to the church. Just why John had been exiled to Patmos we cannot say (1:9). In any case he claimed that God used his exile as the occasion of giving him a series of visions that would trace the conflict between the Kingdom of God and the power of Satan, the final victory of God's Kingdom, and the consummation of his redemptive purpose.

IV. *Methods of Interpretation.* Revelation is the most difficult of all New Testament books to interpret, primarily because of the elaborate and extensive use of symbolism. How are these strange, often bizarre, symbols to be understood? Several distinct methods of interpretation have emerged. Many interpreters find valuable elements in more than one method, so there is considerable overlapping. But four distinct methods can be identified.

Preterist. The view which prevails in critical and scholarly circles is that the Revelation belongs to a distinct genre of Jewish-Christian writings called "apocalyptic," which are "tracts for hard times." Judaism produced such books as *Enoch, The Assumption of Moses, The Apocalypses of Ezra,* and *Baruch,* which exhibit similar literary characteristics to the Revelation, particularly in the use of symbolism, and a similar type of eschatological hope. These writers were discouraged because of the evils of historical experience and the persecutions of God's people at the hands of godless nations. While they were led to despair of history, they continued to hope in God and to look forward to his salvation. They believed that God would soon arise from his throne to shatter the rule of the wicked nations, destroy all evil, and establish his Kingdom on the earth. This would occur by a shattering cosmic visitation which would completely displace the fallen evil order by the glorious Kingdom of God. The apocalyptists looked upon their own days as the worst and the last, since the end of the age was immediately to come. However, their apocalyptic predictions, of course, were not fulfilled, and as genuine prophecies of future events the Jewish apocalypses are worthless. They are important only in understanding the religious hopes of the people whose culture produced them.

Interpreted in this way, the Revelation expresses the hopes

of the early Christians of Asia that they were about to be delivered from their troubles at the hands of Rome. In the preterist view, imperial Rome was the beast of chapter 13, and the Asian priesthood promoting the worship of Rome was the false prophet. The church was threatened with practical extinction in the face of impending persecution, and John wrote to confirm the faith of believers that even though terrible persecution was at the door, God would intervene, Christ would return, Rome would be destroyed and the Kingdom of God shortly established. Of course, Christ did not return, Rome was not overthrown, and the Kingdom of God was not established. But prophetic prediction is not an element of the genre of apocalyptic. The book fulfilled its purpose in strengthening and encouraging the first-century church. For those who accept the claim of Revelation to be a prophecy, this view is quite inadequate.

Historical. This method views the Revelation as a symbolic prophecy of the entire history of the church down to the return of Christ and the end of the age. The numerous symbols of the book designate various historical movements and events in the western world and the Christian church. Obviously, such an interpretation could lead to confusion, for there are no fixed guidelines as to what historical events are meant. One of the most prevailing features of this interpretation has been the view that the beast is the Roman papacy and the false prophet the Roman Church. This view was so widely held that for a long time it was called the Protestant view. This view has little to commend it, for the Revelation would in that case have little to say to the churches of Asia to which it was addressed.

Idealist. This method avoids the problem of trying to find any historical fulfillment of the symbols of Revelation and sees only a symbolic portrayal of the spiritual cosmic conflict between the Kingdom of God and the powers of satanic evil. The beast represents satanic evil wherever it breaks out to oppress the church. That there is some truth in this method is illustrated by chapter 12, which portrays a mighty conflict in heaven between Satan and the angels. However, it is a fact that Revelation belongs to the genre of apocalyptic, and apocalyptic symbolism is primarily concerned with the events in history which lead to the end of the age and the coming of the Kingdom of God. Therefore, we must look further.

Futurist. This method interprets Revelation largely as a prophecy of future events depicted in symbolic terms which lead up to and accompany the end of the world. The futurist view has taken two forms which we may call the moderate and the extreme futurist views. The latter is also known as Dispensationalism. The seven letters are seen as seven successive ages of church history symbolically portrayed. The character of the seven churches depicts the chief characteristics of the seven periods of church history, the last of which will be a period of decline and apostasy (Laodicea). The rapture of John symbolizes the rapture of the church at the end of the age. Chapters 6-18 depict the period of the great tribulation — the last short but terrible period of church history when the Antichrist will all but destroy God's people. In the dispensational view God's people are Israel, restored to Jerusalem, protected by a divine sealing (7:1-8), with a rebuilt temple (11:1-3), who suffer the wrath of Antichrist. The church is no longer on earth, for it has been caught up to be with the Lord in the air.

A moderate futurist view differs from the extreme futurist view at several points. It finds no reason, as does the latter, to distinguish sharply between Israel and the church. The people of God who face fearful persecution are the church. Again, there is no reason to see in the seven letters a forecast of seven ages of church history. There is no internal evidence whatever for such an interpretation; these are bona fide letters to seven historical churches. However, this view agrees that the primary purpose of the book is to describe the consummation of God's redemptive purpose and the end of the age.

The objection again seems valid that if the book is conceived to deal primarily with events which lie in the distant future, its message had little relevance for the first-century churches to which it was addressed. This is an argument which cannot be pressed too far, or else it will empty many of the Old Testament prophecies of any relevance. The prophets spoke not only of contemporary events; they constantly related contemporary historical events to the last great event at the end of history: the Day of the Lord when God will visit his people to redeem them and to establish his Kingdom.

This brings us to a characteristic of Old Testament prophecy which is also characteristic of the Revelation and which solves this problem of distance and relevance. As we have just pointed out, the prophets had two foci in their prophetic perspective: the events of the present and the immediate future, and the ultimate eschatological event. These two are held in a dynamic tension often without chronological distinction, for the main purpose of prophecy is not to give a program or chart of the future, but to let the light of the eschatological consummation fall on the present (II Pet. 1:19). Thus in Amos' prophecy the impending historical judgment of Israel at the hands of Assyria was called the Day of the Lord (Amos 5:18, 27), and the eschatological salvation of Israel will also occur in that day (9:11). Isaiah pictured the overthrow of Babylon in apocalyptic colors as though it were the end of the world (Isa. 13:1-22). Zephaniah described some (to us) unknown historical visitation as the Day of the Lord which would consume the entire earth and its inhabitants (1:2-18) as though with fire (1:18; 3:8). Joel moved imperceptibly from historical plagues of locust and drought into the eschatological judgments of the Day of the Lord.

In other words, the imminent historical judgment is seen as a type of, or a prelude to, the eschatological judgment. The two are often blended together in apparent disregard for chronology, for the same God who acts in the imminent historical judgment will also act in the final eschatological judgment to further his one redemptive purpose. Thus, Daniel viewed the great eschatological enemy of God's people as the historical king of Greece (Antiochus Epiphanes of the Seleucid Kingdom — 11:3), who yet took on the coloration of the eschatological Antichrist (Dan. 12:36-39). In the same way, our Lord's Olivet Discourse was concerned with both the historical judgment of Jerusalem at the hands of the Roman armies (Luke 21:20ff.) and the eschatological appearance of Antichrist (Matt. 24:15ff.). Rome was a historical forerunner of Antichrist.

Thus, while the Revelation was primarily concerned to assure the churches of Asia of the final eschatological salvation at the end of the age, together with the judgment of the evil world powers, this had immediate relevance to the first century. For the demonic powers which will be manifested at the end

13

in the great tribulation were also to be seen in the historical hatred of Rome for God's people and the persecution they were to suffer at Rome's hands.

Therefore, we conclude that the correct method of interpreting the Revelation is a blending of the preterist and the futurist methods. The beast is both Rome and the eschatological Antichrist — and, we might add, any demonic power which the church must face in her entire history. The great tribulation is primarily an eschatological event, but it includes all tribulation which the church may experience at the hands of the world, whether by first-century Rome or by later evil powers.

This interpretation is borne out by several objective facts. First: it is the nature of apocalyptic writings to be concerned primarily with the consummation of God's redemptive purpose and the eschatological end of the age. This is the theme of the Revelation: "Behold, he is coming with the clouds, and every eye will see him" (1:7). Second: it is the nature of apocalyptic symbolism, whether canonical or noncanonical, to refer to events in history leading up to, and associated with, this eschatological consummation. Third: as already noted, the book claims to be a prophecy. We have already seen that the nature of prophecy is to let light shine from the future upon the present.

V. *Structure.* The main contents of the book are easy to analyze. After an introductory chapter follow four series of sevens: seven letters (2-3), seven seals (5:1 — 8:1), seven trumpets (8:2 — 11:19), and seven bowls (15:1 — 16:21). These four series are broken by several interludes which briefly interrupt the flow of the narrative and do not belong to the four series of sevens. The book concludes with the judgment of Babylon, the apostate civilization, the final triumph and consummation of God's Kingdom, and the descent of the heavenly Jerusalem (chaps. 17-21).

In terms of literary structure, the book consists of four visions, each of which is introduced by an invitation to "come and see" what God purposes to disclose (1:9; 4:1; 17:1; 21:9). The book is concluded by an epilogue.

CHAPTER ONE

PROLOGUE AND FIRST VISION

Title. **The Revelation of John.** This is the oldest form of the title of the book. It was not an original part of the book itself but was prefixed to the book early in the history of its circulation. It is an obvious title derived from 1:1. The title found in the King James Version, "The Revelation of St. John the Divine," although appearing in the mass of late Greek manuscripts, is not found before Eusebius in the fourth century.

I. PROLOGUE (1:1-8).

1. SUPERSCRIPTION TO THE BOOK (1:1-3).

Verse 1. **The revelation.** The Greek word, *apokalypsis,* has several meanings. The simple meaning of the word is to uncover something that is concealed (Luke 12:2); but in the New Testament it usually has a distinctly religious connotation, designating the supernatural revelation of divine truths unknown to men and incapable of being discovered by them (Rom. 16:25; Gal. 1:12). In Theodotion's Greek version of Daniel the word is used several times of the divine disclosure through the prophet to the king of events which, in the providence of God, were destined to take place in the future. In the New Testament, what is revealed is the entire good news about God's redemptive plan which is embodied in Jesus Christ; and this redemptive plan is to be consummated in great eschatological events which are also revealed to God's people (Rom. 8:18; I Cor. 1:7; II Thess. 2:8; I Pet. 1:13; 5:1).

19

In the present instance, the revelation was given to John in visions, the content of which he wrote down in the book before us.

This word "apocalypse" has been taken from John's revelation by modern scholarship and applied to the genre of Jewish-Christian literature called "apocalyptic." However, the word is not used here as a technical designation of the book but of its contents: a revealing of the things which must soon take place. Many scholars insist that the Revelation stands on the same level as such Jewish apocalypses as *Enoch, The Assumption of Moses, IV Ezra, The Apocalypse of Baruch,* and others. The Revelation does indeed belong to the same genre of literature, and distinct guidelines can be found from the study of this literature to help us in interpreting the Revelation. These books are similar in their claims to be revelations of events unknown to men, in their use of visions and dreams, in their common use of symbolism which is often bizarre and fantastic, in their common concern about the end of the world and the coming of God's Kingdom, and in their common adherence to an "apocalyptic," i.e., cosmic catastrophic type of eschatology.

However, the Revelation stands apart from Jewish apocalyptic in several notable features. Jewish apocalyptic is pseudonymous; i.e., these writings are attributed to ancient saints in Israel, long since dead, to validate them. John is unique in bearing the name of a contemporary author well known by the addressees. Jewish apocalypses are pseudo-predictive; i.e., the writer takes his stand at a point in past history and then rewrites history under the guise of prophecy by the use of symbols. John takes his stand in his own day and looks forward to the consummation of God's redemptive purpose. The apocalypses tend to be pessimistic; i.e., they despair of God's acting in history, considering it to be under the baleful influence of evil satanic spirits. All hope is focused on the future. While John shares the interest in the future, the future depends upon what God has done in contemporary history in the redemption wrought in the death of Jesus of Nazareth. This is portrayed by the Lion, who is the slain Lamb. History is the scene of redemption; only the crucified one can solve the riddle of history. In all these traits, John reflects his prophetic character and stands apart from Jewish apocalypses. Furthermore, it is a fact of great significance that, while the Revelation is replete with verbal allusions to the Old Testament, it is completely lacking in similar allusions to the known Jewish apocalyptic writings.

Of Jesus Christ. Grammatically, these words are capable of being interpreted in two different ways, either as an objective or a subjective genitive. A few commentators take it in the former sense, and the phrase does indeed appear in this sense elsewhere in the New Testament (Gal. 1:12). John received a revelation of Jesus Christ, who is the object and the content of the revelation. This makes good sense, and it is true that the events disclosed to John result only because of the lordship of Christ in the world. But in its present context the phrase must be considered a subjective genitive. The object of the revelation is the last things which God gave Christ, who in turn shows **to his servants what must soon take place.** God the Father is the ultimate source and fountainhead of all revelation; God the Son is the agent through whom this revelation is imparted to men. This is true even of the exalted Christ. That the Son receives what he is and has from the Father is a New Testament truth in general which is particularly emphasized in the Gospel of John (John 3:35; 5:20ff., 26; 7:16 and 8:28). We are reminded of our Lord's saying, "But of that day or that hour no one knows, not even the angels in heaven, nor the Son, but only the Father" (Mark 13:32).

The words "what must soon take place" contain an echo of Daniel 2:28. Although John seldom quoted the Old Testament in a formal way, his book is filled with obvious allusions to the prophetic writings. Here is a fact whose significance many modern critics overlook. John's mind was saturated with the Old Testament, and he expected such passing allusions to be meaningful to his readers. However, there is not a single similar proven allusion to any known Jewish apocalyptic writings. This suggests that the Revelation is not, as many have said, simply a piece of Jewish apocalyptic which has been "baptized" into the Christian church. John's background was far more the Old Testament prophets, even though he made use of apocalyptic symbolism.

In Jewish apocalyptic we find a significant deterministic factor, almost giving the impression sometimes that the course of events was so inflexibly predetermined that God himself was bound by them. Since events were predetermined, it would be possible for one who had insight to calculate times and seasons and to figure out when the end would come. The New Testament is entirely free from this spirit of calculation: "Of that day or that hour no one knows" (Matt. 24:36). However, God is sovereign; he has a redemptive plan which in his own time *must* be carried out. Nothing can hinder the sure consummation of God's Kingdom.

These events are "soon" to "take place" (cf. 11:18; 22:10). These words have troubled the commentators. The simplest solution is to take the preterist view and to say that John, like the entire early Christian community, thought that the coming of the Lord was near, when in fact they were wrong. Our Lord himself seems to share this error in perspective in the saying: "This generation will not pass away before all these things take place" (Mark 13:30). Others have interpreted the phrase to mean "these events must soon begin"; others "they must certainly begin"; still others "they must swiftly take place"; that is, once the events begin, the end will come quickly.

However, the simple meaning cannot be avoided. The problem is raised by the fact that the prophets were little interested in chronology, and the future was always viewed as imminent. We pointed out in the introduction that the Old Testament prophets blended the near and the distant perspectives so as to form a single canvas. Biblical prophecy is not primarily three-dimensional but two; it has height and breadth but is little concerned about depth, i.e., the chronology of future events.[1] There is in biblical prophecy a tension between the immediate and the distant future; the distant is viewed through the transparency of the immediate. It is true that the early church lived in expectancy of the return of the Lord, and it is the nature of biblical prophecy to make it possible for every generation to live in expectancy of the end. To relax and say "where is the promise of his coming?" is to become a scoffer of divine truth. The "biblical" attitude is

[1]See p. 13.

"take heed, watch, for you do not know when the time will come" (Mark 13:33).

Verse 2. The revelation is imparted by the Son through the further mediation of **his angel.** Angels play a prominent role in this book, but it is rather remarkable that the angel does not appear as the imparter of visions until chapter 17 (17:15; cf. 19:9; 21:9; 22:16). The revelation is not human speculation; it is the **word of God** and **the testimony of Jesus Christ.**

In the New Testament the "word of God" is almost always the spoken word rather than the written word. Elsewhere in the Revelation "the word of God" is the gospel (1:9; 6:9; 20:4); here, it designates the contents of the revelation given to John. The word of God is thought of in the Bible not merely as a means of communicating truth, but as an active, dynamic entity. In the beginning God spoke and it was done (Ps. 33:9). God's word goes out into the world to accomplish what he purposes (Isa. 55:11). At the end God's word will go forth and his redemptive purposes be brought to consummation. It is significant that the only weapon of the conquering Christ is the sword that issues out of his mouth — his word (Rev. 19:15).

"The testimony of Jesus Christ" is a subjective genitive, i.e., the testimony borne by Jesus Christ. The revelation is a word from God which is witnessed to by Christ (cf. 22:16, 18, 20). This witness may include not only the immediate witness of Christ to the revelation granted to John but also the witness of his life on earth and his redeeming mission when the word became flesh (John 1:14).

Verse 3. **Blessed.** There are seven beatitudes in the book: 1:3; 14:13; 16:15; 19:5; 20:6; 22:7, 14. Here, a beatitude is pronounced upon those Christian congregations where John's revelation was to be read aloud. That this is the meaning is proved by the words, **those who hear.** This is not a reference to private reading and study but to public worship. The early church took over the Jewish practice of reading in the congregation (Exod. 24:7; Neh. 8:2; Luke 4:16; Acts 13:15; 15:21; II Cor. 3:15). Paul expected his letters to be read in the assemblies (Col. 4:16; I Thess. 5:27). The Revelation was given not merely to impart information about the future but

23

to help God's people in the present, who must therefore keep
what is written in the words of the prophecy. Here is a remi-
niscence of Jesus' words in Luke 11:28, "Blessed are those who
hear the word of God and keep it." The Revelation contains
many exhortations to faith, patience, obedience, prayer, and
watchfulness. That this book is a *prophecy* places it on a par
with the Old Testament prophets.

2. GREETING AND SALUTATION (1:4-5a).

Verse 4. John to the seven churches that are in Asia. This
sentence sets our book apart from Jewish apocalyptic at one
important point; it is the usual form of introduction used
in the ancient world in writing letters. This firmly anchors
our book in history. The seven churches were seven actual,
historical congregations in the Roman province of Asia. Why
were seven churches selected to be the recipients of the Revelation? John must have been acquainted with other churches,
e.g., Colossae (Col. 1:2; 2:1), Hierapolis (Col. 4:13), and Troas
(Acts 20:5). Shortly after this time, Ignatius wrote letters to
the churches of Magnesia and Tralles. There is no hint in
the seven letters that they represent seven successive periods
of church history. However, seven was one of John's favorite
numbers and seems to have the symbolism of fullness or completeness. John chose these seven churches with which he was
well acquainted so that they might be representative of the
church at large. Seven is not a sacred number. Antichrist has
seven heads and seven diadems (13:1). The significance here
is of diversity within a basic unity. John thus indicated that
while his revelation was addressed in particular to seven
churches known to him, its message was also for the whole
church in general.

Grace and peace is the usual Christian greeting; it is found
frequently in the New Testament epistles. **From him who is**
is a phrase impossible to translate into idiomatic, equivalent
English; it is an allusion to the Greek form of Exod. 3:14.
The full phrase denotes the eternity of the God who also acts
on the scene of human history. **From the seven spirits** means
from the Holy Spirit in his sevenfold fullness (cf. 3:1; 4:5;
5:6). Some have seen here a reference to angelic beings; but
since the preceding phrase refers to God the Father and the

following phrase to God the Son, it is certain that John included a reference to God the Holy Spirit, thus including all persons of the Godhead. In other places the New Testament speaks of the Holy Spirit in his plurality of functions (cf. Heb. 2:4; I Cor. 12:11; 14:32; Rev. 22:6). The source of the idea appears to be Zech. 4, where the prophet described a candlestick with seven lamps which are the eyes of the Lord ranging over the whole earth. The meaning of the vision was, "Not by might, not by power, but by my Spirit, says the Lord of hosts" (Zech. 4:8).

Verse 5a. Jesus Christ is the one who has borne a faithful witness to God's redemptive purpose and work (cf. above on 1:2). He is the **firstborn of the dead** (see Col. 1:18). The word "firstborn" may be a reference to the simple fact that Jesus was the first to rise from the dead, and as such is the first fruits of the resurrection (I Cor. 15:20). However, the word may bear the idea of sovereignty more than chronology; he fills the role of the firstborn son. So in Ps. 89:27: "I will make him the firstborn, the highest of the kings of the earth." By virtue of his resurrection, Jesus has been exalted to the position of firstborn son. This is supported by the phrase that follows: he is also **the ruler of kings on earth.**

Here is one of the central affirmations of the New Testament, which apparently is contradicted by hard political experience but which every Christian confesses. Outwardly, it appeared that Rome ruled without rival, with sovereign might. Human history through the centuries can be interpreted as the clash of nations and the rule of the strongest. It has not been nor is it now true that good has always triumphed and right has always won the day. But behind the chaotic events of history, the believer recognizes that Jesus Christ, who chose the way of obedience and humiliation, has in fact been exalted to God's right hand where he sits as Lord, ruling over the rulers of the earth. His second coming, from one point of view, is to be understood as making manifest to the world the sovereignty which is already his.

The more particular reason for the reference at this point was undoubtedly the emerging tendency to deify and worship the Roman emperor. The emperors were beginning to use the titles of deity. Julius Caesar, Augustus, Claudius, Vespasian, and Titus had been officially declared divine after their death by the Roman Senate, and the last three had used the term *DIVUS* (divine) on their coins. Domitian, the emperor when John wrote, had advanced this tendency by requesting that he be addressed as *Dominus et Deus* (Lord and God). Emperor worship was particularly popular in Asia, especially in Ephesus. In the face of this threatening situation John reminded the churches of a fact which must ever be a touchstone for their conduct, that back of all human political authority stands the sovereignty of him who is in fact, although unseen, ruler over the kings of the earth.

3. A DOXOLOGY TO CHRIST (1:5b-6).

Verse 5b. John next wrote a doxology to the Redeemer Christ. Here we meet the first of numerous places where the modern critical Greek text has been able to correct defects found in the Textus Receptus which stood behind the King James Version. The King James Version reads "washed us from our sins"; the Revised Standard Version reads **freed us** or "loosed us" **from our sins by his blood.** The theological difference here is not great, but we should always be concerned with the accuracy of the text. The King James Version was based upon only a few late manuscripts. Since then a great mass of manuscripts has been discovered, the best of them going back to the middle fourth century A.D. Many of the important differences of translation between the King James and the Revised Standard translations are due to the differences between an inferior and a superior Greek text.

The tenses of the verbs in the doxology are significant. He **loves us.**[2] Christ's love is a permanent abiding fact. He **freed us from our sins by his blood:** a finished work of redemption. Here is the one unambiguous evidence of the fact that God is a God of love who conveys his love to men through his Son. "God shows [or displays] his love for us in that while we were yet sinners Christ died for us" (Rom. 5:8). The early Christians were facing possible persecution when it would seem that God's love was obscured and only evil was dom-

---

[2]The AV has a past tense, "he loved us," but the RSV reflects the best text.

inant; but the love of God, in spite of all evil experiences, is assured by an event in history — the death of Jesus Christ.

The Greek idiom in turn reflects a Hebrew idiom, so that we might well translate, "he has freed us from our sins at the price of his blood." Elsewhere John wrote, "by thy blood thou didst redeem men to God" (5:9). In the Bible, *blood* is a metaphor drawn from the slaughter of the sacrificial lamb to represent sacrificial death, particularly at the Passover, when God freed Israel from bondage to Egypt. The sacrifice of Christ on his cross was the cost of loosing men from bondage to their sins.

Verse 6. The connection with the Passover lamb is made clear in this verse. **He made us [to be] a kingdom, priests to his God and Father.** At the Passover, God commissioned Israel to be "a kingdom of priests and a holy nation" (Exod. 19:6). The question here is whether the church is called a kingdom because it is a people under a king, or because it fulfills a kingly function. This appears to be settled in Rev. 5:10. Christ has made men "a kingdom and priests to our God, and they shall reign on earth" (see Rev. 20:6; 22:5). God's people are a kingdom not merely because they are the people over whom God reigns, but because they are to participate in the messianic reign of Christ. Here are the clearest references in the New Testament where the church is called a kingdom, and it does not provide adequate exegetical support to identify the church with the Kingdom of God. Believers are a kingdom because they will fill the role of kings along with the messianic King — Jesus. Jesus had promised his disciples a share in his rule. (See Matt. 5:2-5; 19:28; Luke 22:30.)

Believers are also *priests*. This does not mean that the church serves as mediator between God and the rest of mankind; it means that believers have no need of further mediation because they have access to the immediate presence of God where they perform the priestly functions of offering sacrifices of thanksgiving, worship, and praise to God (Rom. 12:1; Heb. 13:15; I Pet. 2:5). This verse unites the church and Old Testament Israel in a bond of continuity. The church is the new and true Israel, inheriting the spiritual privileges of the Old Testament people of God. "But you shall be called priests of the Lord, men shall speak of you as ministers of God" (Isa. 61:6).

4. THE THEME OF THE BOOK (1:7).

Verse 7. This reiterates the theme of the book: the second coming of Christ and the events which lead up to and accompany that great consummation. This verse is a conflation of Dan. 7:13 and Zech. 12:10, 12, a combination which also appears in Matt. 24:30. It is impossible to determine whether there is any interdependence between the Revelation and Matthew at this point. The important point in this passage is that the return of the Lord will be a public, visible event.

Every eye will see him. In the days of his flesh, his messiahship was not self-evident. When Jesus was on trial before the Sanhedrin, he was asked by the high priest, "Are you the Christ, the Son of the Blessed?" (Mark 14:61). If this was true, how could such an important fact be in doubt? Jesus answered, "I am; and you will see the Son of man sitting at the right hand of power, and coming with the clouds of heaven" (Mark 14:62). His reply says in effect: "Today you can challenge my messiahship, but the day will come when it will no longer be in doubt but will be evident to everyone." It is idle to speculate how this event will occur and how it will be possible for Jesus to be visible to the whole world at once. What the passage means to say is that the lordship which is his now, but recognized only by believers and confessed only by faith, will become inescapably evident to the whole world. It is interesting to note that this event is nowhere described in terms of this verse in the Revelation. The return of Christ is pictured in chapter 19 where he comes riding on a battle horse to overthrow the enemies of God.

Every one who pierced him. Probably this ought not to be taken to mean primarily or exclusively those who physically crucified Jesus, but all those in every age who share the indifference and the hostility that lay behind the act. The crucified one is to be recognized as king and judge of the world.

The expression **all the tribes of the earth will wail on account of him** is difficult. Ordinarily this idiom should mean that the crucified one has become the object of their sorrow; i.e., they are grieving because they have crucified him. This would mean that men will be convicted for the evil of their terrible crime, and in repentance will seek God's forgiveness. However, there is in the book of Revelation no indication of the repentance of the wicked. On the contrary, the judgments of God only serve to confirm the wicked in their wickedness (9:20; 16:9, 11). Probably, therefore, we are to understand that Christ is not the object but the occasion of their grief; they wail on account of him because of the terrible judgment which he is to inflict upon them.

5. THE DIVINE IMPRIMATUR (1:8).

Verse 8. Before John received his first vision, he was given a reaffirmation of God's sovereign lordship over history. **Alpha and Omega** are the first and last letters of the Greek alphabet and therefore include all that is contained between them. God is the absolute beginning and the end, and therefore Lord of all that happens in human history. He is at the same time the eternal one, the transcendent one, who is unaffected by the conflicts of history, the one **who is and who was and who is to come.** As the one who is to come, he will yet visit men to bring history to its divinely decreed consummation. **The Almighty** can be better translated "the All-Ruler."

II. THE FIRST VISION (1:9 — 3:22).

1. THE REVELATOR: THE GLORIFIED CHRIST (1:9-20).

John next described the occasion of the revelation and related the first vision, a vision of Jesus, now exalted and glorified, which is the background and condition of the entire disclosure of "what must soon take place."

Verse 9. John was commanded to send the visions he was to receive to the seven churches of Asia. He was well known to them and stood in a bond of fellowship with the Asian Christians as their **brother.** He shared with them the **tribulation and the kingdom.** These are the two main concerns of the book: the tribulations which the church was to experience, and the coming of the Kingdom. Tribulation is the lot of God's people in this age. "In the world you have tribulation" (John 16:33). "Through many tribulations we must enter the kingdom of God" (Acts 14:22). Back of human history are mighty spiritual powers in conflict with each other — the Kingdom of God and the power of Satan. The church stands between the two. The church is the people to whom the Kingdom has come and who will inherit the Kingdom when it comes; but as such, it is the object of satanic hatred and is destined to suffer tribulation. Tribulation here includes all the evil which will befall the church, but especially the great tribulation at the end, which will be only the intensification of what the church has suffered throughout all history. Be cause of these anticipated evils, **patient endurance** is needed. "He who endures to the end will be saved" (Matt. 24:13).

Yet all of these hardships are experienced **in Jesus.** Here is John's parallel to Paul's frequent expression, "in Christ," signifying the believer's spiritual union with his Lord. It is interesting that following the salutation in 1:5, where the Lord is referred to as Jesus Christ, throughout the rest of the book he is referred to simply as Jesus. (The King James Version has "Jesus Christ" several times, but this rendering is based on an inferior text.) The use of the simple name "Jesus" calls attention to his life in the flesh.

John **was on the island called Patmos.** The language employed here suggests that John was no longer on Patmos at the time of writing the book. Apparently he received the visions on Patmos but composed the book at some later time. Patmos was one of a group of small islands southwest of the coast of Asia. It was about ten miles long and six miles wide — a bare, rocky volcanic island with hills rising to about a thousand feet. There are references in Roman literature to support the view that such islands were used for the banishment of political offenders. There is no evidence that John's exile was any part of a general persecution of the church in either Rome or Asia. However, the governor had the authority to send people into exile for political reasons, and from its earliest days the church had been liable to the accusation of political sedition (see Acts 17:7). In the time of Emperor Nero, Christians were marked out as adherents of a new and — from the Roman point of view — potentially dangerous religion. Before Nero, the Christian movement was usually viewed as a movement within Judaism. In the present in-

stance, John apparently had been accused to the governor of
Asia of sedition because of **the word of God and the testimony
of Jesus,** i.e., because of his preaching of the gospel of Jesus
the Messiah. Others interpret the passage to mean that he
was in Patmos in order to receive the word of God and thus
write the Revelation; still others, that he was in Patmos for
the purpose of preaching the gospel.

Verse 10. He found himself **in the Spirit on the Lord's day.**
Some interpreters see in the latter expression a reference to
the eschatological Day of the Lord, as though John was trans-
ported in ecstatic imagination to the end of history so that he
might witness the great events of that day unfold. It is far more
likely that we see here the emerging language referring to
the Lord's day as the Christians' distinctive day of religious
devotion. We know from other references that the first day of
the week was of great importance to Christians. They gathered
together to break bread on the first day of the week (Acts 20:7)
and made offerings of love gifts on the first day (I Cor. 16:2).
Here we find the first evidence that the day was viewed as
being particularly consecrated to the Lord, because it was the
day of his resurrection. The emergence of Sunday observance
in place of the Jewish sabbath was a gradual historical process,
and here we have the beginning of that process.

John's use of "in the Spirit" here is not to be confused with
Paul's idiom "in the Spirit," which is the normal state of the
Christian walk (Rom. 8:9). The phrase here means to be
caught up in an ecstatic experience, to enter into a trance
(see Acts 11:5; 22:17). Paul described one such experience in
II Cor. 12:2, when he was "caught up to the third heaven" and
"heard things that cannot be told." Such trancelike visions
were frequently experienced by the Old Testament prophets,
but they were not the only media of revelation. Often the
prophets spoke the word of God as a deep conviction grip-
ping their innermost being; and in the New Testament the
phrase "the word of God" is most frequently used to refer to
the oral tradition of the gospel, as in verse nine. In John's case,
the events of the end were disclosed to him in ecstatic visions.
He heard an unidentified **voice** — it might have been the voice
of Christ, but probably the voice of an angel (see 4:1) — com-
manding him to write what he was about to see in a book and

send it to the seven churches, which were then listed. Unlike modern books, which are made of leaves of paper bound together, an ancient book consisted of a long strip of papyrus rolled up in a scroll. Furthermore, before the invention of printing in relatively modern times, all books had to be written by hand.

Verse 12. Turning to see the source of the voice, John was granted his first vision — that of the exalted Christ. He first saw **seven golden lampstands.** In the holy place of the Jewish temple stood a single candelabrum bearing seven lamps (Exod. 25:36ff.). A seven-branched candelabrum played an important role in Zechariah's vision, apparently to represent Israel (Zech. 4:2). In John's vision the lampstands represented the church, which had now become the the light of the world. However, John saw seven separate lampstands, representing the different churches. In New Testament times the church was not, like the nation Israel, outwardly a single people. In the New Testament view each local church is to be viewed as the church universal in all its fullness. That the unity of the church is not found in organization but in its relationship to Christ is pictured in verse 16, where Christ held seven stars in his right hand. The seven stars were the heavenly counterparts of seven churches, while the seven lamps were the actual churches. It was their function to give light in the world (Matt. 5:14). Should the light fail, the lampstand was removed (Rev. 2:5).

Verse 13. **In the midst of the lampstands** John saw **one like a son of man.** Daniel, in his vision of the coming of God's Kingdom, saw God seating himself upon his throne, surrounded by hosts of serving angels. "And, behold, with the clouds of heaven there came one like a son of man, and he came to the ancient of days" (Dan. 7:13). Later, the "Son of man" became a fixed messianic expression to designate the heavenly Savior; and it was Jesus' favorite title to designate his own person and mission. The present reference goes back directly to Daniel, and serves not so much to designate Jesus as the heavenly King as to point out that while he is like a man, he is not merely a man; he is a supernatural being. In the vision Jesus was dressed in a **long robe . . . with a golden girdle;** this was the garb of the high priest (Exod. 28:4; 39:29).

However, prophets could be similarly garbed (Zech. 3:4), so it is not clear whether this is intended to designate specifically our Lord's high priesthood, or merely the dignity of his person.

Verse 14. **His head and his hair were white as white wool, white as snow.** This is not meant to represent Jesus' sinlessness or his holiness, but his deity. Christ shares this feature with God the Father himself (Dan. 7:9), whose raiment is white as snow and the hair of his head like pure wool. In Daniel, these features belonged to the "ancient of days." John used them to show that Christ shares eternal existence with the Father. **His eyes were like a flame of fire.** This feature occurs again: to the church at Thyatira, Christ was the one with eyes like a flame of fire (2:18), which seems to symbolize his all-searching omniscience. In 19:12, this is a characteristic of the conquering Christ who destroys his enemies. We may conclude that it symbolizes omniscience combined with holy wrath directed against all that is unholy.

Verse 15. **His feet were like burnished bronze, refined as in a furnace.** This may mean that his feet were glowing as though they were still in the furnace, or that they were like bronze that has passed through the furnace of purification. It is not clear whether this is designed to represent any particular characteristic, or merely to add to the magnificence and strength of the portrayal. **His voice was like the sound of many waters,** i.e., mighty.

Verse 16. **In his right hand he held seven stars.** This signifies his care of the churches (1:20; see John 10:28).

From his mouth issued a sharp two-edged sword. The sword of the Spirit is the word of God (Eph. 6:17). The word of God is sharper than any two-edged sword and is invincible in the achievement of its purpose (Heb. 4:12). The only weapon of warfare used by the conquering Christ in chapter 19 was a sword proceeding out of his mouth (Rev. 19:5). Taken literally, this would indeed be a grotesque picture; but understood symbolically, it expresses a sublime truth. He shall speak, and it shall be done. This transcends all human imagination and speculation. It is, however, analogous to the account of the creation: God spoke, and it was done (Gen. 1:3).

His face was like the sun shining in full strength. This is John's way of describing the glory of the exalted Christ. In the time of his incarnation, he was burdened with weakness and human frailty, endured the temptations and testings common to man, and finally succumbed to death itself. This same Jesus is now exalted in power and great glory.

Verses 17-18. So overwhelming was the vision that John fell prostrate to the ground **as though dead.** This was a common reaction to the manifestation of the divine glory (cf. Isa. 6:5; Ezek. 1:28; Dan. 8:17; 10:9, 11). We are reminded of the basic biblical truth, which we so easily overlook and forget, that none but the pure in heart can see God and live. However, John was revived by a hand laid upon him and given the assurance that he had nothing to fear. While he was in the presence of the divine Christ, who like the Father is **the first and the last** (see 1:8; Isa. 44:6; 48:12), he was also in the presence of one who for the sake of man shared their fate and **died,** and who is now the **living one.**

By his resurrection Christ did not merely return to the glorious realm whence he had come; he entered a new life in which death has been conquered forever. He not only came back to life; he is **alive for evermore.** He was not only raised up from the dead; he became the conqueror of death itself and has the **keys of Death and Hades.** Keys in Jewish thought were a symbol of authority (Matt. 16:19). Hades designates the intermediate state of the dead and is the Greek equivalent of the Old Testament Sheol. Death has now lost its terror, for Christ has gained the keys so that he can unlock the gates of the grave and lead the dead into eternal life.

Verse 19. John's commission was now repeated; he was told: **Write what you see,** i.e., the vision of the glorified Christ, **what is,** i.e., the state of the seven churches of Asia in chapters 2-3, and **what is to take place hereafter,** i.e., the consummation of God's redemptive purpose and the coming of the Kingdom of God. This begins with the breaking of the seven seals in chapter 6 and continues to the end of the book.

Verse 20. The first vision concluded with an explanation of the **mystery of the seven stars . . . and the seven golden lampstands.** The essential truth is that as Christ stands among the seven golden lampstands, he stands ever in unbroken fellowship with the churches on earth, persecuted though they may be. At the same time he holds them in his hand; this pictures his keeping and protecting power of a church in persecution.

The expression, **the angels of the seven churches,** represented by the seven stars in the hand of Christ, is difficult, especially since each of the seven letters was addressed *to the angel* of each respective church. This fact has led many commentators to conclude that the *angel* stood for the bishop of the church. This would be a good solution for the problem except for the fact that it violates the New Testament usage. *Aggelos* was not used of Christian leaders, and in the seven letters, neither angels nor bishops were rebuked. Another meaning of *aggelos* is "messenger," and the "angels" are taken to be the seven messengers who carried the letters to the seven churches of Asia. If this is so, it is difficult to see why the letters were addressed to the messengers rather than to the churches themselves. The proper meaning of the word is *angel,* and the natural idea is that churches on earth have angels in heaven who represent them. However, the feature of angels symbolizing or representing men is lacking in all apocalyptic literature. Some have felt that the angels are guardian angels of the churches. It is best to understand this as a rather unusual symbol to represent the heavenly or supernatural character of the church.

CHAPTER TWO

THE LETTERS TO THE
SEVEN CHURCHES

2. THE SEVEN LETTERS (2:1 — 3:22).

Before John describes what he has seen in his visions, he writes messages to seven of the churches in Asia. The many allusions to local history, topography, and conditions in these churches lead to the inescapable conclusion that John was personally and intimately acquainted with them. The letters are not structured in strict epistolary form; they are special messages addressed to the seven churches. The book as a whole is in the form of a letter. Furthermore, the phrase repeated seven times, "He who has an ear, let him hear what the Spirit says to the churches," suggests that the message in each letter is intended for a wider audience than for the local church alone.

The seven letters are structured after a common plan. Each letter is introduced by a brief characterization of Christ as he has been portrayed in the first chapter. Usually this characterization is adapted to the situation in the local church. This is followed by words of praise for the good qualities to be found in the particular church. One exception is Laodicea, where nothing is found to praise. Next come words of criticism for the faults of each church. Again, criticism is lacking in the letters to Smyrna and Philadelphia where nothing is found to blame. Each letter concludes with a word of promise, particularly to those who conquer.

(1) The Letter to Ephesus (2:1-7).

Verse 1. **Ephesus** was both the foremost city of Asia and the home of the most important church in the province. Today Ephesus is situated about eight miles from the gulf of Ephesus in a swampy plain, but in the first century it was the most important seaport of Asia Minor. Ephesus was also a religious center. It had long been the home of the Mother Goddess who was identified by the Greeks with Artemis (Acts 19:35). To this goddess was dedicated a huge temple which was known as one of the wonders of the ancient world. This temple also became the site of the worship of the goddess Roma and of the Roman emperor. The Asiarchs of Acts 19:31 were the foremost men of the city from whose ranks were selected annually the high priests of the cult of "Rome and the Emperor." Ephesus was also the home of all kinds of superstitious practices and was famous throughout the world for the magical arts (see Acts 19:19).

The church in Ephesus apparently was founded by two outstanding Christians, Aquila and Priscilla. They had come from Corinth with Paul to Ephesus (Acts 18:18), and remained in Ephesus after Paul journeyed on to Antioch. Some two or three years later, Paul returned to Ephesus and spent two years preaching and teaching the gospel. While there is no evidence that Paul visited any other cities in Asia, his work in Ephesus became the center of evangelism for the entire province of Asia (Acts 19:10). Later, the work in Ephesus was carried on by Paul's companion Timothy (I Tim. 1:3) and, according to traditions in Irenaeus and Eusebius, after Paul's death, by the apostle John. Ephesus was quite certainly one of the cities to which Paul addressed the circular letter which we call Ephesians.[1] In the first years of the second century, Ignatius, bishop of Antioch, wrote his first and longest letter to the Ephesians in which he praises them for their unity and blameless Christian conduct and for living in harmonious love under their bishop, Onesimus.

The words of him who holds the seven stars in his right hand, who walks among the seven golden candlesticks. The

[1]As the RSV indicates in Eph. 1:1, the words of address "who are at Ephesus" are not found in the best Greek texts.

letter to Ephesus is prefaced with a reference to Christ which
involves an element of encouragement. The Greek verb used
here for "holds" differs from that used in 1:16. This is a
stronger word, indicating a firm grasp, indicating that Christ
holds his churches firmly in his hand, that they should not be
snatched away (see John 10:28). The words also indicate the
constant vigilance and watchful presence of Christ not only
over Ephesus but over all the churches.

Verse 2. **Works** is a broad term indicating not only good
deeds but the entire course of life and conduct. Two nouns,
toil and **patient endurance**, stand in apposition to "works." The
good works of the Ephesians consisted in their firm opposition
to false teachers who had arisen in Ephesus (see Acts 20:29-30),
and in their steadfast refusal to be led away by their teachings.
Their good works are further described in the strong statement that they **cannot bear evil men.** This does not refer to
the evil conduct of their profane neighbors but to the false
teachers in the church.

They have **tested those who call themselves apostles but are
not.** By such careful scrutiny, most have **found** these teachers
to be false. These words reflect an entirely different situation
in New Testament times from that which prevails in the
modern organized church. Many itinerant preachers and
teachers arose in the early church who claimed to be the
mouthpiece of the Holy Spirit and to speak for God. When
Paul admonished the Thessalonians not to quench the Spirit
(I Thess. 5:19), he recognized the validity of the prophetic
gift. However, it was necessary to "test the spirits" (I John 4:1;
see I Thess. 5:20) to determine whether or not such teachers
really conveyed the word of God.

Not only were there false prophets but also men who falsely
claimed to be apostles. The question of the role of apostles
in the early church is not an easy one to solve; but there seem
to have been two orders of apostles: the original twelve who
retained a distinctive role (21:14) and a larger indeterminate
number who were itinerant missionaries, such as Paul, James,
Barnabas, Silas, Andronicus, and Junias (Acts 14:14; I Cor.
15:7; Gal. 1:19; Rom. 16:7). Among this larger group were
false apostles who used their professed role as apostles for
selfish purposes rather than for edifying the church; and such

false apostles were among Paul's chief opponents in the Corinthian church (II Cor. 11:5, 13; 12:11).

The church in Ephesus was outstanding because of its ability to distinguish between true and false apostles and its refusal to tolerate those who were false. That this was a deeply rooted characteristic of the church is witnessed by the fact that Ignatius commends the Ephesians because no false teaching could gain a hearing among them (Ignatius, *Ephesians* 19).

Verse 3. Their patient endurance and bearing up for the name of Christ suggest that the problem of false teachers faced by the Ephesian Christians was no temporary crisis but one that exerted a severe test of their steadfast adherence to the gospel. Here was a church outstanding for her doctrinal purity.

Verse 4. Although their struggle with false teachers had made no inroads in the sound doctrine of the Ephesian Christians, it had had serious effects on some aspects of their Christian conduct; it had led them to abandon **the love** they **had at first.** Here was a failure which undermined the very foundation of the Christian life. The Lord had taught that mutual love was to be the hallmark of Christian fellowship (John 13:35). The Ephesian converts had knówn such a love in their early years; but their struggle with false teachers and their hatred of heretical teaching had apparently engendered hard feelings and harsh attitudes toward one another to such an extent that it amounted to a forsaking of the supreme Christian virtue of love. Doctrinal purity and loyalty can never be a substitute for love.

Verse 5. The loss of love was no trivial matter; it is treated as though it involved a fall from the Christian life. The Ephesians are warned to **remember** the fervor of their first Christian experience, to **repent** because they have fallen into sin, and to **do the works** they did at first, i.e., works of love. As Paul wrote to the Corinthians, all the good works done in the name of Christ are empty if they are not motivated by love (I Cor. 13:1-3). Unless the Ephesians repent, Christ **will come** to them and **remove** their **lampstand from its place.** Some interpreters see here a reference to the judgment to be inflicted by Christ at his second coming, but it is more likely that these words refer to some kind of visitation which will bring a historical judgment upon the church so that destruction will befall it and it will cease to exist as a church.

Verse 6. The false teachers resisted at Ephesus are further defined as the **Nicolaitans.** These constituted a heretical sect in the early church about which we know nothing apart from the references in the Revelation. Ancient church fathers, beginning with Irenaeus, speculated that they formed a heretical sect which was founded by Nicolaus, a proselyte of Antioch (Acts 6:5) who was one of the seven. But we have no sure information to this effect. John refers again to these false teachers in the letter to Pergamum where he gives us more information about them.

Which I also hate: the exhortation to recover their first love does not carry with it an implication of doctrinal laxity. The hatred of the Ephesians for such false doctrine is in itself admirable, for the glorified Christ himself expresses hatred for such heretical teaching. What is rebuked is the influence of the struggle with heresy.

Verse 7. Each of the seven letters concludes with this admonition to hear what the prophet writes. In these admonitions John addresses his exhortations not only to the local church but to the entire Christian community. The emphasis upon hearing rather than reading points to the fact that the contents of the Revelation were designed to be read in public worship.

The Spirit is the Spirit of Christ (Rom. 8:9) who interprets the voice of Christ (2:1) to the prophet. The New Testament establishes a close and intimate relationship between the glorified Christ and the Holy Spirit — so intimate that Paul can say, "The Lord is the Spirit" (II Cor. 3:17). The glorified Christ speaks to his church through the Spirit, and it is at the same time the voice of the Spirit and the voice of Christ.

The letter concludes with a promise to **him who conquers.** This note of victory resounds in each of the seven letters. Although the Revelation forecasts the terrible domination of evil in the person of Antichrist in the last days, it is in reality a prophecy of the victories to be won by Christ and his church. The idea of conquering suggests warfare. The Christian life is an unrelenting warfare against the powers of evil. The victory is not a physical or worldly one; it is a victory analogous to the victory won by Christ himself, even though it involved his death on the cross. "He who conquers, I will grant him to sit with me on my throne, as I myself conquered and sat down with my Father on his throne" (3:21). A later vision, after the appearance of the beast and his fierce persecution of the church, sees the martyrs standing before the throne of God with harps in their hands singing a chant of praise to God; they are described as "those who had conquered the beast" (15:2). In other words, their very martyrdom was their victory, for they had conquered every satanic effort to turn their loyalty and devotion away from Christ and had remained true. The conqueror, then, is the victim of persecution whose death is not loss but is in reality his victory. Love and loyalty to Christ will conquer fear of suffering and death.

The conqueror is promised that he will **eat of the tree of life.** The Revelation concludes with a beatitude upon those "who have the right to the tree of life" (22:14). This language is a biblical way of expressing the promise of eternal life in the consummated Kingdom of God; it is not a special blessing awarded to a particular group of Christians; all believers will find their names written in the Lamb's book of life (20:15; 21:27). Why then does John seem to make the promise of eternal life a particular blessing only for the conquerors? The answer is that every disciple of Jesus must be in principle a martyr and be ready to lay down his life for his faith. Jesus himself taught more than once that those who would follow him must be ready to take up their cross (Mark 8:4; Matt. 10:38), and the cross is nothing less than an instrument of death. The Revelation pictures a life and death struggle between Christ and Antichrist for the hearts of men; and the conqueror is he who is unswervingly loyal to his Lord even though it costs him his life.

Paradise is one of the Bible's ways of describing the dwelling place of God. Paul spoke of being caught up in ecstasy to Paradise where he heard wonderful things (II Cor. 12:2). In the present passage, Paradise is equivalent to the heavenly Jerusalem which is to descend from heaven to earth at the consummation of God's Kingdom when God himself takes up his dwelling among men (21:10; 22:4).

41

(2) The Letter to Smyrna (2:8-11).

Verse 8. **Smyrna** was situated some thirty-five miles north of Ephesus, and like that city was also a prosperous seaport town. Its wealth and prosperity led it to contend with Ephesus for the honor of being the foremost city of Asia. Smyrna had supported Rome long before she had become a world power, and as early as 195 B.C. had erected a temple to the goddess of Rome. This naturally made Smyrna a seat of emperor worship, and in 26 B.C., when several cities of Asia were competing for the honor of building a temple to the Emperor Tiberius, Smyrna alone secured this privilege. This fact enhanced her claim to be the first city of Asia.

The letter reflects the fact that Smyrna contained a substantial colony of Jews who were aggressively hostile to Christianity and who exercised considerable influence with the civil authorities. Some years later, the Jews joined the gentiles to form a mob and to call for the death of the bishop of the church, Polycarp. They actively assisted in his martyrdom by burning and prevented the Christians from getting possession of his body (*Martyrdom of Polycarp*).

When and by whom the church was founded, we do not know. We may assume that it was the fruit of Paul's missionary work in Asia which centered in Ephesus (Acts 19:10). Apparently, the church was healthy and spiritually prosperous, for the letter contains no word of criticism or condemnation.

The description of Christ repeats words from the initial vision in 1:17: **the words of the first and the last, who died and came to life.** These words suggest that members of the church were threatened with persecution and possible martyrdom; in the face of such an experience, the church is reassured that her Lord is the conqueror of death.

Verse 9. **I know your tribulation and your poverty (but you are rich).** This statement stands in sharp contrast to the church in Laodicea which professed to be rich but in fact was poor (3:17). Apparently tribulation and poverty are linked together, and we may assume that the poverty of the Smyrneans was not due alone to their normal economic condition but to confiscation of property, looting by hostile mobs, and to the difficulty of earning a living in a hostile environment. The letter to the Hebrews refers to such persecution of Christians which involved the plundering of their property (Heb. 10:34).

The spiritual condition of the Smyrnean church stands in sharp contrast to their economic condition. Spiritually, they are rich, even though they suffer economic poverty.

Slander is incorrectly translated by the AV as "blasphemy," which is a literal rendering of the Greek word. However, its proper meaning is not blasphemy of the name of God but slanderous accusations against men. We do not have the historical resources to reconstruct precisely what this slander involved, but we may get a hint from the somewhat later writing, *The Martyrdom of Polycarp*. After Polycarp refused to renounce his Christian faith and swear by the genius of Caesar, a mob consisting of both heathen and Jews "cried out with uncontrollable wrath and a loud shout, 'This is the teacher of Asia, the father of the Christians, the destroyer of our gods, who teaches many neither to offer sacrifice nor to worship' " (xii.2). The seeds of this kind of problem are to be seen in the earliest church when Paul was accused by the Jews before the city authorities in Thessalonica of "having turned the world upside down" and "acting against the decrees of Caesar, saying that there is another king, Jesus" (Acts 17:6-7). This accusation created such a dangerous situation that Paul found it expedient to leave Thessalonica. We may conclude that in Smyrna the Jews found grounds for effective accusation of Christians before the Roman authorities which made them appear to be violators of Roman law.

Those who say that they are Jews and are not. Clearly, the opponents of the church are Jews. In the form of this expression, John makes an important distinction between outward and inward Judaism. These "Jews" are without question Jews by race and religion, who met together in the synagogue to worship the Lord. But in reality, inwardly, they are not Jews, because they have rejected Jesus as their Messiah and confirmed their rejection by persecuting his church. Who, then, are the true Jews? John does not offer an explicit answer, but the implication is clear: true Jews are the people of the Messiah. Paul says the same thing very clearly: "For he is not a real Jew who is one outwardly, nor is true circumcision something external and physical. He is a Jew who is one inwardly, and real circumcision is a matter of the heart, spiritual and not literal" (Rom. 2:28-29). That this "Judaism of the heart" is not to be limited to believing Jews but includes believing gentiles is clear from Paul's words to the Philippians: "For we are the true circumcision, who worship God in spirit, and glory in Christ Jesus" (Phil. 3:3). We must conclude, then, that John makes a real distinction between literal Israel — the Jews — and spiritual Israel — the church.

A synagogue of Satan. Throughout the Hellenistic world, Jews gathered on the sabbath for the worship of God in their synagogues. Paul in his missionary journeys in Asia Minor and Greece always went to the Jewish synagogue to gain a hearing for his proclamation of Jesus as the Messiah. However, because the Jews have rejected their Messiah, they are no longer a synagogue of the Lord but in reality a synagogue of Satan. "Synagogue" is used once in the New Testament of the Christian assembly (Jas. 2:2).

Verse 10. The Jews had such influence with the Roman authorities that some sort of persecution was impending. Some of the Christians would be thrown into **prison.** In the ancient world, prison was not so much a place of punishment as a place of detention awaiting trial. The trial might issue in vindication or in some sort of punishment, including death.

Tested. Imprisonment and possible death were perceived as the work of **the devil** and involved a test of the validity of Christian profession. Everyone who professed discipleship to Jesus must be ready to go to prison and if need be to lay down his life for his Lord. Martyrdom would prove beyond doubt the reality of his faith. Every Christian must **be faithful unto death.**

The number **ten days** has no particular symbolic significance beyond that of indicating a relatively short period of persecution. In the case of the Smyrneans, John does not expect an extensive universal persecution but a local one of short duration.

As in verse 7, the **crown of life** is not a promise of a special reward for the martyrs. All who belong to Christ will receive a crown of life. God has promised this crown to all who love him (Jas. 1:12). The figure of the crown is not borrowed from royalty but from the festivity of athletic games. Such contestants strove "to receive a perishable wreath [the same Greek word is used], but we an imperishable" (I Cor. 9:25). John introduced the promise of the crown of life in this context to remind the Smyrneans that although they suffered physical death, they were assured of the prize of eternal life. The crown itself is eternal life.

Verse 11. **The second death.** The first death is the death of the body which all men, believers and unbelievers alike, must suffer. The second death is the eternal death. The phrase occurs again in 20:6, 14 and 21:18, where the fate of the lost is described in terms of a lake of fire and brimstone. Jesus himself had taught, "and do not fear those who kill the body but cannot kill the soul; rather fear him who can destroy both soul and body in hell" (Matt. 10:28).

(3) The Letter to Pergamum (2:12-17).

Verse 12. **Pergamum,** while not as important a commercial city as Ephesus and Smyrna, was nevertheless more important as a political and religious center. It had become a prominent city after the death of Alexander the Great in 133 B.C. The last king of Pergamum, Attalus III, bequeathed his territory to Rome, and Pergamum was made the capital city of the Roman province of Asia. Pergamum was the first city of Asia to support openly the imperial cult. In 29 B.C. a temple was dedicated "to the divine Augustus and the goddess Roma," and thus Pergamum became the chief seat in Asia of the worship of the emperor. Observance of this worship became a test of loyalty to Rome, for the imperial cult was the keystone of the imperial policy, and refusal to take part in the official cult was considered high treason.

Pergamum was also a center for many other deities. In the city was an acropolis, about a thousand feet high, upon which had been erected many temples to pagan deities. The acropolis was crowned by a hugh altar dedicated to Zeus, and by a temple of Athena. Pergamum was also the center of the worship of Asclepius, the serpent-god of healing, and was famed for its college of medical priests. Thus Pergamum was a stronghold of both pagan religion and emperor worship and provided an unusually difficult environment for a Christian church.

45

Christ is represented as the one **who has the sharp two-edged sword,** an allusion to the vision of Christ in 1:16. In the present instance, this sword is his word of judgment on a church which has grown lax in its attitude toward pagan practices (vs. 16).

Verse 13. Several explanations have been suggested for the phrase **where Satan's throne is.** Possibly it refers to the prominence of the city as a center of pagan worship. Or it could refer to the worship of Asclepius, the serpent-god of healing, whose serpent symbol might well remind Christians of Satan. Again, it might refer to the prominent altar of Zeus in the acropolis which overshadowed the city. It is most likely, however, that John used the phrase because Pergamum was the center of the imperial cult with its worship of the emperor, which was becoming the greatest danger to the Christian church.

You hold fast my name. In spite of the fact that the church was surrounded by so many pagan deities, the believers in Pergamum are commended because they have held fast to their Lord. We should remember that most of the converts in Pergamum had come from paganism, and undoubtedly the social and religious pressure to abandon Christ and to turn back to their pagan worship was severe.

You did not deny my faith. The tense of the verb points to some definite situation in the recent past when members of the church were faced with the challenge of denying their faith in Christ. Whether there had been an outbreak of persecution because of alleged disloyalty to Rome, we do not know. In any case, one martyrdom had occurred, and **Antipas my witness, my faithful one,** had been killed because of his faithfulness to his Lord. We have no information about Antipas apart from this verse: whether he was killed as the result of an outbreak of mob violence or as the result of a judicial sentence by the local authorities, we do not know. However, the tone of the letter suggests the latter. If so, Antipas is one of the first martyrs at the hands of Roman officials for refusal to conform to emperor worship. It is clear, however, that Rome had not yet engaged in a policy of seeking out and executing all who evaded the imperial cult.

The Greek word used here for "witness" is *martys,* which

later came to bear the connotation of martyr; possibly it
carries this meaning in the present context. In 17:6, the
same word is translated "the martyrs of Jesus." By standing
faithful to the point of death and suffering martyrdom, the
Christian bore his most effective witness to his Lord.

Verse 14. **But I have a few things against you.** Although
the Pergamum Christians had held fast to Jesus' name and did
not renounce their faith in him under the pressure of threatened persecution, they allowed pagan morals to influence them.
A party had arisen in Pergamum which held **the teaching of
Balaam.** Balak, king of Moab, threatened by the Israelites,
had invited the prophet Balaam to curse them. Balaam had
been restrained by God and to Balak's disgust had blessed
rather than cursed (Num. 22-24). Subsequent to this, however, Israel had let herself become involved in harlotry and
in the idolatrous worship of Baal of Peor (Num. 25:1-3), and
this sin was attributed to the advice of Balaam (Num. 31:16).
In our text Balaam is a prototype of those who promote compromise with paganism in idolatry and immorality.

Our understanding of the phrase **eat food sacrificed to idols**
must be taken from its context. A single Greek word is translated "food sacrificed to idols." It can refer either to meat
purchased in the public market which had formerly been
sacrificed in a pagan temple and later sold to the market, or
it can refer to feasts conducted in the temples in honor of the
various gods. The problem of these meats which Christians
must buy in the public market had arisen in Corinth, and
Paul dealt with it at length, declaring that nothing is unclean
of itself, and that unless it is offensive to a man's conscience,
he does no wrong in eating such meat (I Cor. 7:7-13). At the
same time, Paul says that it is impossible to drink the cup of
the Lord and the cup of demons (I Cor. 10:21), and in this
case he must have reference to actual participation in temple
feasts which amounted to worship of the deity involved. Such
seems to be the situation in Pergamum. It would be difficult
to understand this prohibition as a restriction against buying
meat in the open market; rather, it refers to active participation in feasts in the temples in honor of the pagan deities.
Probably the argument was put forward that the Christian
knows that such alleged gods really have no existence and

47

therefore no wrong is done in participating in temple feasts. One can maintain his loyalty to Christ and participate in such pagan feasts provided that he does not acknowledge the existence of such alleged deities. Some interpreters think the words **practice immorality** are synonymous with idol worship and designate spiritual fornication, as the idea often appears in the Old Testament (Isa. 1:21; Ezek. 23:37). However, it is equally possible that this refers to the sin of fleshly immorality. Background for this is the fact that sexual laxity was not considered a serious sin by the Greeks and Romans. This may be illustrated by the decision of the first church council in Jerusalem (Acts 15) which met to decide the terms of relationship between Jewish and gentile Christians. Among the admonitions to the gentile Christians was the encouragement to abstain from "unchastity" or sexual laxity (Acts 15:20). From the point of view of our western culture, this seems like a strange exhortation, for we almost automatically assume that a Christian will live by a high moral standard. But it was not so in the ancient world. Not far from Antioch where the first gentile church arose was a beautiful spot called Daphne, adorned with fair edifices, and containing a temple dedicated to Apollo and Diana. The temple area was surrounded by a thick grove of cypresses and bay trees, and was beautified with numerous lovely fountains. It became a favorite retreat for the wealthy citizens of Antioch, and even Roman governors frequented the place. Daphne was famous for her corps of temple prostitutes; and the phrase *Daphnici mores* became a synonym for immoral practices. Against this pagan background, it is entirely credible that a party arose in Pergamum which advocated a lax attitude toward pagan customs, including both temple feasts and sexual immorality.

Verse 15. **The teaching of the Nicolaitans.** The language suggests that we are not to think of the Nicolaitans as constituting another sect, but as giving further definition of the "teaching of Balaam." It was the Nicolaitan heresy which promoted laxity toward the pagan practices.

Verse 16. **Repent then,** that is, of laxity toward the teaching of the Nicolaitans. The entire church is summoned to repent for a sin of which only a few were actually guilty. The sin of

the Ephesians was harsh intolerance; the sin of the Pergamum
church was tolerance and laxity.

I will come to you soon. As in verse 5, this probably does
not refer to the second advent of Christ when faithful believers
will be given access to the tree of life (vs. 7) and will receive a
crown of life (vs. 10); rather, it refers to some historical
visitation which will bring judgment upon the whole church.

Verse 17. **To him who conquers** a promise of reward is held
out, that is, to those who resist the teaching of the Nicolaitans
and who remain true to Christ.

Hidden manna. Probably John's thought is drawn to the
manna because of the allusion to Balaam, in whose time Israel
was being fed with manna. Hebrew tradition held that a pot
of manna was preserved in the ark (Exod. 16:32-34; Heb. 9:4),
and when the temple was destroyed, Jeremiah (*II Macc.* 2:4ff.)
or an angel (*Apoc. Baruch* 6:5-10) rescued the ark with the
manna, and they were miraculously preserved until the
messianic times, when the manna would become once again
food for God's people. John uses the idea metaphorically to
indicate admission to the messianic feast, which is elsewhere
called the marriage supper of the Lamb (19:9). The manna
is referred to as hidden, perhaps because it was hidden in a
pot of gold and "laid up before God" (Exod. 16:23); or else
because it is thought of as hidden now in the presence of God
but destined to be revealed in the messianic age.

A white stone. In the ancient world, white stones had a
variety of uses. A white stone signified acquittal by a jury, a
black stone condemnation. White stones were used as tickets
of admission to public festivals. This meaning fits the context
best. The white stone is a symbol of admission to the
messianic feast.

It is not clear whether the **new name** is the name of Christ
or a new name given to the holder of the stone. In either case,
it means certainty of entrance to the messianic banquet.

(4) The Letter to Thyatira (2:18-28).

Verse 18. **Thyatira** was the least important of the seven
cities of Asia; it was not a religious or political center, but
owed its importance altogether to trade. It did possess a few
temples, but it was not a strong seat of emperor worship and

49

the state cult. There were also few Jews in Thyatira to trouble the church. Thyatira was noted for her trade guilds, about which we have considerable knowledge from inscriptions. One of these guilds dealt in purple cloth, and it is probable that Lydia of Philippi was a representative of this guild (Acts 16:14). These trade guilds enjoyed common meals which were probably dedicated to some pagan deity, and from this source arose the problem of the Christians in Thyatira. It would be nearly impossible for a citizen to participate in trade and industry without membership in the appropriate guild, and the question naturally arose whether a Christian could properly participate in such meals. Many Christians would argue that the alleged gods had no real existence, and therefore participation in such meals involved no compromise of one's Christian witness. The question was complicated by the fact that such social meals would often end in unbridled licentiousness. Here is the same problem we have met in other churches. Ephesus had declared herself strongly opposed to all such compromise with pagan practices; in Pergamum, a small party in the church had advocated full participation in heathen social life. The problem in Thyatira, as we shall see, assumed a new and dangerous form.

The Son of God. This is the only occurrence of this title in the Revelation, but God is called the Father of Christ in 1:6; 2:27; 3:5, 21; 14:1. Only in 21:7 is God called the Father of believers. Probably the title anticipates the use of Psalm 2 which is quoted in verse 27.

Who has eyes like a flame of fire and whose feet are like burnished brass. This allusion to 1:14 designates Christ as the one whose eyes flash with anger and who is prepared to tread under his feet the enemies of the Christian faith. This stern portrayal prepares us for the equally stern words in verses 26-27.

Verse 19. **I know your works, your love and faith and service and patient endurance.** Probably the four words of approbation are an explanation of the good works of this church. Possibly service is the manifestation of *love,* and patient endurance of *faith.* Here is a church which has much to commend it. Its love has not grown cold as in Ephesus, and the vast majority of the church have let their faith lead them to

patient endurance in the face of the problems the church
faced in a pagan environment.

Your latter works exceed the first. This church had manifested admirable growth in the Christian virtues; her love and
faith had steadily increased.

Verse 20. You tolerate the woman Jezebel. The problem in
this church was that even though the vast majority were increasing steadily in love and faith, they were tolerant of evil
teaching. There had arisen in the church a woman of whom
Jezebel was the prototype. As Jezebel, Ahab's queen, had supported idolatry (I Kings 16:31), so this woman with her
pernicious teaching was leading some away from the faith.

Who calls herself a prophetess. Prophets were highly regarded in the early church, and are mentioned in close relationship with the apostles (I Cor. 12:28; Eph. 4:11). In Romans
12:6 prophecy heads the list of the gifts of the Spirit. The
office of prophet was not primarily that of predicting future
events, although that might be included (Acts 11:27); it was
rather that of inspired teacher. We must remember that the
early church did not possess the New Testament as we do with
its inspired account of the words and deeds of Christ, and the
meaning of his death and resurrection. Partly to fill this need
for trustworthy teaching, the Holy Spirit often illuminated
prophets to set forth the word of God. Paul has left us an
extended account of the role and function of prophets in I
Corinthians 14. Prophets, together with the apostles, constituted the human medium for the revelation of divine truth
(Eph. 3:5). This false Jezebel claimed to be a prophetess,
having special revelations from God which qualified her to be
an authoritative teacher. Obviously, she was a member of the
church and sought followers from among the Thyatiran
Christians.

You tolerate. The problem in Thyatira was an unhealthy
tolerance. They recognized the presence of the false prophetess;
they recognized also the evil character of her teaching, but
they tolerantly refused to deal with her. Here is the opposite
situation from that in Ephesus. The Ephesians had tested
those who called themselves apostles and had rejected pseudo-
apostles, but this conflict had made them harsh and censorious.

Here is a church abounding and increasing in love and faith
which is tolerant of false prophets to her own detriment.
**Teaching and beguiling my servants to practice immorality
and to eat food sacrificed to idols.** The error of this Jezebel
was the same as that of the Nicolaitans in Pergamum: full
accommodation to pagan mores. The reason why the problem
assumed such acute form in Thyatira was that membership
in the trade guilds involved participation in pagan meals and
often led to immorality.

Verse 21. **I gave her time to repent.** These words obviously
refer to some incident in the past, unknown to us, when God
had used some situation to rebuke the false prophetess and
to summon her to repentance. Possibly John himself had
ministered in the church at Thyatira and had rebuked this
woman, but without success.

Verse 22. **I will throw her on a sickbed.** The Greek simply
reads "bed," but the translators have correctly rendered the
Old Testament idea which means to fall sick (Exod. 21:18).
Probably a contrast between a bed of sickness and a bed of
adultery is intended. God promises to punish Jezebel with
some affliction of physical sickness.

Into great tribulation. These words involve Hebrew poetic
parallelism and promise the same affliction for those who have
accepted the woman's teaching and have tried to adjust their
Christian profession to the practices involved in membership
in the trade guilds.

Verse 23. **I will strike her children dead.** The text distinguishes between those who join in adultery with the prophetess
and those who are called her children. The punishment of the
latter is much more severe than the former: death. Apparently
John intends us to distinguish between those who are still
struggling with the problem of how to be loyal to Christ
and at the same time to adapt fully to the business and social
mores about them, and those who have unreservedly committed
themselves to the teaching of the false prophetess. Some commentators think that "her children" designates her literal
physical offspring, but this seems unlikely.

All the churches shall know. We must infer that this false
Jezebel was widely known throughout the churches of Asia;
God promises a judgment which will be itself an obvious testi-

mony to the fact that **I am he who searches the mind and heart.**

Verse 24. John proceeds with a promise of assurance to the majority of the church **who do not hold this teaching** of the false prophetess, even though they have tolerated her. Her teaching is described as **the deep things of Satan.** Some interpreters think that the false Jezebel claimed that her teaching would introduce her disciples into satanic mysteries. It is more likely that John wrote ironically; as a prophetess, she claimed to introduce her followers into the deep things of God (I Cor. 2:10; Rom. 11:33; Eph. 3:18), but in reality, they were not such; they were the deep things of Satan, not of God.

The words **any other burden** are perplexing, for the context does not make clear what burden John is laying upon his readers. Many interpreters see an allusion to the decree of the Jerusalem council in Acts 15 which includes prohibitions of eating meats offered to idols and immorality. This is a likely interpretation whether John had the decree in Acts in mind or not.

Verse 25. **Only hold fast what you have.** Instead of adding a new list of demands upon the believers in Thyatira, Christ merely exhorts them to continue in their faithfulness to their Christian profession and to shun the pagan feasts with their accompanying immorality.

Verse 26. **He who conquers and keeps my works.** The victorious Christian who does not accept the teaching of the false prophetess is said to keep the works of Christ himself, i.e., his commandments.

Power over the nations. The idea appearing in 1:6 is made more explicit in the present passage: the saints are to share Christ's messianic rule over the nations. The saints are a kingdom because they will share Christ's kingly reign. Christ promised his disciples that they should inherit the earth (Matt. 5:5). He promised the twelve that in the new world they would sit on twelve thrones judging the twelve tribes of Israel (Matt. 19:28); and the same promise is repeated in Luke 22:30. The same basic idea is found in Paul's assertion that the saints shall judge the world (I Cor. 6:2). The premillennial interpretation of 20:4 sees the fulfillment of this promise in the temporal messianic kingdom which intervenes between the parousia (19:11-16) and the new age when the new heavens and the new earth will displace the old order (21:1ff.).

Verse 27. **He shall rule them with a rod of iron.** These words further explain the power of the conqueror over the nations. The conqueror is promised that he will share the functions of the Messiah himself: "you shall break them with a rod of iron, and dash them in pieces like a potter's vessel" (Ps. 2:9). This phase is repeated in the vision of the coming of Christ: "he will rule them with a rod of iron" (19:15; see also 12:5). A problem occurs in the Greek text, for the word in the Septuagint which translates the Hebrew, "to break" or "shatter," is a word which means basically "to tend a flock" and often has the idea of ruling in the sense of protecting and preserving (see Matt. 2:6; John 21:16; Rev. 7:17). However, the meaning of the word in this context cannot be in doubt, for it is further defined by the phrase that follows: **as when earthen pots are broken in pieces.** The effective establishment of the Kingdom of God cannot be accomplished apart from the destruction of all hostile and recalcitrant powers. The new age cannot be inaugurated without the displacement of the old, fallen, sinful age with its rebellious hosts. In some way not made clear in Scripture, the followers of the Messiah are to share in his triumph over the hostile nations.

Even as I myself have received power from my Father. The victorious rule of Messiah is a gift bestowed on him by his Father by virtue of his sufferings, death, and resurrection (Phil. 2:9-11).

Verse 28. **I will give him the morning star.** This is an obscure saying. Possibly it refers to such passages as Daniel 12:3, where it is promised that "those who turn many to righteousness" shall shine "like the stars for ever and ever." If so, this is a promise of the glory to be bestowed upon the victor. The fact that it is the *morning* star may refer to its prominence in the heavens (Job 38:7). In view of the fact that 22:16 speaks of Christ as the bright morning star, many commentators feel that this is a promise that Christ himself will be given to the victor; but this is a difficult idea.

CHAPTER THREE

THE LETTERS TO THE
SEVEN CHURCHES
(continued)

(5) The Letter to Sardis (3:1-6).

Verse 1. The glory of **Sardis** lay in the past. In the sixth century B.C., she had been the capital city of the kingdom of Lydia and later a center of Persian government. In New Testament times she had sunk to relative obscurity. Her one claim to prominence was that she provided the meeting place of several major Roman roads, and was an important industrial center, the home of woolen and dyed goods. The chief cult in Sardis was that of Cybele, the goddess of one of Asia's most famous mystery religions. Sardis was also zealous in promoting emperor worship. The people of the city were widely known for their luxurious, loose way of life. It is significant that nothing is said in the letter about Jewish hostility, about open persecution, or about heretical teaching. The main problem is that of a deep spiritual apathy, which may have resulted from the softness and love of luxury which characterized the secular society.

The seven spirits of God. As in 1:4, this is an allusion to the fullness of the Holy Spirit. The problem of the church at Sardis was spiritual death; Christ is the possessor of the Holy Spirit who alone can give life.

As in 1:16, the phrase **the seven stars** signifies Christ's concern and care for his churches. Although the church in Sardis had fallen into sad spiritual complacency, she was still the object of Christ's care.

3:2 THE FIRST VISION

I know your works. The spiritual decay in the church at Sardis was not obvious to outward observation. In fact, it was a church well known for good works. It had the name of being alive; it had an outstanding reputation for life and vitality, but in the sight of God it was dead. Here is a picture of nominal Christianity, outwardly prosperous, busy with the externals of religious activity, but devoid of spiritual life and power.

Verse 2. **Awake, and strengthen what remains and is on the point of death.** A more literal translation for "awake" would be "be watching." This admonition was particularly relevant in Sardis, for in the city was an impregnable acropolis which had never been seized by frontal attack; twice, however, in the history of the city, the acropolis had been taken by stealth because of lack of vigilance on the part of its defenders. This admonition suggests that the church was not yet entirely beyond hope. It was not too late to awaken from spiritual lethargy; there still remained a residuum of life which could be revived. But unless such a revival occurs, this small remainder will also fall subject to spiritual death.

I have not found your works perfect in the sight of my God. This church was noted for its good works, which by men were praiseworthy but which before God stood condemned because they were imperfect. They were incomplete, inadequate. The church was not troubled by persecution; it was not disturbed by heresy; it was not distressed by Jewish opposition; it was well known as an active, vigorous Christian congregation, characterized by good works and charitable activities. But in the sight of God, all of these religious activities were a failure because they were only formal and external, and not infused with the life-giving Holy Spirit. Here is a perfect example of purely nominal Christianity which in all outward and formal aspects is outstanding but which in the sight of God is a complete failure.

Verse 3. **Remember then what you received and heard; keep that, and repent.** John recalls the church to its earliest experience of love and devotion to Christ. He recognized that there remained a faithful element in the church, and he called upon the church as a whole to remember the early days when they received the gospel, to hold fast to their primitive devotion, and to repent of the indifference into which they had fallen.

If you will not awake, I will come like a thief, and you will not know at what hour I will come upon you. This is language usually used of the second coming of Christ (16:15; Matt. 24:43; Luke 12:39; I Thess. 5:2; II Pet. 3:10), and emphasizes not the suddenness of the Lord's return but its unexpectedness. Paul indicates that this unexpectedness will be the experience of unbelievers, in contrast to the outlook of believers: "But you are not in darkness, brethren, for that day to surprise you like a thief" (I Thess. 5:4). However, in the present context, the warning is far more suitable to some historical visitation when the Lord will bring upon a lethargic church an unexpected experience which will mean a divine judgment. This interpretation is supported by the fact that this visitation is posited upon the failure of the church to repent—a condition which is not primarily related to the Lord's return.

Verse 4. **Yet you have still a few names in Sardis.** The spiritual torpor in Sardis was not universal; there remained a few persons who had retained their loyalty to Christ.

People who have not soiled their garments. This suggests that the spiritual lethargy of the Sardian Christians was due to the pernicious influence of the pagan environment. Spiritual indifference was due to the fact that Christians, while maintaining outwardly their good works and Christian activities, wished to adapt themselves to the luxury and pleasures of their pagan environment.

They shall walk with me in white. Some commentators see in these words a reference to the resurrection body; but it is more likely that this is a promise of victory and purity in the messianic Kingdom when those who have remained faithful in a pagan and corrupt society will experience the consummation of fellowship with the Lord (see Ps. 104:2; Rev. 7:9, 13).

Verse 5. **I will not blot his name out of the book of life.** The metaphor of a book in the presence of God in which the names of the saints are written occurs frequently (Exod. 32:32; Ps. 69:28; Luke 10:20; Phil. 4:3; Heb. 12:23; Rev. 13:8; 17:8; 20:12, 15; 21:27). As a civic register contained the names of living citizens, so God's book of life contains the names

57

of the saints. The form of the promise in the present passage is an assurance of salvation in the consummated Kingdom of God.

I will confess his name before my Father and before his angels. Here is an echo of Jesus' promise to his disciples: "So everyone who acknowledges me before men, I will also acknowledge before my Father who is in heaven" (Matt. 10:32; see Luke 12:8).

(6) The Letter to Philadelphia (3:7-13).

Verse 7. **Philadelphia** was the youngest of the seven cities of Asia. It supported the pagan cult of Dionysus, but the main problem faced by the church was from the Jews rather than the pagans. Apparently the church was in a healthy condition, for the letter includes no words of censure or criticism. The church was rather a weak one, possessing only a little power (vs. 8), but she had remained faithful to her Lord.

The words of the holy one. "The holy one" elsewhere in the Revelation is a title attributed to God (4:8; 6:10), but it was a common designation of the Lord's Messiah (Mark 1:24; Luke 4:34; John 6:69; I John 2:20), pointing not so much to his sinlessness as to his complete dedication to God.

The true one. The word "true" or "genuine" has two different meanings. In a Greek context, the word designates that which is real, which corresponds to reality. But in a Hebrew context, it designates what is faithful and trustworthy. In the Old Testament, God is he who "keeps faith forever" (Ps. 146:6), i.e., who can always be trusted to keep his promises. When God is described in the Old Testament as the true one (Exod. 34:6), he is the one who is faithful (RSV) to his covenant promise. Isaiah speaks of the "God of truth" (Isa. 65:16), meaning the God who can be trusted to keep his word and is therefore one by whom men can swear to keep their word. In the present context, "the true one" recalls the covenant made with Israel in Old Testament times which God has now faithfully fulfilled with his church in Jesus Christ.

The key of David can be understood only in its Old Testament setting. In Isaiah 22:22, Eliakim received the key of the chief steward of the king's household, and as the representative of the king, he was authorized to exercise full administrative authority in the king's name. The key of David is the key to David's house — the messianic Kingdom. The immediate background of the phrase was the claim of the Jews in Philadelphia that they were the true people of God who held the key to the Kingdom of God. John contradicts this claim by asserting that the key to the kingdom which had belonged to Israel really belongs to Jesus as the Davidic Messiah (5:5; 22:16) and had been forfeited by Israel because she had rejected her Messiah. It is Christ alone and no longer Israel who can give men entrance into the messianic Kingdom.

Who opens and no one shall shut, who shuts and no one opens. These words are a commentary on the key of David. To Christ has been given absolute and exclusive power to give entrance and to exclude from the Kingdom of God. This is, however, a privilege which Christ has shared with his church (Matt. 16:16).

Verse 8. **I know your works.** These good works are not further described; the church in Philadelphia was one so abounding in good works that she was pleasing to the Lord. Although the church had but little power and was small and with very limited influence, its character was such that the letter has only commendation from the Lord, not censure.

I have set before you an open door. This expression is subject to two different interpretations. In view of the context, that Christ is the one who has absolute authority to give admission into the Kingdom of God, this may be a promise that in spite of the obvious conflict being waged with the Jews, the church is promised sure entrance into the eschatological Kingdom of God. **No one is able to shut** the door and bar her from her place in God's Kingdom. However, the idea of an open door appears several times in the New Testament to designate a door of opportunity, especially in preaching the gospel (I Cor. 16:9; II Cor. 2:12; Col. 4:3; Acts 14:27). The thought may well be that though the church is small and weak, Christ has set before her a great opportunity to make the gospel known. In view of the context of the present passage, the former interpretation seems preferable. The Jews in Philadelphia were aggressive in their hostility to the church and claimed that only they—Israel—had access to the door of God's Kingdom. Christ assures his church that the Jews cannot prevail in their purpose to close the door of the Kingdom to the church.

I know that you have but little power is a far more accurate translation than that of the AV, "for thou hast a little strength." The emphasis is not on the little strength that the church possesses, but upon the fact that she has only a little strength. Apparently this church was small, poor, and uninfluential.

You have kept my word and have not denied my name. The church had recently passed through a time of severe trial, probably at the hands of the Jews, in which she had remained faithful to her Lord.

Verse 9. Once again, as in 2:9, the Jewish synagogue, which claimed to be a synagogue of the Lord, is called a **synagogue of Satan.**

Who say that they are Jews and are not, but lie. Once again, John asserts that the true Jews are not those who attend the synagogue to worship God, although they are outwardly Jews by virtue of race and religion. He clearly implies that true Jews are not those who are Jews outwardly but inwardly (cf. Rom. 2:28-29). Rejection of their Messiah has led to the denial of the true spiritual Judaism of the Jewish people.

I will make them come and bow down before your feet. One might think upon the first reading of these words that John referred to some impending historical humiliation of the Jews in Philadelphia before the church. However, there is no intimation that these Jews were any worse than the Jews who troubled the churches in other cities; and in view of the eschatological references in verses 10-11, it is probable that this refers to an eschatological salvation of the Jews.

We find a broad background for this idea in the Old Testament, with the difference that there it is pictured in terms of the triumph of Israel over her enemies and the salvation of the gentiles by faith in the true God of Israel. "The sons of those who oppressed you shall come bowing low to you; and all who despised you shall bow at your feet; they shall call you the City of the Lord, the Zion of the Holy One of Israel" (Isa. 60:14). "They will make supplication to you, saying: 'God is with you only, and there is no other, no god besides him' " (Isa. 45:14). "With their faces to the ground, they shall bow down to God, and lick the dust of your feet. Then you will know that I am the Lord; those who wait for me shall not be put to shame" (Isa. 49:23). "Then the nations will know that I the Lord sanctify Israel, when my sanctuary is in the midst of them for evermore" (Ezek. 37:28). "The nations will know that I am the Lord, says the Lord God, when through you I vindicate my holiness before your eyes" (Ezek. 36:23). These and many other passages look forward to a day of the triumph of Israel over the nations; sometimes it is expressed in terms of the humiliation of the gentiles before Israel, sometimes in the conversion of the gentiles to the faith of Israel.

John reverses the picture. The Jews have surrendered their role as the people of God because they have rejected their Messiah. In their place, the church, largely gentile, has become the true Judaism, the new people of God. However, the Jews hate the church and were often the instruments of bringing persecution upon her. John looks forward to a day when this situation will be changed — when the Jews will acknowledge that the church is indeed the true people of God, and will **learn that I have loved you.**

This is not a new idea in the New Testament. Paul in Romans 9-11 dealt with the problem of Israel and the church. The olive tree is the people of God; natural branches (Jews) were broken off because of unbelief, and wild branches (gentiles) were grafted into the tree, contrary to nature (Rom. 11:17-20). However, if the branches broken off (Jews) do not continue in unbelief, "they will be grafted in, for God has the power to graft them in again" (Rom. 11:23). Then Paul makes an amazing statement: "and so all Israel will be saved" (Rom. 11:26). In light of its context, it is difficult to see how "Israel" can mean anything other than the Jewish people who will yet come to salvation and be grafted back into the olive tree along with the church; when and how this great redemptive event will occur may be given in chapter 11.

Verse 10. **Because you have kept my word of patient endurane.** The Greek says, "Because you have kept the word of my patient endurance." Paul spoke of "the steadfastness of Christ" (II Thess. 3:5), and the thought here is that the fol-

lowers of Jesus share and emulate his steadfastness in the face
of the pressures about them.

**I will keep you from the hour of trial which is coming on
the whole world.** Here is a distinct eschatological reference to
the "messianic woes" which are to precede the return of the
Lord. John viewed the troubles which the church will suffer
in the near future against the background of the consummation of evil and the time of terrible trouble at the end. This
period is referred to elsewhere in the Bible in Dan. 12:2; Mark
13:14 and parallels; II Thess. 2:1-12. This time of great tribulation (Matt. 24:21) will involve two aspects: the persecution
of the church by Antichrist (Rev. 13:7-8), and the outpouring
of divine judgments upon a rebellious and apostate civilization. The danger of martyrdom is nothing the church should
fear. Jesus said that when his disciples are hated and put to
death, "not a hair of your head will perish" (Luke 21:17).
Physical death, even as a martyr, has no eternal significance;
indeed, in the time of Antichrist, the martyrdom of the saints
will prove their salvation. In the very act of martyrdom, they
conquer the beast (Rev. 15:2).

On the other hand, God will pour out his wrath upon the
followers of the beast to try to drive them to repentance before
it is too late (9:20; 16:9, 11). The Greek expression translated
those who dwell upon the earth appears several times in the
Revelation and always designates the pagan world (6:10;
8:13; 11:10; 13:8, 14; 17:8). The outpouring of God's wrath
is pictured symbolically by the plague of the seven trumpets
(8:1 — 9:19) and the seven bowls (16:1-20). Before these terrifying judgments, the people of God are sealed upon their
foreheads that they should not be hurt by these plagues. These
fearful divine judgments are directed upon those who follow
the beast (16:2); those who have the seal of God will be divinely sheltered (9:4). Although the church will be on earth
in these final terrible days and will suffer fierce persecution
and martyrdom at the hands of the beast, she will be kept
from the hour of trial which is coming upon the pagan world.
God's wrath, poured out on the kingdom of Antichrist, will
not afflict his people.

Verse 11. **I am coming soon** is the keynote of the entire
book: the coming of the Lord in power and glory to finish his

great work of redemption and to establish his **Kingdom on the earth.**

Hold fast what you have, so that no one may seize your crown. The church is to face persecution in the midst of which she is summoned to hold fast to her good works of faith and love. We are reminded of the challenge to the Smyrneans: "Be faithful unto death, and I will give you the crown of life" (2:10).

Verse 12. **I will make him a pillar in the temple of my God** is symbolic language which gives assurance of admission into the consummated Kingdom of God. The New Testament says little about a heavenly temple; the sole reference is to the man of lawlessness who would ascend to the temple of God and take the place of God himself (II Thess. 2:4). Paul does speak of a heavenly Jerusalem (Gal. 4:26), but he obviously uses metaphorical language. The Revelation constantly refers to a heavenly temple as the dwelling place of God (7:15; 11:19; 14:15; 15:5; 16:1). However, in the consummated Kingdom of God, there will be no temple, for God himself will be the temple (21:22). The present verse is, then, a promise in symbolic language of the assured place of the overcomer in the final Kingdom of God.

I will write on him the name of my God is a symbol of possession. The name of their God was put on the people of Israel (Num. 6:27). The followers of the beast will bear his name (13:17). The followers of Christ receive his mark on their foreheads to show that they belong to him, not to the beast, and to protect them from the wrath of God (7:3). This mark is the name of Christ himself (14:1). Those who bear the name of God belong to God (22:4).

The name of the city of my God is another symbolic way of expressing citizenship in the new Jerusalem. The idea of a heavenly Jerusalem appears in Gal. 4:26 and in Heb. 12:22. Paul writes that our citizenship is in heaven (Phil. 3:20); he could have said in the heavenly Jerusalem. In the consummation, the heavenly Jerusalem will descend to earth (21:2) and God will take up his residence with men. Those who bear its name are those who will have access to the new redeemed order.

My own new name. When Christ comes as the mighty con-

63

queror, he has a name inscribed which no one knows but himself (19:12). This is a symbolic way of suggesting the glory and majesty of Christ at his revelation, which will be shared by his followers.

(7) The Letter to Laodicea (3:14-22).

Verse 14. **Laodicea** was situated at the convergence of three important roads. Its situation contributed to its becoming a prominent center of banking and industry. Its wealth is illustrated by the fact that when it, together with other cities in Asia, suffered severe damage from an earthquake in A.D. 60-61, it was able to finance its own rebuilding and did not need, like other cities, substantial subsidies from the imperial treasury. The city was famous for a beautiful black woolen cloth used to make clothing and carpets. Laodicea was also the seat of a flourishing medical school which was particularly noted for its ear ointment and for "Phrygian powder" which was used in the manufacture of eye-salve.

Paul had not visited this church at the time of his first imprisonment (Col. 2:1); the church had probably been founded by Epaphras of Colossae (Col. 1:7; 4:12f.). Paul was acquainted with the church, for he wrote a letter to the Laodiceans from Rome (Col. 4:16), which has unfortunately been lost.

The church in Laodicea is obviously quite prosperous and outwardly in excellent condition. The letter makes no mention of persecution from Roman officials, of trouble from the Jews, or of any false teachers within the church. Laodicea was much like Sardis: an example of nominal, self-satisfied Christianity. One major difference is that at Sardis there remained a nucleus who had preserved a vital faith (3:4), while the entire Laodicean church was permeated by complacency. It is probable that many of the church members were active participants in the affluent society, and that this very economic affluence had exercised a deadly influence on the spiritual life of the church.

The words of the Amen. Amen is a Hebrew word expressing the idea of verity. Isa. 65:16 speaks of "the God of Amen," and the Septuagint translates it "the true God" (RSV: "the God of truth"). The idea involved in the expression is not that God is the true God in contrast to false gods, but that God is the faithful one, the reliable and trustworthy one, who can be trusted to keep his covenant with his people. The word applied to Christ guarantees the truthfulness and reliability of his words. This is supported by the following phrase, **the faithful and true witness.** He is true not in contrast to what is false, but true because he can be trusted to communicate truth.

The beginning of God's creation. This phrase in itself is capable of two translations: the "beginning" of creation, or the "source and origin" of creation. The latter is quite certainly the correct meaning, for John clearly regards Christ as eternal. He is the first and the last, the Alpha and the Omega (1:17f.; 2:8; 21:6; 22:13); he is the transcendent one above all creation. The same idea appears in Paul's letter to the Colossians; Christ is the firstborn of all creation (Col. 1:15).

The emphasis upon the fact that it is *God's creation* is a reiterated New Testament theme. God is the ultimate source of creation; Christ is the immediate agent. "All things were made through him" (John 1:3), not by him. "There is one God, the Father, from whom are all things and for whom we exist; and one Lord, Jesus Christ, through whom are all things and through whom we exist" (I Cor. 8:6).

Verse 15. **I know your works.** The letter has no word of commendation for the Laodiceans, neither is there any word of censure for false teaching or immorality. The trouble at Laodicea was that the church members were **neither hot nor cold.** They were not characterized by the coldness of hostility to the gospel or rejection of the faith; but neither were they characterized by a warm zeal and fervor (Acts 18:25; Rom. 11:11). They were simply indifferent, nominal, complacent. **Would that you were cold or hot.** Any condition is better than nauseous lukewarmness.

Verse 16. **I will spew you out of my mouth.** Lukewarm water is revolting and fit only to be spit out. This language sounds like a final and irrevocable rejection of the church by Christ. However, since verses 18-20 are a call to repentance, we must conclude that the Laodicean church is not entirely beyond hope of recovery. The strong language is designed to rouse the church from her spiritual indifference.

Verse 17. **For you say, I am rich, I have prospered, and I need nothing.** The church boasted that it was healthy and prosperous. The Greek of this verse literally rendered is, "I am rich, and I have gotten riches." Not only did the church boast in her supposed spiritual well-being; she boasted that she had acquired her wealth by her own efforts. Spiritual complacency was accompanied by spiritual pride. No doubt part of her problem was the inability to distinguish between material and spiritual prosperity. The church that is prospering materially and outwardly can easily fall into the self-deception that her outward prosperity is the measure of her spiritual prosperity.

Not knowing that you are wretched, pitiable, poor, blind, naked. Here is the actual spiritual condition of the church. She is in reality like a blind beggar, destitute, clad in rags. The word translated "naked" can mean scantily clad.

Verse 18. **Buy from me gold refined by fire** does not, of course, suggest that one can actually buy spiritual blessings with money; this is metaphorical language. The prophet summoned the hungry and thirsty to buy wine and milk without money and without price (Isa. 55:1). Jesus represented the Kingdom of Heaven as a treasure buried in a field which a man acquired by purchase; and as a pearl of great price which a merchant bought with money (Matt. 13:44-45). These are parabolic ways of describing the inestimable value of the blessings of the Kingdom of Heaven. In the present verse, Christ exhorts the church to secure for herself the true riches — gold refined by fire which will not tarnish.

White garments to clothe you. The church is summoned to cover her nakedness with garments of purity and sincerity.

Salve to anoint your eyes, that you may see. This appeal gains its relevance from the fact that Laodicea was noted for her medical college and for the "Phrygian powder" used to make eye-salve. Phrygian physicians might aid men in their physical blindness; only Christ can heal the eyes of those who are spiritually blind.

The balanced construction between verses 17 and 18 is obvious: Christ summons the church to obtain gold for her poverty, white garments for her nakedness, and eye-salve for her blindness.

Verse 19. **Those whom I love, I reprove and chasten.** The strong language with which Christ has described the sad plight of the Laodiceans does not mean that he loved them any less than others. His attitude toward the church was not punitive but disciplinary and corrective. "For the Lord disciplines him whom he loves, and chastises every son whom he receives" (Heb. 12:6).

So be zealous and repent. Although the threat of spewing these nauseously lukewarm Christians out of the mouth (vs. 16) sounds like a final judgment, this appeal shows that there is still hope. If the Laodiceans will anoint their eyes with the eye-salve Christ provides and are thereby enabled to recognize their blind, impoverished state, it will not be too late to replace complacency with zeal, and thereby repent.

Verse 20. **Behold I stand at the door and knock.** The meaning of these words is vigorously debated. Many interpreters feel that they are eschatological and point to the promise of the imminent return of the Lord. It is true that the metaphor of Christ standing at the door is a familiar eschatological concept (Mark 13:29; Matt. 24:33; Luke 12:36; Jas. 5:9). It is also true that the idea of a messianic banquet is often used as a symbol of fellowship in the Kingdom of God (Luke 14:15; 22:29ff.; Matt. 8:11; 22:1-4; 26:29; Rev. 19:9). However, the present context is different. In the passages cited above, Christ gathers his people into the blessing of the messianic Kingdom; here, the context is one of summons to repentance. Therefore, the interpretation is preferable which sees Christ summoning the members of a lifeless, complacent church to spiritual life. Even though the church is in a sad and deplorable state, Christ still stands at the door of the heart of each individual seeking admission. The repentance of verse 19 is implemented by the admission of Christ into the life.

If any one hears my voice and opens the door. Although they bear the name of Christian and formally constitute a Christian congregation, the Laodiceans are in fact spiritually naked and poor and blind, and like any new convert, must respond to the appeal of Christ and open the life to his incoming.

I will come in to him and eat with him and he with me. This promise was given by Christ: "If a man loves me . . . we

will come to him and make our home with him" (John 14:23).
A shared meal in the ancient Jewish world had far more
significance than it has today. It was a symbol of affection, of
confidence, of intimacy. Jesus was criticized by the Pharisees
not merely for associating with publicans and sinners but for
eating with them (Luke 15:2). Peter was criticized by the Jerusalem Christians not for preaching the gospel to a gentile
but for eating with him (Acts 11:3). So the present verse contains a promise of the most intimate fellowship possible.

Verse 21. To the conqueror, Jesus promises that he will
**sit with me on my throne, as I myself conquered and sat down
with my Father on his throne.** This is obviously metaphorical
language describing the ultimate victory of the saints. In
John's first vision, Christ is pictured as standing in the midst
of the lampstands (1:13). In the vision of the heavenly throne
room, he is pictured as a lamb standing before the throne of
God (5:6). Here the victory of Christ is pictured as an enthronement with his Father upon his Father's throne. Usually,
the New Testament speaks of the enthronement of Christ at
the right hand of the Father (Acts 2:34; Rom. 8:34; Eph.
1:20; Col. 3:1; Heb. 1:3; 8:1; 10:12; 12:2; I Pet. 3:22). The
right hand is the position of highest honor. No significance is
to be drawn from the distinction between the enthronement
at the right hand of God and the sharing of the throne of God
itself in the present verse; both involve the same theological
idea. The important fact is that Christ is already enthroned.
His messianic reign is not something which begins at his
parousia; it has already begun, even though it is visible only
to the eye of faith. This is what Peter meant when he announced after the resurrection the ascension of Christ: "God
has made him both Lord and Christ, this Jesus whom you
crucified" (Acts 2:36). Lord and Christ (Messiah) are synonymous terms carrying the same theological content. Because
of his obedience in suffering and death, God has bestowed
upon him the name that is above every name — Lord (Phil.
2:9-11). To be sure, the world does not recognize his lordship
and his heavenly reign, and demonic powers are still allowed
to work through pagan rulers to bring fearful affliction and
persecution to God's people. Here is a message for every church
which faces persecution: the assurance that their evil plight

is only temporary; that even though human experience may seem to contradict it, Christ is already enthroned as Lord and King; and that his kingly rule will soon put all his enemies under his feet (I Cor. 15:25).

The conqueror is assured that he will have a share in this reign in the eschatological consummation. Just how this is to be fulfilled is not altogether clear but probably during the millennium (see note on 2:26). However, the promise is not limited to the millennium, for in the new order of the age to come "they shall reign forever and ever" (22:5).

There is no need to restrict the promise to martyrs as some interpreters do. The promise in each of the seven letters to the conqueror is addressed to all disciples of Christ, with the expectation that all faithful disciples will overcome.

CHAPTER FOUR

THE HEAVENLY THRONE

III. THE SECOND VISION (4:1 — 16:21).

1. THE HEAVENLY THRONE (4:1-11).

After the first vision of the exalted Christ caring for and protecting his churches, the revelation of "what must take place after this," i.e., the coming of God's Kingdom, begins. This revelation will include the destruction of the powers of evil, of Satan, and of death; but before these evil powers are destroyed, they will break forth in a final desperate effort to frustrate the purposes of God by destroying the people of God. However, the terrible conflict that takes place on earth between the church and the demonic powers embodied in an apostate civilization — Rome in the first century and Antichrist at the end — are in reality expressions in historical form of a fearful conflict in the spiritual world between the Kingdom of God and the kingdom of Satan. Therefore, the Revelation proper begins with the ultimate and eternal fact of God enthroned and ruling in his universe. However fearful or uncontrolled the forces of evil on earth may seem to be, they cannot annul or eclipse the greater fact that behind the scenes God is on his throne governing the universe.

Verse 1. John saw in heaven a **door** standing **open,** not that he might be able to look into heaven, but that he might pass in ecstatic state from earth to heaven, there to behold its wonders. Other doors have already been mentioned in our book

which must not be confused with this door: the door of the
Kingdom (3:8), the door of the heart (3:20). This is the door
of revelation. That this is metaphorical language designed to
show what John saw in an ecstatic state is suggested by the
fact that he had already in vision been in heaven where he
beheld the glorified, exalted Christ walking in the midst of
the golden lampstands without any mention having been
made of heavenly doors. The metaphorical, picturesque character of the language is further suggested by the great fluidity
with which the scene changes throughout the Revelation from
heaven to earth. John is caught up in vision to heaven at 4:1
and remains there until the end of chapter nine. In chapter
ten he has returned to earth, for he sees an angel "coming
down from heaven" (10:1), and he remains on earth until
11:13; but in 11:15-19, the scene of the vision is again in
heaven. In chapter twelve the Seer seems to be on earth again,
but 14:18-20 imply his presence in heaven. It is not always
possible to follow the Seer's movements, but the frequent
change of scene makes it evident that this is not important
but is only incidental to the substance of the visions which
John sees, for in a trance-like state, one can move without
difficulty from earth to heaven.

Verse 2. John heard the voice which had already spoken
to him (1:10), summoning him to **come up hither** to receive
further revelations of future events. At once he **was in the
Spirit;** that is, he entered into a trance. This is a bit difficult,
for John had already experienced a trance (1:10) in which
he had beheld the vision of the glorified Christ, and no hint
is given that he had returned to his normal senses. We must
conclude either that this had happened, even though it is not
indicated; or else the words suggest an even more exalted
state than the first. It is possible that the visions in the Revelation were not all received at one and the same time but that
the book embodies the written record of a group of visions
received on Patmos on different occasions.

One school of interpretation finds in the language of this
verse the rapture of the church. John represents all Christians;
the trumpet voice is that which is to be heard at the parousia
(I Thess. 4:16); and the rapture of John stands for the rapture of all Christians at the end of the age. According to this

71

view, the time of the great tribulation when God's people are persecuted by the Antichrist has nothing to do with the church but is the time of "Jacob's trouble" (Jer. 30:7), that is, the Jewish people with whom God is to revive his dealings in the last days. Support of this position is sought in the fact that the word "church" occurs twenty times in the first three chapters but not once after chapter four until 22:17. Further support is sought in the identification of the twenty-four elders (4:4) with the raptured, rewarded church. The older dispensational literature spoke quite dogmatically of the rapture of the church at this place; one of the most recent commentaries admits that this truth is not explicitly taught, but insists that it may nevertheless be assumed.[1] However, the entire question of a so-called pretribulation rapture is an assumption which does not command the support of explicit exegesis of the New Testament.[2] There is no reference in 4:1 to the rapture of the church; the language is addressed exclusively to John and refers only to his reception of the revelations of the book.

Verse 3. John was granted a vision of God seated upon his **throne.** Sometimes the Scriptures speak of God as making heaven itself his throne (Isa. 66:1; Matt. 5:34; 23:22); sometimes, as here, his throne is located in the heavens. Solomon realized that heaven could not really contain God (I Kings 8:27).

The throne itself is not described, neither is the person of the one sitting upon it. When John looked to the throne, what he saw can only be described in terms of the brilliance of precious stones. Every trace of anthropomorphism has been cast off. Daniel pictured God as one ancient of days whose raiment was white as snow and the hair of whose head like pure wool (Dan. 7:9). John saw a brilliance like **jasper,** supposed to be a transparent crystal-like stone, and **carnelian,** a fiery red stone. The throne with its brilliance was surrounded by a **rainbow** which, instead of containing the colors of the prism, was **emerald** green. The word translated "rainbow" can mean either a partial arc or a complete circle like

[1]John F. Walvoord, *The Revelation of Jesus Christ* (Chicago: Moody, 1966), p. 103.

[2]See George E. Ladd, *The Blessed Hope* (Grand Rapids: Eerdmans, 1956).

a solar halo. No indication is given as to the relationship of the rainbow to the throne — whether it encircled the throne vertically or horizontally.

It is doubtful if any special symbolic meaning is intended by the choice of these three stones. They are sometimes associated together in classical literature. They were placed in different positions on the high priest's breastplate (Exod. 28:17ff.); they are third, sixth, and fourth in the twelve foundation stones of the Holy City (Rev. 21:19). Some take the crystal jasper to represent God's holiness, the fiery red carnelian to represent the consuming fire of his judgment, the emerald green to represent his mercy. While this may be a possible application, there is no hint that such ideas were in John's mind. Rather, we are reminded that different manifestations of light are often used in the Bible to represent the presence and the glory of God. Israel was led by a pillar of fire at night; the presence of God in the Holy of Holies was represented by the shekinah glory. We can only conclude that the majesty of what John beheld was so great and ineffable that he despaired of trying to describe it in any but symbolic terms. It is possible that the rainbow is meant as an allusion to the bow given to Noah as a promise of mercy that God would never again let his judgment fall upon the entire race. As such it may be taken as a sign of patience of the ruler of the world toward sinful men until the last judgment falls upon the whole world. This is a possible inference, but we cannot say with any certainty that this meaning is actually intended.

Verse 4. **Round the throne were twenty-four thrones, and seated on the thrones were twenty-four elders, clad in white garments, with golden crowns upon their heads.** Their function was to fall down before the throne and worship him who sits on it, to cast their crowns before the throne, and to adore the Creator (4:10). These twenty-four elders have been very diversely understood. One of the oldest interpretations is that they represent the ideal church in heaven in anticipation of the final state. The number twenty-four is said to represent the twelve patriarchs and the twelve apostles — the church of both the Old and the New Testaments. This is an ideal picture realized potentially in the resurrection and ascension of

Christ (Eph. 2:6). The reality awaits the return of the Lord and the day of the resurrection.

Another view is that we have a representation of the church which was raptured with John's response to the call to John in 4:1, "Come up hither." The church is seen in the white robes of Christ's righteousness, wearing the victors' crowns (II Tim. 4:8), and rewarded for their works (I Cor. 3:14) by being seated on the thrones. However, there is nothing in the context which suggests that the elders represent the church, either ideal or raptured, and some features tell against such an identification. They stand in close proximity to the four living creatures; in fact, the four creatures are closer to the throne than the elders. In 5:8, they join together with the four creatures in worship of the Lamb and offer bowls of incense, which are the prayers of the saints. This same function is performed by one who is explicitly designated an angel in 8:3. In other words, they perform some kind of mediating function of expediting the prayers of the saints to the throne of God. Again, one of the elders performs an angelic function in 7:13-14 which is not suitable for the redeemed, and John addresses him with a title of respect, "Sir," which is inappropriate of a fellow believer.

Support for the identification of the elders with the raptured church is sought in the AV rendering of 5:9, where the elders sing a new song to the Lamb who "hast redeemed us to God by thy blood out of every kindred, and tongue, and people, and nation; and hast made us unto our God kings and priests: and we shall reign on the earth." In this form of the song, the elders appear to be the church, for they are identified as those redeemed by the blood of the Lamb who are to share Christ's millennial reign.

If this were a correct reading, the reasoning would be sound; but this is another of the numerous instances in the Revelation where the Greek text behind the old King James Version is defective. Practically all modern English translations recognize the correct form of the Greek: "For thou . . . by thy blood didst ransom men for God from every tribe and tongue and people and nation, and hast made them a kingdom and priests to our God, and they shall reign on earth." Far from supporting the identification between the elders and the church, this song of the elders clearly sets them apart from the redeemed. The elders themselves are not the redeemed, but they sing of those who are redeemed. Again, in 14:3, the elders are set over against those who have been purchased out of the earth who sing a new song which the elders cannot learn.

There is no difficulty in understanding the twenty-four elders as a body of angels who help execute the divine rule in the universe. White clothing is the garb of angels (John 20:12; Matt. 28:3; Acts 1:10; Mark 16:5). Paul refers to certain ranks of angels as thrones, principalities, rulers (Col. 1:16; Rom. 8:38; Eph. 3:10). In the Old Testament, God is sometimes pictured surrounded by a council of heavenly beings. "God (is) feared in the council of the holy ones, great and terrible above all that are about him" (Ps. 89:7). God will reign on Mount Zion, "and before his elders he will manifest his glory" (Isa. 24:23). Micaiah "saw the Lord sitting on his throne, and all the hosts of heaven standing beside him on his right hand and on his left" (I Kings 22:19). So we may conclude that the twenty-four elders are a company of angels who serve as a sort of heavenly counterpart to the elders in Israel (Exod. 24:11), who are pictured as helping to execute the divine rule.[3] They worship God because he is about to bring history to its goal, judge the dead, and reward "thy servants, the prophets and the saints" (11:16). Possibly the number twenty-four is derived from the fact that there were twenty-four priestly orders in the Old Testament. However, the elders appear to carry out no distinctive priestly functions. Their song praises God both for creation (4:11) and for the redemption of men (5:9). The number twenty-four is not used in the Revelation in any other connection.

This interpretation is supported by the vision in 7:9-11. First we have a great multitude of the saved which no man can number; then the various concentric ranks of heavenly beings round about the throne: first the angels, then the elders, and finally the four living creatures. See also a similar order of the heavenly beings in 19:1-4. The elders are grouped with other angelic beings in distinction to the redeemed.

[3]For an extended discussion of this problem, see N. B. Stonehouse, *Paul Before the Areopagus* (Grand Rapids: Eerdmans, 1957), chap. IV.

Verse 5. The majesty and glory of the divine presence are enhanced by **flashes of lightning, and voices and peals of thunder.** These are common manifestations of the divine presence in the Old Testament (Exod. 19:16; Ezek. 1:13), symbolizing the divine power and glory (Ps. 18:13-15; Job 37:2-5).

The presence of the Holy Spirit is represented by **seven torches of fire** which burn **before the throne.** We have already met the symbolism of seven to denote the fullness of God's Spirit (1:4). Here, the Holy Spirit is mentioned probably not so much with reference to his regenerative and sanctifying work as to his work in the creation and preservation of the natural world (Gen. 1:2; 2:7; Ps. 104:29f.).

Verse 6a. **Before the throne there is as it were a sea of glass, like crystal.** Here is the language of simile: the sea before the throne was not made of glass, but is something like glass. The background of the picture is found in the Old Testament. In the vision of God granted to the elders of Israel, "there was under his feet as it were a pavement of sapphire stone, like the very heaven for clearness" (Exod. 24:10). In Ezekiel's vision, "Over the heads of the living creatures there was the likeness of a firmament, shining like crystal, spread out over their heads.... And above the firmament over their heads there was the likeness of a throne" (Ezek. 1:22, 26). Before Solomon's temple stood a brazen sea (I Kings 7:23).

This glass sea is mentioned only once more in the Revelation. John saw the likeness of a sea of glass mingled with fire, with the victorious martyrs standing beside the sea of glass bearing their tokens of victory, singing the song of Moses and the song of the Lamb (15:2-3).

The significance of this glass sea has been diversely interpreted; no clear hint as to its symbolic meaning is given in our book. Some see it as a symbol of the distance that separates God in his holiness from the fallen evil world — the majestic repose and eternal purity of the divine world. Some place the emphasis on its transparency and find a symbol of God's omniscient vision of all that happens in the world; nothing hinders God's gaze from penetrating to the depths. A recent commentator understands it very differently. Since the final redeemed order of the new heaven and the new earth will have no more sea (Rev. 21:1), the sea belongs to the old fallen order and represents, like the experience of Israel at the Red Sea, the barrier which the redeemed must pass through in the new exodus from earthly experience to the redeemed world of God. The glass sea stands before the throne as a mute reminder that the whole creation is affected by the taint of evil.[4]

The easiest interpretation is to see in the glass sea a picturesque element adding to the majesty of the divine presence.

Verses 6b-8. **And round the throne, on each side of the throne, are four living creatures, full of eyes in front and behind: the first . . . like a lion, the second . . . like an ox, the third . . . with the face of a man, the fourth . . . like a flying eagle.** Each of the four living creatures had six wings and was full of eyes all round and within. It is quite clear that these four living creatures are analogous to the seraphim of Isa. 6:1-3 and the cherubim of Ezek. 10:14. Their form is closer to Ezekiel's cherubim, each of which had four faces — those of a man, a lion, an ox, and an eagle — and four wings, whereas John's living creatures each have a single head and six wings. Isaiah's seraphim had six wings each. The fullness of eyes represents ceaseless vigilance and unlimited intelligence, and the wings suggest swiftness of movement. It seems quite likely that the four different heads are intended to represent different aspects of nature: the wild beasts, domesticated animals, human beings and flying creatures. This in turn may be interpreted in two different ways. Either the cherubim represent the praise and adoration extended to the Creator by the totality of his creation; or else they represent angelic beings who are used by the Creator in executing his rule and his divine will in all the orders of his creation. They are created spirits who are thought of as mediating the divine energy and power in all the world. The fact that they sing a song of adoration,

> **Holy, holy, holy, is the Lord God Almighty,**
> **who was and is and is to come!**

suggests that both interpretations may be correct.

From early times, these four creatures have been thought

[4]See G. B. Caird, *The Revelation of St. John The Divine* (New York: Harper and Row, 1966), pp. 65ff.

to represent the four gospels. Irenaeus (second century) thought that the lion represented John, the ox Luke, the man Matthew, and the eagle Mark. Victorinus (third century), followed by the great Jerome (fourth century), changed the order. The lion was Matthew, the man Mark, the ox Luke, and the eagle John. Such interpretations are interesting but entirely without foundation or support in the text.

The relationship of the creatures to the throne is not altogether clear. The text reads, literally, "in the midst of the throne and around the throne." It is not clear whether the four creatures stood under the throne supporting it, like Ezekiel's cherubim (Ezek. 1:22), or whether they stood in the midst of each of the four sides.

They join in exalting the holiness of God, as do Isaiah's seraphim (Isa. 6:3). That they worship God not only as the eternally existing one, who was and is, but also as the coming one suggests the longing of creation for deliverance from the bondage to decay to share the glorious liberty of the children of God (Rom. 8:21; cf. Rev. 21:1).

Verses 9-11. The four cherubim and the twenty-four elders join in worship and adoration of the Creator, but there is a slight difference in their songs. The cherubim praise God for his essential nature as the eternal one — "who was and is and is to come" — while the twenty-four elders praise him for the glory of his created works:

for thou didst create all things,
and by thy will they existed and were created.

The last clause is rather difficult, for it seems to suggest that all things existed before they were created. It may designate two different things not related in any sequence or order: the being vs. the non-being of all things, i.e., the simple fact of their being, and then the fact of their creation. Another way of solving the problem is to interpret "they existed" to mean "they existed in the mind and will of God, and therefore were actually created." Another solution is to interpret the connective as what is called an epexegetic construction: i.e., a connective of two corollaries. "And by thy will they existed, yea, they were created." In any case, the song asserts that behind all creation is the active sovereign will of the Creator.

CHAPTER FIVE

THE SEALED BOOK

2. THE SEVEN SEALS (5:1 — 8:1).

(1) The Sealed Book (5:1-14).

Verse 1. **And I saw in the right hand of him who was seated on the throne a scroll written within and on the back, sealed with seven seals.** While the RSV renders the word *biblion* by "a scroll," there is disagreement among scholars as to the form of the book. The most common form of ancient books, whether papyrus or leather, was that of a scroll. Pieces of fragile papyrus about ten inches wide were pasted together making a long strip of material. Ordinarily writing was confined to the inside of the scroll. The leaf form of books came into use in the second century. A minority of commentators have argued that this book was a leaf book, the seven seals binding together groups of leaves. In this way, as each seal was broken, a part of the book could be read. A major difficulty with this view is that if this is the case, the entire contents of the book should be exhausted with the breaking of the seven seals, whereas in fact the breaking of the seals seems to be only preparatory to the opening of the book.

The most natural way to understand the book is in accordance with the RSV translation. It is a scroll, sealed along the outside edge with seven seals of wax. This is important for a correct interpretation of the nature of the book. It is significant that the breaking of the seals is accompanied by

79

plagues in history of a general kind: war, famine, pestilence, and martyrdom (the first seal is not so self-evident as to its meaning), and the sixth seal introduces the end itself. The seventh seal has no specific content like the first six; in fact, we must conclude that the seven trumpets constitute the content of the seventh seal. This leads to the suggestion that the breaking of the seven seals and the following events do not constitute the contents of the scroll but are preliminary and preparatory to the actual opening of the scroll. This corresponds to the view that the scroll is sealed on its outside edge with seven seals, and that the scroll itself is not opened and its contents disclosed until all seven seals have been broken.

There are several interpretations of the scroll itself. Many interpreters appeal to the fact that in the Roman world seven seals was the usual way of attesting the validity of a last will and testament. A will was witnessed by seven witnesses and seven seals were attached to the seven threads that secured the testament. In life, the execution of a will assumed the death of the testator; and while God does not die, early Christian faith made much of the idea of the inheritance which believers enjoyed and which was grounded on the death of God's son (Heb. 9:15ff.). Viewed in this way, the scroll is the symbol of the promise of the Kingdom of God which God's people are to inherit. This irrevocable disposition of God occurred long ago, has been documented and sealed, but not yet executed (I Pet. 1:4). The contents of this inheritance have been proclaimed through the prophets, through Jesus and the Holy Spirit in the early church, and are to a certain extent known. However, the full realization of this inheritance is future, when the returning Christ opens the testament and executes it.

This view is attractive, but it faces a major difficulty; namely, that the seals as well as the trumpets do not have to do with the Christians' inheritance but with the plagues of judgment which God will pour out upon a rebellious civilization. An adequate interpretation of the scroll must make room for the inclusion of God's judgmental acts as well as the positive aspect of the inheritance bestowed upon the saints.

A second view identifies the scroll as the Lamb's book of life which appears several times in the Revelation (3:5; 13:8;

17:8; 20:12, 15; 21:27). The fullness of the writing contained in the book points to the multitude of names included in it (Rev. 7:9). The breaking of the seals indicates the disclosure of the names of the redeemed. This view is difficult, for it does not correspond with the events which accompany the breaking of the seals, and there seems to be no reason in the context for introducing the book of life at this place.

A third view which goes back to ancient times is that the scroll is the Old Testament viewed as fulfilled in the New Testament. Jesus went into the synagogue at Nazareth and after reading from the scroll of Isaiah, he announced, "Today this scripture has been fulfilled in your hearing" (Luke 4:21). Thus Christ is the one who is able to bring the entire volume of the Old Testament prophetic hope to its divinely ordained fulfillment.

The clue to the meaning of the book is found in the experience of Ezekiel, who in preparation for his prophetic ministry to Israel was given a written scroll, which, like John's scroll, was full of writing on both sides. Ezekiel's scroll contained "words of lament and mourning and woe" (Ezek. 2:10). He was then told to take the scroll and eat it, and thus he would be able to prophesy to Israel (Ezek. 2:1-10).

The easiest identification of John's scroll is that it contains the prophecy of the end events, including both the salvation of God's people and the judgment of the wicked. It is God's redemptive plan for the denouement of human history, the overthrow of evil, and the gathering of a redeemed people to enjoy the blessings of God's rule. Although John, surprisingly, does not describe the actual opening of the scroll, the breaking of the sixth seal brings us to the end of the world — the last day; and in view of the fact that the opening of the seventh seal is accompanied by no specific event like the first six, we may conclude that the contents of the scroll consist of the material in Revelation 7:1 — 22:21. The events accompanying the breaking of the seals are not the end itself, but the events leading up to the end, while the contents of the scroll are that complex of events, both redemptive and judicial, which will accompany the end of this world and the introduction of the world to come.

The details mentioned in connection with the scroll are all-important. The scroll, like Ezekiel's scroll, was "written within and on the back." This was not a common practice in the ancient world but was sometimes done; such a book was called an opisthograph. This represents the fullness of the divine foreknowledge and counsels. History will not end until the purposes of God have come to their full consummation; when God's purposes are complete, the end will come.

Verses 2-3. The fact that the book was sealed with seven seals is not insignificant. Seven in John is the number of completeness. The scroll is completely sealed and its contents hidden from every human eye. **No one in heaven or on earth or under the earth was able to open the scroll or to look into it.** Here is a simple but profound biblical truth which cannot be overemphasized: apart from the person and redeeming work of Jesus Christ, history is an enigma. For centuries since Augustine and his *City of God,* a Christian view of history as having a divinely ordained goal which was inseparable from the redemptive word of Christ has colored western thought. Since the Enlightenment, many philosophers have rejected the Christian view of life, and for them history has become a problem. The evolutionary view of inevitable progress is hardly popular today. Some of our greatest minds have been prophets of doom who see nothing but darkness ahead. The problem of the meaning, purpose and goal of history has become one of the most disturbing and difficult questions of our time. The secularistic, pessimistic attitude even penetrates the thinking of Christian theologians, and one of them has written, "We cannot claim to know the end and goal of history. Therefore, the question of meaning in history has become meaningless."[1]

In the face of this modern dilemma, the fact that the scroll is so tightly sealed that no human eye can read its contents is highly significant. Christ, and Christ alone, has the key to the meaning of human history. It is therefore not surprising that modern thinkers are pessimistic; apart from the victorious return of Christ, history is going nowhere.

It is equally significant that the scroll rests "in the right hand of him who was seated upon the throne" (vs. 1). The whole story of human history rests in the hand of God. What

[1]Rudolf Bultmann, *History and Eschatology* (Edinburgh: University Press, 1957), p. 120.

simpler or more sublime way of picturing God's ultimate sovereignty over all history could be found than this picture of the scroll resting in the hand of God? However strong evil becomes, however fierce be the satanic evils that assail God's people on earth, history still rests in God's hand.

Verses 4-5. John's grief that no one was found worthy to open the book was tempered by the words of one of the elders: **weep not; lo, the Lion of the tribe of Judah, the Root of David, has conquered, so that he can open the scroll and its seven seals.** These two phrases pointing to the conquering Christ sum up the totality of the Old Testament messianic hope. "The Lion of the tribe of Judah" alludes to one of the first messianic prophecies in Genesis 49:9-10: "Judah is a lion's whelp; from the prey, my son, you have gone up. He stooped down, he couched as a lion, and as a lioness; who dares rouse him up? The scepter shall not depart from Judah, nor the ruler's staff from between his feet, until he comes to whom it belongs; and to him shall be the obedience of the peoples."

We know from contemporary Jewish literature that the figure of a lion was used to designate the conquering Messiah (*IV Ezra* 11:37; 12:31), even though the metaphor is not found elsewhere in the New Testament. The reference in Genesis is obviously not to a humble, suffering Messiah but to one who wields the sceptre as a ruling king.

"The Root of David" is an allusion to Isaiah 11:1: "There shall come forth a shoot from the stump of Jesse, and a branch shall grow out of his roots." The royal family of David, the son of Jesse, is likened to a tree which has fallen; but out from its roots springs forth a new tree to restore the kingly rule of David. The verses that follow (Isa. 11:2-9) give us one of the most vivid prophecies of the promised triumphant messianic King. "With righteousness he shall judge the poor, and decide with equity for the meek of the earth; he shall smite the earth with the rod of his mouth, and with the breath of his lips he shall slay the wicked" (vs. 4). This verse is a vivid summary of the Old Testament promise of a divinely endowed messianic King who will be so mightily equipped that he will destroy all evil, deliver God's people from their affliction by evil powers, both spiritual and political, and establish a new order on earth in which peace, righteousness,

and blessedness reign. The important thing to emphasize is
that the biblical hope is not one of spiritual salvation alone,
of the salvation of the individual from his guilt and his
sin. While individualistic salvation is included, the primary
emphasis is upon the salvation of the people of God as a
society dwelling on the earth and their deliverance from all
evils — spiritual, social, political, and physical. "They shall
not hurt or destroy in all my holy mountain [Jerusalem], for
the earth shall be full of the knowledge of the Lord as the
waters cover the sea. In that day the root of Jesse shall stand
as an ensign to the peoples; him shall the nations seek, and
his dwelling shall be glorious" (Isa. 11:9-10).

John is assured that this mighty Messiah has already won
a great victory. The King James Version renders this phrase
inadequately: "he hath prevailed." The Revised Standard
Version does better with the rendering, "he has conquered."
The verb literally says, "he has won a victory." Here is a great
mystery. In some way extending far beyond our understanding, the death of Christ on the cross was a victory over the
enemies of God's people. The New Testament puts greater
emphasis on the spiritual nature of God's enemies than does
the Old Testament, but the difference is one of emphasis, not
of kind. The great enemies of God's people are Satan, sin, and
death. Satan will not be finally destroyed until he is cast into
the lake of fire after the return of Christ; but by his incarnation, death, and resurrection, Christ has already defeated the
powers of Satan. He partook of human nature "that through
death he might destroy him who has the power of death, that
is, the devil, and deliver all those who through fear of death
were subject to lifelong bondage" (Heb. 2:14-15). This victory
over Satan, accomplished through the incarnation, is frequently alluded to in the New Testament, even in the gospels
(Matt. 12:29; Luke 10:18; John 12:31; 16:11). This victory is
not only over Satan but over the entire host of evil spiritual
powers. "He disarmed the principalities and powers, and made
a public example of them, triumphing over them in him"
(Col. 2:15).

In the same way, Christ's victory is a conquest over the
power of death. He has already "abolished death and brought
life and immortality to light through the gospel" (II Tim.

1:10). The New Testament teaches that because of his incarnation, death, resurrection, and ascension, Christ has won a victory by virtue of which he is already reigning at the right hand of God as messianic King. "When he had made purification for sins, he sat down at the right hand of the Majesty on high" (Heb. 1:3). Peter interpreted the ascension of Jesus with the words of David, "The Lord [God] said to my Lord [Messiah], 'Sit at my right hand, till I make thy enemies a stool for thy feet'" (Acts 2:34-35). *The future and final victory of Messiah is but an extension of the rule he now enjoys by virtue of the victory already won.* At the end he will destroy "every rule and every authority and power. For he must reign until he has put all his enemies under his feet. The last enemy to be destroyed is death" (I Cor. 15:25-26). The book of Revelation does not emphasize the present messianic reign of Christ as do other New Testament writers, but the basic elements of this theology are summed up in the single word, *he has won a victory.* It is also implicit in the description of Christ as the one who died but who is alive forevermore, who has the keys of Death and Hades (Rev. 1:18). It is also probable that the victory of Christ already won over Satan is pictured in the mighty drama of the war in heaven and the overthrow of the great dragon (Rev. 12:7-11).

Verse 6. When John turned to look at the Lion, he did not see a Lion, but **a Lamb standing, as though it had been slain.** The final victory of Christ as the Lion of the tribe of Judah — as the conquering Messiah — is possible only because he has first suffered as the Lamb.

Here is a great mystery, which the New Testament affirms but does not explain because it involves ineffable realities at the point where God's spiritual world intersects man's historical world. Christ's worthiness and ability to break the seals of the scroll of human history and destiny are dependent on the victory he won in his incarnate life. If he had not come in humility as suffering Savior, he could not come as conquering Messiah.

The significance of the lamb is a common one in the Old Testament. At the Passover, when God delivered Israel from Egypt, each family took a lamb and killed it in the evening, sprinkling the blood of the lamb on the doorposts and lintel of each house, and then eating the flesh of the roast carcass. That night, the Lord passed through the land of Egypt to slay the firstborn son in every household, except those who had been sprinkled with blood. "The blood shall be a sign for you, upon the houses where you are; and when I see the blood, I will pass over you, and no plague shall fall upon you to destroy you, when I smite the house of Egypt" (Exod. 12:13). The annual sacrifice of the Passover lamb together with the feast became the most important festival in Israel, recalling the time when God delivered his people from bondage and constituted them a nation.

The metaphor of a lamb is central in the great prophecy of the suffering servant in Isa. 53. Isaiah saw one who is humble and despised, who would be abused and maltreated, who would redeem his people by suffering, bearing their transgressions and their iniquities in his own person. His sufferings would lead him to the point of death. "He was oppressed, and he was afflicted, yet he opened not his mouth; like a lamb that is led to the slaughter, and like a sheep that before its shearers is dumb, so he opened not his mouth" (Isa. 53:7). He was cut off from the land of the living, he made his grave with the wicked, he made himself an offering for sin, he poured out his soul in death, and was numbered with the transgressors, bearing the sin of many and making intercession for the transgressors.

The Jews did not know what to do with this prophecy of the servant of God who suffered the fate of a slaughtered lamb. It could not be a prophecy of Messiah, for by definition, Messiah was to be a victorious, conquering king who would overthrow the powers of evil, not be crushed by them. There is no clear evidence that the suffering, lamblike servant was ever applied to Messiah in pre-Christian times by Judaism, for the role of the conquering, reigning King and that of the meek, rejected, suffering servant seem to be mutually exclusive. In this connection, it is important to note that Isaiah himself does not attribute these sufferings to the Messiah, but to the Servant of the Lord (Isa. 52:13; 50:10; 49:3, 5, 6).

The mission and ministry of Jesus disclosed something not previously understood, viz., that Messiah has a twofold role to fulfill. First, he must come in humility and meekness to suffer and die; then at the end of the age he must return in power and glory to put all his enemies under his feet. The fact that the reigning King must be first a crucified Savior was not made clear in the Old Testament. The prophecies of the conquering King of Isaiah 11, the reigning son of man of Daniel 7, and the suffering servant of Isaiah 53 all appear in the Old Testament, but in their Old Testament contexts, they are unrelated to each other and appear to be three independent prophecies. The fact that Messiah must be crucified was not only unforeseen by the Jews; it continued to be a stumbling block (I Cor. 1:23). However, it was the heart of the Christian faith. John's Gospel asserts that he is both the Messiah, King of Israel (John 1:49), and the Lamb of God who takes away the sin of the world (John 1:29). Jesus himself had asserted this fact after his resurrection. "Was it not necessary that the Christ [Messiah] should suffer these things and enter into his glory?" (Luke 24:26). Philip interpreted the prophecy of the suffering servant as referring to Jesus (Acts 8:32-35), and Peter spoke of the salvation wrought by the precious blood of Christ as that of a lamb without blemish or spot (I Pet. 1:19).

This central fact of New Testament theology is beautifully pictured by John's vision of the Lion, who is a slain Lamb. *Why* in the providence and purpose of God it must be that the Lion of the tribe of Judah can only win his final victory over his foes by first filling the role of the slain Lamb is not explained. In ordinary Christian thinking, we are primarily concerned with the cross as the place where Jesus bore our sins and accomplished atonement for sinners. John's emphasis is that only by virtue of Jesus' sacrifice as the Lamb of God can he fill the role of the messianic King and bring human history to its denouement in the Kingdom of God.

The Lamb had the appearance of having been slain; that is, with its throat cut as though it had been slaughtered. By this, John points to the sacrificial death of Christ, not primarily to his weakness and humility. Yet he is standing; he has been slain, but he still lives (cf. 1:18).

The **seven horns** represent the fullness of power which the Lamb possesses. A horn is a common symbol of strength in the Old Testament, occurring first in Deut. 33:17, and appearing frequently in the Psalms (Pss. 18:2; 112:9). The risen Jesus asserted, "All authority in heaven and on earth has been given to me" (Matt. 28:18).

The Lamb also has **seven eyes;** this denotes his fullness of vision, his omniscience. Background for this is Zech. 4:10, where the seven lamps in the prophet's vision "are the eyes of the Lord, which range through the whole earth." The seven eyes of the Lord are the seven eyes of the Lamb; they are also identified as the **seven spirits of God sent out into all the earth.** The eyes of the exalted Christ are like a flame of fire (1:14) and the seven spirits blaze like torches before the throne of God (4:5). In this symbolic way, John pictures the relationship between Christ and the Holy Spirit. In the earlier vision the symbol of the Spirit — seven torches of fire (4:5) — stand before the throne, thus picturing the relationship of the Spirit to God the Father. Here the seven spirits are sent out into all the earth on a worldwide mission. The nature of this mission is not explained, but we are reminded of similar sayings in the New Testament, particularly in the Gospel of John. The Spirit is the Spirit of the Son whom the Father has sent to dwell in the hearts of men (Gal. 4:6). The Father will send the Paraclete in Jesus' name to teach them all things (John 14:26). The Spirit is also sent by the exalted Jesus from the presence of the Father to bear witness to himself (John 15:26). In fact, Jesus said that the disciples would be better off with his Spirit with them than they had been with his incarnate presence (John 16:7). The inseparable relationship between the Son and the Spirit is seen in John 14:18 where Jesus describes the coming of the Spirit in terms of his own presence with the disciples: "I will come unto you" (John 14:18).

The position of the Lamb is a bit difficult to determine. He stood **between the throne and the four living creatures and among the elders.** The words literally are, "in the midst of the throne and of the four living creatures and in the midst of the elders." It is not clear whether this places the Lamb between the throne and the angelic beings surrounding it, as the RSV translates it, or whether it intends to place the Lamb in the midst of all, the centerpiece of the entire scene. Elsewhere the Lamb is spoken of as being "in the midst of the throne" (Rev. 7:17); and in the letter to Laodicea, the glorified Christ is seated with the Father on his throne (Rev. 3:21).

Verse 7. **He went and took the scroll from the right hand of him who was seated upon the throne.** This is John's way of picturing what he has stated at the beginning of the book: "The revelation of Jesus Christ, which God gave to him to show to his servants what must soon take place" (Rev. 1:1). It is the Father who imparted the revelation of the last things to the Son, who in turn will bring the end to pass.

Verse 8. When the Lamb took the sealed scroll, all heaven broke forth in a hymn of praise to the Lamb. Perhaps the order of the several angelic hosts is here important in helping to determine the identity of the twenty-four elders. They stand close to the four creatures, and are in turn surrounded by hosts of angels. This supports the view that the elders are angelic beings. Furthermore, no distinction is made between the four living creatures and the elders; they **fell down** together **before the Lamb** and apparently joined together in the song of praise to the Lamb.

Each holding a harp, and with golden bowls full of incense. It is not clear whether these words apply to both the elders and the living creatures, or to the elders alone. Most commentators limit them to the elders, but the wording suggests that both groups are included. A harp or lyre was the traditional instrument of worship and singing the Psalms (Pss. 33:2; 98:5; 147:7). On two other occasions, John refers to the lyre as the instrument of heavenly music (14:2; 15:2). Golden bowls (or saucers) full of incense are a symbol of the prayers of the saints (Ps. 141:2; Luke 1:10). Incense was used in Old Testament times and in the temple worship. An altar of incense stood before the inner veil, and fresh incense was offered daily to God. There is no evidence that incense was used in Christian worship in the first three centuries. In some way, angelic beings are thought of as assisting the prayers of the saints to rise to God. This is again pictured in 8:3, when an angel came to the golden altar upon which were the prayers of all the saints. The reference to **the prayers of the saints** at this point seems to be their prayers for the coming of the Kingdom. "Thy Kingdom come, thy will be done on earth as it is in heaven" is an age-long prayer of the church which is now about to be answered.

"Saints" is the most common term used by John to designate God's people (8:3, 4; 11:18; 13:7, 10; 14:12; 16:6; 17:6; 18:20, 24; 19:8; 20:9), and this is also one of the most common Pauline terms to designate Christians. According to the dispensational interpretation, the saints who are persecuted by the beast (13:7, 10), who are to be martyrs in the great tribulation (17:6), who are finally to be delivered by God (18:20), are not the church, but converted Israel. According to this view, the church has been raptured at the beginning of the tribulation. However, the limitation of "saints" to converted Jews is not a natural use of the word. In the present verse, "saints" appear to designate all of God's people on earth who have prayed for the coming of God's Kingdom; and the foremost among such saints must be believers who constitute the church. The natural meaning of the use of "saints" in 11:18 where the time has come "for the dead to be judged, for rewarding thy servants, the prophets and saints and those who fear thy name, both small and great" is the whole body of believers. The collocation of the two terms, "prophets and saints" (11:18; 16:6; 18:24), and especially of the terms "saints and apostles and prophets," is only meaningful when applied to the church, for Judaism did not have apostles. The Bride who is prepared for the wedding feast by adorning herself in fine linen, which is "the righteous deeds of the saints" (19:8), is surely the church.

Verse 9. **And they sang a new song.** This is an echo from the Old Testament worship where Israel is frequently exhorted to sing unto the Lord a new song (Pss. 33:3; 98:1; 144:9; 149:1). Originally the phrase denoted a fresh song of praise, not necessarily one quite different from those which had been previously sung. However, the phrase can also designate a special song composed for some great occasion. In Isa. 42:10, a new song is sung because "the former things have come to pass, and new things I now declare" (Isa. 42:9); that is, a new order is about to begin with a new cycle of blessings. So in the present instance, a new song is sung because the new redeemed order of God's Kingdom is about to be inaugurated. Revelation is characterized by new things: a new name for the redeemed (2:17; 3:12); the new Jerusalem (3:12; 21:2); new heavens and a new earth (21:1); all things made new (21:5).

The new song stands in contrast to the songs already mentioned by John which were sung in worship and adoration of God the Creator (5:8, 11). The new song is sung to the Lamb as redeemer, who is worthy to break the seals and open the scroll, i.e., establish God's Kingdom, because of his redeeming death. His worthiness is not based in particular on his deity, upon his relation to God, upon his incarnation, or his perfect human life, but upon his sacrificial death.

The Greek word translated **slain** is used of the death of Christ only in the Apocalypse (Rev. 5:6, 9, 12; 13:8) but is an echo of Isa. 53:7, where the same root is found: he was "led to the slaughter." The word is also used of the martyrdom of believers in Asia (6:9; 18:24).

Salvation is here pictured as a **ransom,** or purchase. This is a Pauline word (I Cor. 6:20; 7:23; Gal. 3:13; 4:5) and has as its background the possibility of a slave purchasing his freedom from bondage by a certain sum of money. This was accomplished by the deposit of the money in a certain temple under the fiction that the god of the temple purchased the slave from his human owner. The former owner received the money from the temple and the slave received his purchased freedom, although formally he remained the property of the god. Christ has purchased men **for God** "from the earth" (14:3) so that they become the possession of God and find release from the bondage of sin and death, evil and suffering that has plagued earthly existence. The cost of the purchase is Christ's **blood.** The Greek idiom employed can well be translated "at the cost of thy blood" (cf. 1:5).

The objects purchased are **men . . . from every tribe and tongue and people and nation.** Here John's vision extends beyond his own immediate horizon to include the entire world — peoples to whom the gospel had not yet reached. John sees in the mission of the church a worldwide fellowship extending far beyond the shores of the Mediterranean and the rule of the Caesars. The church must always remember its true ecumenical nature.

Verse 10. The result of Christ's ransom is a people who have been made a **kingdom and priests to our God,** who **shall reign on earth.** This is a repeated emphasis in the Revelation. It is one of the main keynotes at the beginning of the book: Christ "made us a kingdom, priests to his God and Father" (1:6). It is heard again at the consummation when Christ returns to raise the dead: "They shall be priests of God and of Christ, and they shall reign with him a thousand years" (20:6).

The idea of priesthood means full and immediate access into the presence of God for the purpose of praise and worship, and the idea of a kingdom means that the redeemed will not merely be God's people over whom he reigns; they will actually be granted the privilege of sharing his reign. Jesus promised that the meek would inherit the earth (Matt. 5:5), and Paul's message included the promise that the saints would one day reign (I Cor. 4:8).

A textual problem is involved in the Greek word translated as "shall reign," for it occurs in the manuscript tradition both as a present tense and as a future. The present tense is preferred by many textual critics. If so, it may refer to the fact that the church is already a kingdom in the sense that believers have been raised up to be seated in the heavenly places with Christ (Eph. 2:6). However, the spiritual ascension with Christ in the New Testament emphasizes the believers' present victory over sin and death rather than the idea of sharing Christ's lordship and heavenly reign. In light of the clear reference in 20:6, the RSV, followed by the NEB, appears to be correct in choosing the future tense, and viewing the kingly reign of the saints as belonging primarily to the consummation. It includes both the millennial kingdom (20:4) and the final redeemed order in the new heavens and new earth (22:5).

Another textual problem is important in this verse. The AV translates "thou hast redeemed us to God . . . and made us . . . kings and priests; and we shall reign on earth." The RSV renders the verbs in the third person. This is very important for determining the identity of the elders. If the King James Version is right, the elders are identified with the redeemed, but if the Revised Standard Version is right, the elders are sharply and clearly distinguished from the redeemed. In terms of our knowledge of the history of the text, there is hardly any question as to which reading is correct, for this is one of several places where the King James Version is clearly incorrect because it was based upon a late inferior Greek text. It is surprising to find any modern commentary still following the incorrect King James Version. The elders sing praise to the Lamb not for their own redemption but for the redemption of the church.

The particular significance of the song at this point is that

Christ by the shedding of his blood on the cross has brought into existence a new redeemed humanity; and therefore his redemptive work must include the breaking of the seals and the opening of the scroll, i.e., the establishment of the Kingdom of God that the redeemed may inherit the Kingdom promised to them. The coming of the eschatological Kingdom is an essential part of the redemptive work of Christ; what he did on the cross remains forever unfinished until the ransomed enter into their kingly reign with Christ and until faith is changed to sight when God comes to dwell in the midst of his people (21:3).

Verse 11. John then saw unnumbered hosts of angels adding their song of praise to that of the four living creatures and of the elders.

Verse 12. They extol the worthiness of the Lamb to receive **power and wealth and wisdom and might and honor and glory and blessing.** These seven attributes leave nothing wanting in the ascription of praise; all that belongs to God the Father also belongs to the Lamb because of his redemptive work.

Verse 13. Now all creation joins with the angelic hosts in praise and worship: **every creature in heaven and on earth and under the earth and in the sea, and all therein.** This is poetic language describing the universality of the redemption wrought by Christ and should not be taken to mean that all men and all spiritual beings, including the demonic hosts of evil, will be brought within the blessings of Christ's salvation. It is an expression of the fact that the lordship of Christ is to be universal, that "at the name of Jesus every knee should bow, in heaven and on earth and under the earth, and every tongue confess that Jesus Christ is Lord, to the glory of God the Father" (Phil. 2:10-11). Through Christ God has been pleased "to reconcile to himself all things, whether on earth or in heaven, making peace by the blood of his cross" (Col. 1:20). The worship and adoration of all creation is no more a song of personal redemption than is the song of the four living creatures and of the elders. It is an assurance that through Christ God will restore order and peace to his fallen universe.

The song of creation is addressed both to God the Father and to the Lamb, **to him who sits upon the throne and to the**

Lamb. We are reminded that the exalted Christ has sat down with his Father upon his throne (3:21). Here are the raw materials of a trinitarian theology. John, as a Jew, was an inflexible monotheist; there is and can be only one God. Yet the Father is God, and the Son shares equally the divine prerogatives and the worship and adoration which God alone can receive. It is because of this high Christology along with unswerving monotheism that the church later formulated its trinitarian theology: one God existing in three persons. John does not reflect upon it, nor offer any explanation for it. He simply records what he together with the early church experienced.

CHAPTER SIX

THE SIX SEALS

(2) The Six Seals (6:1-17).

The fifth chapter centered attention upon the sealed book of destiny in the hand of God, and stressed the truth, central in the Revelation, that only the Lamb, by virtue of his sacrificial death, is able to break the seals and open the book. John next relates what he saw in his vision: the actual breaking of the seals and—we may assume—the opening of the book. We have already indicated that the breaking of the seals does not represent stages in the opening of the book but is only preliminary to the actual opening. The book itself contains two things which complement each other: the establishment of the Kingdom of God and the gathering of his saints into his Kingdom; and the judgment of God upon the evil demonic powers which have oppressed his people. The book of destiny explains the bitter hatred and the violent hostility of the forces of evil against God's people and the sufferings the latter are to endure just before the end comes. However, God will judge these evil powers and finally destroy them. Before the final judgment falls, God will pour out a series of woes upon those who are seduced by these evil powers. These judgments will not only manifest the wrath of God against all evil and rebellion but will also have the merciful purpose of driving the wicked to their knees in repentance before final judgment falls and it is too late.

The breaking of the seven seals is preliminary to the actual opening of the book and the events of the end time. It pictures the forces that will be operative throughout history by which the redemptive and judicial purposes of God will be forwarded. They are not a part of the great tribulation itself, but are preparatory and preliminary to the great tribulation. This conclusion is reinforced by the fact that the breaking of the sixth seal clearly brings us to the threshold of the end; the five seals must precede it.

a. The First Seal (6:1-2).

Verse 1. John saw (in vision) the Lamb break the first seal, and he heard one of the four living creatures say, as with a voice of thunder, **Come.** Many copyists of the Greek manuscripts understood this to be a summons to John to come and behold the sequel to the breaking of the seal, and so they added the words, "and see." The AV follows this inaccurate rendering. However, the best Greek texts contain only the summons, "Come." The late variant is also found in verses 3, 5, 7.

A different interpretation is that the admonition "Come" is parallel to the same summons in 22:17, "The Spirit and the Bride say, 'Come.' And let him who hears say, 'Come.'" Thus interpreted, it is a repeated summons for Christ to come in power and victory. This view is based on the assumption that the four living creatures represent the powers of nature, which is yearning for the final redemption to be accomplished at the return of the Lord (Rom. 8:22), and so nature is represented as calling upon Christ to come. However, such a summons in this context of the breaking of the first four seals is difficult. The most natural understanding of the repeated summons, *"Come,"* is that the four living creatures call forth the four horsemen.

As the Lamb breaks each of the first four seals, four horses ride forth on the earth as instruments of the divine purpose: the first is white, the second red, the third black, and the fourth pale. The background for this symbolism is found in Zech. 6:1ff. where the prophet is given a vision of four chariots drawn by horses of different colors: red, black, white, and dappled gray. These four chariots ride out to the four winds to patrol the earth as instruments of God's wrath upon the enemies of his people.

Verse 2. The significance of the second, third, and fourth

horsemen is not in doubt. The second is war, the third is scarcity, the fourth is death in the form of pestilence and violence. The identity of the first horse with its rider is widely disputed. John saw a **white horse, and its rider had a bow; and a crown was given to him, and he went out conquering and to conquer.** Most interpreters insist that the first horseman must be understood consistently with the other three; and since the other three are evil powers of destruction and death by which God executes his judgment, the white horse must be similar in kind. Usually, this horse is said to be conquest in general, while the red horse is war in particular. Some feel that the clue to the interpretation is the rider's bow—an instrument of war in the ancient world for which the Parthians were particularly noted. The Parthians were a warlike people living in Asia southeast of the Caspian Sea in the region of what is today Iran. They were famous in war as horsemen for the swiftness of their mobility and their skill in the use of the bow and arrow. They had been subdued by the Persians and later by the Greek kings (Seleucidae) of Syria; but about 250 B.C., they revolted from the Seleucids and throughout New Testament times they stood threateningly just outside the boundary of the Roman Empire to the east as one of Rome's most dangerous foes. The crown worn by the rider is thought to be a symbol of conquest; the horseman rides forth triumphantly as a conqueror to win ever fresh conquests.

One of the main difficulties with this interpretation is that it does not do justice to the *white* garb of the rider and the *white* horse on which he rides; and in the identification of the other three horsemen the color is of great significance. In a Roman triumphal procession, the victorious general did not ride a white horse, but was generally seated in a four-horse car.

Other interpreters have pointed to the obvious similarity between this horse and rider and the vision of the conquering Christ in 19:1-11. Christ there rides a white horse, and he wears on his head many diadems. However, a representation of the victorious coming of Christ is out of place in this context, and it is furthermore difficult to conceive of Christ returning in summons to the call of one of the four living creatures.

The color white may be taken, however, as the clue to the identity of the first horseman, for in the Revelation, white is always a symbol of Christ, or of something associated with Christ, or of spiritual victory. Thus the exalted Christ has white hair white as wool (1:14); the faithful will receive a white stone with a new name written on it (2:17); they are to wear white garments (3:4, 5, 18); the twenty-four elders are clad in white (4:4); the martyrs are given white robes (6:11) as is the great numberless throng (7:9, 13); the son of man is seen on a white cloud (14:14); he returns on a white horse accompanied by the armies of heaven who are clad in white and ride white horses (19:11, 14); in the final judgment, God is seen seated on a white throne (20:11). In view of this extensive evidence, we may look for some interpretation of the white horse that connects it with something associated with Christ and the spiritual life. This is further supported by the fact that, unlike the second to the fourth seals, the first has no woe connected with it.

A further clue to the meaning of the seals may be found outside the Revelation. Many commentators have pointed out that there is a similarity between the structure of the seven seals and the Olivet Discourse in Mark 13 and Matthew 24. Mark 13:5-13 describes what are called "the beginning of sufferings," or better, "the beginning of woes." The Kingdom of God will not be established at once, but the future will be a period of wars and rumors of wars, conflict, earthquakes, and persecutions even to the point of death. Matthew adds that there will also be famines (Matt. 24:7). These preliminary evils, which characterize the "beginning of woes," are to be followed by a short time of great tribulation (Mark 13:19) such as the world has never seen, when the "abomination of desolation" (AV), the "desolating sacrilege" (RSV)—the Antichrist—will terribly afflict the people of God. After this will occur the coming of Christ and the gathering of the saints into the Kingdom of God.

The same basic structure of thought appears in the Olivet Discourse and in the Revelation: a time of preliminary troubles marked by evils in human society and in nature (the seven seals), followed by a short but terrible time of great tribulation (the seven trumpets and bowls, and the beast). There is, however, in the preliminary evil period one positive note, somewhat differently reported by Mark and Matthew: "and the gospel must first be preached to all nations" (Mark 13:10); "and this gospel of the kingdom will be preached throughout the whole world, as a testimony to all nations; and then the end will come" (Matt. 24:14). The course of the age is not to be one of unrelieved evil when God's people are surrendered helplessly and passively into the hands of hostile powers. While the Kingdom of God will not be established until the return of the Son of man, the age will be one of tension: tension between evils which characterize history and afflict particularly the followers of Jesus, and the active and aggressive proclamation of the gospel of the kingdom by those same disciples.

This truth is well portrayed by John in the vision of the white horse. The rider is not Christ himself but symbolizes the proclamation of the gospel of Christ in all the world. The details with which the first horseman is described do not weaken this conclusion. A bow is often used in Scripture as a symbol of divine victories. "Thou didst strip the sheath from the bow, and put arrows to the string. . . . Thou didst bestride the earth in fury, thou didst trample the nations in anger. Thou wentest forth for the salvation of thy people, for the salvation of thy anointed" (Hab. 3:9, 13; see also Isa. 41:2; 49:2-3; Zech. 9:13; Ps. 45:4-5). The crown is a symbol whose meaning is expressed in the words "he went out conquering and to conquer." This does not necessarily mean complete and utter conquest, but it does mean that the proclamation of the gospel will win its victories. It will be preached effectively in all the world; and in spite of an evil and hostile environment characterized by human hatred, strife, and opposition, the gospel will make its way victoriously in all the world.

Here is a word of confidence, combined with a realistic note, for the church of the first century and every other age. How can any people be devoted to a cause which they believe will experience only defeat? The first generation of believers suffered, and at the hands of some of the later emperors they met determined efforts to root them out and to destroy them completely. But in spite of every form of opposition, the church effectively and victoriously established the gospel in all the Roman world until the Empire ceased its violent opposition. We do not look for the coming of God's Kingdom and the righting of the world's evils short of the return of Christ; but we are, as the modern bearers of the gospel of the kingdom, expectant of seeing victories won by the power of this gospel.

b. The Second Seal (6:3-4).

Verses 3-4. After the breaking of the second seal, one of the living creatures summoned forth a **red** horse whose rider **was permitted to take peace from the earth,** and **he was given a great sword.** This is obviously a symbol of warfare and bloodshed. The time when John lived, the late first century, was not a time particularly characterized by warfare. In fact, the might of the Roman armies had crushed effective resistance so that peace reigned from Armenia to Spain. The great Pax Romana gave to the Mediterranean world several centuries of peace which the western world has never since experienced. However, it was a peace based on force, and the might of Rome was everywhere represented by the presence of her legions. In principle, warfare and conquest were the dominant policy and will remain so until the return of the Lord.

c. The Third Seal (6:5-6).

Verse 5. The **black horse** with its rider carrying a **balance** or a pair of scales in his hand represents scarcity. The balance was used for the purpose of measuring out grain.

Verse 6. John heard a voice which reflected conditions of great scarcity if not actual famine: **a quart of wheat for a denarius, and three quarts of barley for a denarius.** A denarius was a silver coin worth about sixteen cents, but it was the average day's pay of a working man. Grain was the main food in the ancient world, and barley was the food of poor people because it was less expensive than wheat. A quart of wheat was the average daily consumption of a man. This pictures a situation where scarcity prevails, when it would take all that a man could earn — a denarius — to buy enough of the cheapest food for a small family. In ordinary times, a denarius would purchase twelve to fifteen times as much food.

The voice added, **do not harm oil and wine.** Many commentators understand this to mean that the luxury foods, oil and wine, would suffer no lack in times of scarcity; the poor would suffer but the wealthy would not find themselves in want. However, it is more likely that these words place a limitation on the degree of scarcity, for while fine wines might be a luxurious food of wealthy people, oil and cheap wine were among the common necessities of life of poor people. "Grain, oil and wine" is a common phrase in the Bible representing the ordinary necessities of life (Deut. 7:13; 11:14; 28:51; II Chron. 32:28; Neh. 5:11; Hos. 2:8, 22; Joel 2:19; Hag. 1:11). These were the staple foods in Bible lands. They were all essential to the normal life of these countries and were not real luxuries. Therefore, the black horse represents a condition of dire want, but not one of acute famine conditions. This is not a situation which belongs to the actual time of the great tribulation, but to the beginning of woes.

d. The Fourth Seal (6:7-8).

Verses 7-8. The **pale horse** represents **death** from **famine, pestilence,** and **wild beasts.** The Greek word *chloros* often means green, and is an adjective often used with grass, leaves, trees. The word by itself can mean vegetation. However, a green horse does not suit the present context. The word can also mean pale grey, the ashen color of fear; and here it seems to mean the pallor of death. It does not represent death in general, but death which is caused by the three particular things mentioned.

Hades followed the pale horse of death. It is not clear how we are to picture this, whether Hades is conceived of as riding a second horse, as walking along behind on foot, which is hardly likely, or as being mounted on the same horse behind Death. In any case, the idea is clear. Hades means the underworld or the grave, and Hades accompanies Death to swallow up all those who are struck down by famine, pestilence and by wild beasts. Death by the sword differs from the plague of the second horseman, war, in that it can include all kinds of violent deaths by the sword, such as murder, as well as war. The inclusion of famine as one of the causes of death suggests that this plague is similar to the black horse — scarcity — the difference being that the plague is more intense. However, it is still of limited scope, for ths rider is given power only **over a fourth of the earth.**

e. The Fifth Seal (6:9-11).

The first four seals have pictured in vivid symbolic terms the forces by which God will prosecute his redemptive and judicial purposes throughout the course of the age. In other words, it has pictured the character of the age and its relationship to the Kingdom of God. The proclamation of the kingdom will be carried out effectively, but in a hostile environment, which in spite of the presence of the gospel of the kingdom will be characterized by war, suffering caused by material and economic need, and death. This is to say that the Kingdom of God will not be established in all its fullness during the present age — a teaching which is clearly paralleled in our Lord's Olivet Discourse in Matthew 24 and Mark 13.

Verse 9. Another fact which the church must face as it pursues its mission of proclaiming the gospel of the kingdom is persecution and martyrdom. This is set forth in a very vivid way. John **saw under the altar the souls of those who had been slain for the word of God and for the witness they had borne.** The mention of the altar raises a difficult question. Was it the altar of burnt offering which stood outside the temple proper in the court of the priests? Or was it the altar of incense which stood inside the temple building before the curtain which separated the Holy Place from the Holy of Holies? This is the first mention of the altar; there is no reference to it in chapter 4 which pictured heaven as the throne room of the heavenly king, filled with hosts of adoring angels. Where does the altar stand with reference to the throne? How can heaven be pictured as both a throne room and a temple at the same time?

It is precisely the fluidity of apocalyptic thinking which makes this possible. Apocalyptic pictures are not meant to be photographs of objective facts; they are often symbolic representations of almost unimaginable spiritual realities. In fact, God does not sit upon a throne; he is an eternal Spirit who neither stands or sits or reclines. The picture of God seated upon his throne is a symbolic way of asserting the kingship and sovereignty of the Deity.

Some interpreters insist that the altar must be the altar of incense, for since the sacrifice of Christ on the cross, there is no more room for sacrifice. Such thinking does not adequately take into account the symbolic nature of apocalyptic language. Heaven is both the throne room of God and his temple; and the altar is the altar of sacrifice, even though Christ's death put an end to all sacrifice. Isaiah "saw the Lord sitting upon a throne, high and lifted up; and his train filled the temple" (Isa. 6:1). The altar is also pictured as standing in the temple (Isa. 6:6). Psalm 11:4 says, "The Lord is in his holy temple, the Lord's throne is in heaven." There is no problem in mixing the symbols and conceiving of heaven both as God's temple in which stood God's throne, even though there is no earthly equivalent for the blending of the two features. (Heaven is conceived of as God's temple in such passages as Pss. 18:6; 29:9; Hab. 2:20; Mic. 1:2.) Therefore we need not press the question of the position of the altar or of its relationship to God's throne.

The altar is mentioned in 8:3, 5; 9:13; 11:1; 14:18; and 16:7. In 8:3, 5, the altar stands before the throne and appears to be the altar of incense representing the prayers of the saints. In 11:1, the altar appears to be the altar of sacrifice which stood in the court of the priests. In the present instance, the altar is clearly the altar of sacrifice where sacrificial blood was poured. The fact that John saw the souls of the martyrs *under the altar* has nothing to do with the state of the dead or their situation in the intermediate state; it is merely a vivid way of picturing the fact that they had been martyred in the name of their God. In the Old Testament ritual blood of sacrificial victims was poured out at the base of the altar (Lev. 4:7). The souls of martyrs are seen under the altar as though they had been sacrificed upon the altar and their blood poured out at its base. Christian thought often employs the language of sacrificial death. Facing death, the apostle Paul wrote, "For I am already on the point of being sacrificed" (II Tim. 4:6). At an earlier date, also facing possible death, he had written, "Even if I am to be poured as a libation upon the sacrificial offering of your faith, I am glad" (Phil. 2:17). Thus Christian martyrs are viewed as sacrifices offered to God. In fact, they were slain on earth and their blood wet the ground; but in Christian faith, the sacrifice was really made in heaven where their souls were offered at the heavenly altar.

It is doubtful if John is thinking of any particular historical martyrdom or group of martyrs. We have already seen that by the time John wrote, martyrdom had not become a widespread or common experience of the church. Nero waged a brief localized persecution against Christians in Rome, and in John's time Domitian persecuted a few families in Rome, apparently because they were Christians. John does foresee that in the end time the beast or Antichrist will wage fierce persecution against the church, almost to the point of its destruction. Here John appears to have in mind all Christian martyrs of every age, perhaps those of the end time in particular. One of the repeated emphases of the entire New Testament is that it is the very nature of the church to be a martyr people. When Jesus taught that a man to be his disciple must deny himself and take up his cross (Matt. 10:38; 16:24), he was not speaking of self-denial or the bearing of heavy burdens; he was speaking of willingness to suffer martyrdom. The cross is nothing else than an instrument of death. Every disciple of Jesus is in essence a martyr; and John has in view all believers who have so suffered.

These martyrs "had been slain for the word of God and for the witness they had borne" (cf. 1:9; 12:11, 17; 19:10; 20:4). The *word of God* is the gospel which God has given to men and by which they are saved, which includes the great facts of the resurrection and the lordship of Christ. No Christian could confess the lordship of Christ and at the same time bow to the lordship of a human sovereign such as Caesar. In the story of the *Martyrdom of Polycarp* (9), he was promised freedom if he would revile Christ and swear by Caesar. This tendency toward the persecution of Christians was already abroad in the Roman world, even though it did not become a general principle until considerably later.

Grammatically, "the witness they had borne" can mean the witness they had given to Christ; but from a study of this repeated phrase (see above), it more likely means the witness which had been borne by Jesus, which they had accepted, and for which they were put to death.

Verse 10. From these souls under the altar ascends a cry to God. **O Sovereign Lord, holy and true, how long before thou wilt judge and avenge our blood on those who dwell**

upon the earth? The expression "Sovereign Lord" is a translation of a single Greek word. It is not the common word for Lord in the New Testament — *kyrios* — but one of the common titles for God in the Greek Old Testament, *despotes,* designating the divine sovereign rule over all things. God is appealed to as the one who is *holy,* i.e., transcendent above all evil and who therefore cannot finally tolerate the evils which have been perpetrated upon the martyrs. He is also the *true* one, that is, the one faithful to his covenant promises who will finally save his people, even though they have suffered martyrdom, and bring them into the full redemption of the Kingdom of God. The souls of these martyrs which rest under the altar lift a cry to God for vindication. The phrase "those who dwell upon the earth" is repeated often in the Revelation, and designates mankind in its rebellion and hostility to God (cf. 3:10; 11:10; 13:8, 12, 14; 14:6; 17:8).

The prayer of these souls can be interpreted either as a prayer of vengeance or a prayer of vindication. There are indeed instances in the history of early Christian martyrdom when the martyrs did not show the spirit of Jesus and of Stephen, praying forgiveness on those who persecuted them. On the contrary, the martyrs sometimes threatened their tormentors with the judgment of the coming wrath. The Scripture warns against such a spirit of vengeance, forbidding personal revenge, and admonishing afflicted Christians to give food to hungry enemies and drink to those who are thirsty. They are to show love to tormentors and leave all vengeance to God who will judge righteously (Rom. 12:19). In the light of this, some interpreters have understood the prayer of the martyrs to be a Jewish prayer for vengeance rather than a truly Christian prayer.

There is, on the other hand, a recurring note of vindication throughout the Scriptures. God said to Abel because of his murder of Cain, "The voice of your brother's blood is crying to me from the ground" (Gen. 4:10). Our Lord himself told a parable about righteous people who suffer at the hands of the wicked and whose only vindication is God: "Will not God vindicate his elect, who cry to him day and night? Will he delay long over them? I tell you, he will vindicate them speedily" (Luke 18:7). The fact that the prayer comes from under the altar where martyr blood is conceived of as having been sacrificed suggests that it is the blood of the martyrs crying for vindication, not the martyrs themselves crying for personal vengeance. They pray that the divine vindication on wicked men who have slain the righteous, which is certain because God is the holy and true one, may also be speedy.

Verse 11. The **white robe** given to the martyrs is not an intermediate body or the resurrection body. If this were the meaning of the white robes, the martyrs would have received them at death. The white robe is a symbol of blessedness and rest, even though the state of final and perfected blessedness awaits the return of Christ and the resurrection of the body. The souls of the martyrs are seen as still resting beneath the altar; they have not yet entered into the enjoyment of the full presence of God. The martyrs must **rest a little longer** until the consummation of their blessedness; but in the meantime, they are in a state of rest.

They must wait in patience **until the number of their fellow servants and their brethren should be complete.** This statement is surely not to be understood in any mathematical way, as though God had decreed that there must be a certain number of martyrs, and when this number was slain, the end will come. It does indicate that John knows the end is not immediately to come, but that there is to ensue a time when the church would experience further martyrdom.

f. The Sixth Seal (6:12-17).

Verses 12-14. With the opening of the sixth seal, John beheld a set of phenomena which in prophetic and apocalyptic language is the usual way of describing the end of the world. In view of the fact that many interpreters understand these words symbolically to designate social and economic and political upheavals, the Old Testament prophetic background needs to be emphasized. In the day of the Lord when God will finally visit the earth in both judgment and redemption, the entire earthly order will be shaken. Joel prophesies, "The sun shall be turned to darkness and the moon to blood before the great and terrible day of the Lord comes" (Joel 2:31). Again, "The day of the Lord is near.... The sun and the

moon are darkened and the stars withdraw their shining"
(Joel 3:15). Haggai wrote, "Once again in a little while I will
shake the heavens and the earth, the sea and the dry land"
(Hag. 2:6). Isaiah sees the day of the Lord as a time when
"the stars of the heavens and their constellations will not give
their light; and the sun will be dark at its rising, and the moon
will not shed its light" (Isa. 13:10). In another place, Isaiah
wrote, "All the host of heaven shall rot away, and the skies
roll up like a scroll, all their host shall fall as leaves fall from
the vine, like leaves falling from the fig tree" (Isa. 34:4).
Jeremiah described this same event, "I looked on the earth
and lo, it was waste and void, and to the heavens, and they
had no light. I looked on the mountains, and lo, they were
quaking, and all the hills moved to and fro. . . . For thus says
the Lord, The whole land shall be a desolation; yet I will not
make a full end. For this the earth shall mourn, and the
heavens above be black" (Jer. 4:23-28).

The same cosmic catastrophic language is found in our
Lord's Olivet Discourse. Immediately after the short period
of the great tribulation, "the sun will be darkened, and the
moon will not give its light, and the stars will fall from
heaven, and the powers of the heavens will be shaken" (Matt.
24:29). Immediately after this cosmic disturbance will appear
the Son of man on the clouds of heaven to gather the elect into
the Kingdom of God. The language used by John is so similar
to the prophecy in Matthew 24 that it is difficult to believe
that John was not familiar with it.

There is a profound theology underlying this language of
cosmic catastrophe at the end of the age. It illustrates the
transcendence of God and the dependence of his creation
upon its creator. The Old Testament constantly pictures the
divine visitations of God to his people in terms of a theophany,
i.e., in terms of majesty and power and glory so great that the
physical world is shaken. The most notable illustration of
this in the Old Testament is the visitation at Mount Sinai.
However, this is not all. The Old Testament pictures the
physical world in some way as sharing man's fate, as having
fallen under the burden of violence, decay and death, and
therefore subject to the divine judgment and in need of the
divine salvation. The language of cosmic catastrophe at the

end of the age when God finally visits his creation in the day of the Lord is the Bible's picturesque way of describing the divine judgment falling on the world. The language is "semi-poetic": i.e., it is symbolic language which can hardly be taken with stark literalness.[1] How, for instance, in light of our modern knowledge of astronomy can we conceive of the stars falling upon the earth? Since we know that the blue vault of the sky is in reality an optical illusion, how can we imagine the heavens being rolled up like a scroll?

However, the language is not merely poetical or symbolic of spiritual realities but describes a real cosmic catastrophe whose actual character we cannot conceive. Out of the ruins of judgment will emerge a new redeemed order which John calls new heavens and a new earth (Rev. 21:1).

Verses 15-17. Those who experienced this catastrophe recognized it as the end of the world. All sorts of men, high and low, small and great, **hid in the caves and among the rocks of the mountains,** seeking to cover themselves **from the face of him who is seated on the throne, and from the wrath of the Lamb, for the great day of their wrath has come, and who can stand before it?** Back of this is the language of one of the first "apocalyptic" passages of the Old Testament, Isa. 2:19, where the day of the Lord is described as a time when "men shall enter the caves of the rocks and the holes of the ground, from before the terror of the Lord, and from the glory of his majesty, when he rises to terrify the earth."

The expression "the day of the Lord" is an inclusive term, which can encompass the entire period that will end this age and inaugurate the age to come. It will be a day of judgment for the wicked — a day of wrath — but a day of redemption for the righteous. In the New Testament, it is called the day of the Lord (II Thess. 2:2), the day of Christ (Phil. 1:10), the day of the Lord Jesus Christ (I Cor. 1:8), or the day of the Lord Jesus (II Cor. 1:14). It is also the day of wrath (Rom. 2:5) and the day of redemption (Eph. 4:30). No distinctions can be made between these various terms as though there were different days which can be distinguished from one another.

[1]The present author has worked out this problem in some detail in his book *Jesus and the Kingdom* (Waco, Texas: Word Books, 1964), chap. 2.

In the present instance, the cosmic catastrophe convinces men that the day has come and the Lord is about to appear.

However, John does not go on to describe the end itself and the coming of the Lord as we might expect. Instead, he continues to relate certain events which immediately precede the end. In fact, when the seventh seal is broken (8:1), there is no single woe which follows; instead, John relates the sounding of the seven trumpets and the woes which accompany them, and then the emptying of the seven bowls and their woes. This is consonant with our understanding of the seven seals. We have interpreted the seals to represent forces which will be at work throughout the course of the age and which are only preparatory to the opening of the book. The breaking of each of the seals does not witness the opening of part of the book, chapter by chapter as it were; all of the seals are preliminary to opening the book. The sixth seal brings us to the threshold of the opening of the book and the great events of the end. The breaking of the seventh seal makes it possible for the book to be opened and its contents disclosed. The book contains the prophecies of the end of the world; but the end is not a single event but consists of a whole complex of events. It includes the outpouring of God's wrath upon a rebellious civilization, the judgment of the Antichrist and the destruction of his hosts, as well as the resurrection of the dead and the establishment of the Kingdom of God. So we may conclude that the sixth seal brings us to the threshold of the end; and then John stands back, as it were, to tell the story of the end in greater detail. The breaking of the seventh seal opens the book and begins the story of the events of the end time; this is the substance of the remainder of the Revelation.

CHAPTER SEVEN

THE TWO MULTITUDES

The first six seals, representing events preliminary to the
end or the "beginning of woes" (Matt. 24:8), have now been
broken and the time has come for the breaking of the final
seal, the opening of the book, and the story of the end itself.
The end is a complex of events which will include the culmi-
nation of the struggle between the people of God — the church
— and the satanically inspired beast or Antichrist. It will tell
of the outpouring of God's wrath upon the Antichrist and the
civilization that has supported him, and finally the deliverance
and salvation of God's people in the Kingdom of God.

Before John begins the story of the actual end, he pauses
to employ a technique which he uses several times to interrupt
the flow of his narrative. He inserts an interlude, painting
a picture which is essential background to the flow of the
narrative. In the present instance, as the church stands on
the threshold of her time of great tribulation, she is reassured
that God will safely see her through her terrible ordeal. When
the breaking of the sixth seal was followed by signs of the
end, men cried out in terror, "The great day of . . . wrath has
come, and who can stand before it?" (6:17). The answer to
this question is now given. Those whom God has sealed will
be safely preserved from the outpouring of divine wrath, even
though they suffer martyrdom.

(3) Interlude: The Two Multitudes (7:1-17).

This interlude contains a vision of two multitudes. The first is a company consisting of twelve thousand of each of the twelve tribes of Israel. The second is a great innumerable company from all tribes and peoples and tongues, i.e., gentiles, who are martyred in the great tribulation.

a. The 144,000 (7:1-8).

Verse 1. John now pictures the earth as though it were a great square with an angel standing at each of the **four corners.** They are **holding back the four winds of the earth, that no wind might blow on earth or sea or against any tree.** These angels have power to harm the earth and the sea and the trees, supposedly by letting loose the four winds.

Verses 2-3. However, John saw **another angel ascend from the rising of the sun,** i.e., from the east in the direction of Palestine, who had the **seal of the living God,** and he called to the four angels, admonishing them not to harm the earth **till we have sealed the servants of our God upon their foreheads.**

This is John's picturesque way of referring to the plagues which are shortly to fall on mankind and the protection of God's people from these plagues. We meet here again the fluidity of apocalyptic language. We would expect that after the sealing of God's servants, the four angels at the four corners of the earth would be released and the four winds bring their torments. But the four angels are not referred to again. In their stead, we meet seven angels, each with a trumpet, upon whose sounding plagues fall on the earth. We cannot too often emphasize that apocalyptic language does not convey its message in precise photographic style, but more in the style of modern surrealistic art with great fluidity and imagination. The message of these verses is simply that the judgment of the first plagues is to be withheld until God's people are sealed.

Verses 4-8. John heard the number of those sealed: twelve thousand from each of twelve tribes of Israel. The purpose of this sealing is made clear from a later reference. After the sounding of the fifth trumpet, a plague of locusts falls upon the earth, but the infliction of the plague is not universal. It falls only on "those of mankind who have not the seal of

God upon their foreheads" (9:4). God is about to visit the
earth in wrath, afflicting an apostate and rebellious society
with fearful plagues before the final judgment falls. In the
midst of this apostate society is God's people; but the wrath
of God does not fall on them; they are sealed and thus delivered from the wrath.

John's vision is reminiscent of Israel in Egypt. God visited
the Egyptians with a series of ten plagues to try to bend the
stubborn Pharaoh before the divine will. Israel found herself in the midst of Egypt, but God protected Israel from the
plagues which afflicted the Egyptians. The tenth plague
brought death to every firstborn male in every household in
Egypt, but the Israelites were directed to kill a lamb and
sprinkle blood over the door; and when the angel of death
passed through the land, he passed over every house protected
by the mark of the blood.

This interpretation of the meaning of the sealing of the
144,000 is confirmed by the statement in 16:2 at the beginning of the bowl judgments. They are not poured out on all
men but only on those men who bore the mark of the beast
and worshipped its image. In the time of the great tribulation, God will protect his people from the outpouring of his
wrath even though they must suffer tribulation at the hands
of the Antichrist.

Certainly this sealing is a spiritual fact and not a visible
bodily phenomenon. The sealing of God's servants is different
in meaning from the sealed book in 5:1-5. That book was
sealed to hide its contents from the eyes of men; the 144,000
are sealed to protect them from the ensuing evils. An analogous idea is found in the spiritual sealing by the Holy Spirit
of all Christians, who "were sealed with the promised Holy
Spirit, which is the guarantee of our inheritance until we
acquire possession of it" (Eph. 1:14; cf. also II Cor. 1:22;
Eph. 4:30). This sealing of believers is an assurance of spiritual safety on the grounds of divine ownership. It is an
inner spiritual fact which cannot be observed with the outward eye. So will God's people in the tribulation be sealed
and protected from his wrath.

The identity of the 144,000 is not an easy problem. The
most natural way to interpret them is to see them as the Jew-

ish people and to find in this symbolism the salvation of Israel. The problem of the unbelief of the Jewish people in light of the promises of God was an acute problem in the early church, and Paul devoted three chapters in his epistle to the Romans (9-11) to this question. Some critics have recognized these three chapters to constitute the central section of that epistle. Paul insists that God's promises are not annulled, for there is a believing remnant of Jews who have inherited the promises. However, the majority of Israel have been guilty of unbelief and therefore have been broken off from the people of God, for whom Paul uses the metaphor of an olive tree. Their place has been taken by believing gentiles who have through faith been grafted into the olive tree. However, God is not through with Israel; they are still a "holy people" (Rom. 11:16); and it will be God's purpose finally to provoke Israel to jealousy and bring them back to faith. For the present, Israel is hardened in unbelief "until the full number of the Gentiles comes in" (Rom. 11:25). But this salvation of the gentiles will provoke Israel to jealousy (Rom. 11:11, 14), and in this manner "all Israel will be saved" (Rom. 11:25). Paul is here speaking from the perspective of redemptive history. He obviously cannot mean that all Jews who ever lived will be saved. He means that there will come a day when the entire family of living Jews — "all Israel" — will be saved.

Many interpreters understand this passage spiritually and apply the words "all Israel" to the gentile church. This view makes Paul merely assert that God's entire people will be saved — that spiritual Israel will be complete. This interpretation does not suit the context. There is a movement throughout Romans 9-11 from literal Israel to the gentile church, and in its context, "all Israel" must refer to an entire generation of living Jews. God has not finally cast off his people; when the full number of the gentiles have been saved, God will turn again to Israel, and they too will experience a nationwide salvation.

Many interpreters understand the 144,000 to represent converted Israel. The sealing of the 12,000 from each of the twelve tribes of Israel is John's picturesque way of saying the same thing that Paul says: "All Israel shall be saved."

113

This is obviously a possible interpretation, but it is faced with an acute difficulty, for the 144,000 are not sealed in salvation but for protection from the plagues. Furthermore, in verse 3, they are called the "servants of God." They are not converted at this time, they have already been converted. Furthermore, if these are converted Jews, it is difficult to understand why they should be sheltered from the sufferings of the tribulation when great unnumbered multitudes of gentiles are permitted to suffer martyrdom.

Another view, close to the one just cited, is that this is a saved Jewish remnant who are to be witnesses to the "gospel of the kingdom," i.e., the coming of God's Kingdom, during the great tribulation after the church has been raptured. In this case, the second multitude is a great host of gentiles who are supposed to be saved as a result of the preaching of the Jewish remnant, but who in turn are martyred by the Antichrist. This view, however, depends upon the theory that the church has already been raptured — a theory for which we have found no evidence. Furthermore, this view is beset with certain internal contradictions. This dispensational view teaches that the church will be raptured at the beginning of the great tribulation, and that the chief objects of the wrath of the beast or Antichrist will be the Jewish nation restored to Palestine. This interpretation believes that Antichrist will make a seven-year treaty with the nation Israel, only to break it in the middle of the "week of years" and then turn in anger to try to destroy his former allies (cf. Dan. 9:27). This standard dispensational view must face the difficulty that it is not the Jews but a great host of gentile believers who are martyred by falling victim to the hatred of Antichrist (chap. 13).

There are good reasons to believe that by the 144,000 John means to identify spiritual Israel — the church. This view is suggested by certain irregularities in the list of the twelve tribes of Israel. As a matter of fact, John's list agrees with no known list of the enumeration of the twelve tribes of Israel. Many interpreters insist that these twelve tribes must be interpreted literally and therefore designate literal Israel. However, when interpreted literally, *these twelve tribes do not*

represent actual Israel. A brief survey of several of the Old
Testament listings will make this clear.

Revelation 7	Genesis 49	Ezekiel 48
Judah	Reuben	Dan
Reuben	Simeon	Asher
Gad	Levi	Naphtali
Asher	Judah	Manasseh
Naphtali	Zebulun	Ephraim
Manasseh	Issachar	Reuben
Simeon	Dan	Judah
Levi	Gad	Benjamin
Issachar	Asher	Simeon
Zebulun	Naphtali	Issachar
Joseph	Joseph	Zebulun
Benjamin	Benjamin	Gad

The prophecy in Ezekiel 48 tells of the final salvation
of Israel and the eschatological division of the land of
Palestine. If John means to relate the eschatological salvation
of Israel, we would expect him to follow the list of Ezekiel;
but this he does not do. The irregularities in John's list are
these: the tribe of Dan is altogether omitted; the tribe of
Ephraim is also omitted, but it is included indirectly because
Joseph was the father of both Ephraim and Manasseh. This
means that in reality, the tribe of Manasseh is included twice.

No satisfactory explanation of this irregular list of names
has been offered, unless it be this: John intends to say that
the twelve tribes of Israel are not really literal Israel, but
the true, spiritual Israel — the church. Some interpreters have
tried to avoid the greatest difficulty — that of the omission
of Dan (which is the first tribe mentioned in the eschatological people of Ezekiel 48) — by suggesting that the Antichrist
was expected to arise from the tribe of Dan. This tribe is
therefore considered to be apostate and excluded from the
people of God and their inheritance of the land. This view
can be traced back as far as Irenaeus.[1] It founders, however,
on the fact that Dan is included in the salvation of the eschatological people in Ezekiel 48.

The New Testament clearly conceives of the church as the

[1]*Against Heresies,* V.30.2.

true, spiritual Israel. To be sure, the word "Israel" is never used of the church, unless it is so used in Gal. 6:16; but the exegesis of this verse is disputed. However, it is beyond debate that "if you are Christ's, then you are Abraham's offspring, heirs according to the promise" (Gal. 3:29). Again, Abraham is "the father of all who believe" (Rom. 4:11), whether they be circumcised or uncircumcised. "He is not a real Jew who is one outwardly, nor is true circumcision something external and physical. He is a Jew who is one inwardly, and real circumcision is a matter of the heart, spiritual and not literal" (Rom. 2:28-29). "We are the true circumcision who worship God in spirit and glory in Jesus Christ" (Phil. 3:3). If believers are the true sons of Abraham, the true circumcision, then we must conclude that the church is the true spiritual Israel, even though the word itself may not be used of the church. This we believe to be confirmed by the expression, "the Israel of God," in Gal. 6:16.

That John also shares this distinction between outward, literal Israel and inner, spiritual Israel is clear from two earlier references. In Smyrna were "those who say that they are Jews and are not, but are a synagogue of Satan" (2:9; cf. also 3:9). That is, there are men who are actually and outwardly Jews — literally Israel — but in reality they are not true Jews — spiritual Israel — but follow the ways of Satan rather than God.

If then John distinguishes between literal and spiritual Israel, it would be possible for him to speak of the twelve tribes of Israel and by so doing intend to designate those who are true Jews — the church. And he indicates this intention by listing the twelve tribes in a form not identical with empirical Israel.

This interpretation makes the best sense of the passage and suggests the relationship between the two multitudes. They represent the same people — the church — seen in two stages of her history in the end times: first, standing on the threshold of the great tribulation, and later having passed through this time of tribulation, martyred but victorious. We are reminded of our Lord's words in which he described the fate of his disciples: "You will be delivered up even by parents and brothers and

kinsmen and friends, and some of you will be put to death. . . .
But not a hair of your head will perish" (Luke 21:16, 18).

The two multitudes represent the church seen in the light of
the two aspects of the great tribulation: God's wrath, and the
persecution of the beast. The church is sealed that it may be
protected from the plagues which express God's wrath upon
the Antichrist and his followers; but the church in the great
tribulation will suffer persecution and death as she has
throughout her entire history.

The meaning of the number, 12 x 12,000 is not difficult. As
usual in the Revelation, the number is symbolic and affirms
that the full number of the people of God will be brought
safely through the time of tribulation; not one of the people of
God will be lost.

b. The Innumerable Multitude (7:9-17).

The church is pictured a second time from an entirely different perspective. The first multitude is pictured as standing on
the threshold of the tribulation; the second multitude is seen
after the tribulation is over, saved in the Kingdom of God. The
most difficult question is whether or not they are represented
as having been martyred. They have come out of the great
tribulation (vs. 14) and have washed their robes and made
them white in the blood of the Lamb. There is no positive indication in the passage that they are martyrs. However, they are
seen standing before the throne; that is, they have suffered
death and now stand in the presence of God and before the
Lamb. If they have died in great tribulation, the presumption
is that they have been martyred, for the great tribulation will
be a time of intense martyrdom.

This idea appears several times in the New Testament and
goes back to Dan. 12:1. "And there shall be a time of trouble
[Greek, tribulation] such as never has been since there was a
nation till that time." Our Lord re-echoed these words of
Daniel: "For then there will be great tribulation, such as has
not been from the beginning of the world until now, no, and
never will be. And if those days had not been shortened, no
human being would be saved; but for the sake of the elect those
days will be shortened" (Matt. 24:21-22). Paul described the
evil personage who will oppose the people of God as "the man

of lawlessness . . . the son of perdition, who opposes and exalts himself against every so-called god or object of worship" (II Thess. 2:3-4). John devotes an entire chapter to this Antichrist, calling him the beast who, supported by the false prophet, will demand universal worship. The beast "was allowed to make war on the saints and to conquer them" (Rev. 13:7). He was granted authority over all peoples on the earth. The false prophet demands that all men worship the beast; those who do not conform are put to death (Rev. 13:15).

The theology behind the great tribulation is the age-long conflict between God and Satan. One of the main motifs in our Lord's ministry was his conflict with Satan and demonic powers. By his incarnation and earthly mission, our Lord has rendered a decisive defeat to the devil (Matt. 12:28-29; Luke 10:18; Heb. 2:14) that men may be delivered from darkness and brought into the Kingdom of Christ (Col. 1:13). While delivered from the spiritual power of Satan, the church is not spared from tribulation and persecution, which expresses the fierce hatred of Satan for the people of God. In fact, tribulation — persecution — is the normal expectation of the church in the world (John 16:33; Acts 14:22; Rom. 8:35). The great tribulation will be but a concentration of the same satanic hostility which the church has experienced throughout her entire existence when Satan, in one final convulsive effort, tries to turn the hearts of God's people away from their Lord.

A parallel to the vision of the great unnumbered multitude is found in chapter 14 where, immediately after the great tribulation, a proleptic vision is given of the 144,000 standing on Mount Zion, i.e., heavenly Jerusalem, in the Kingdom of God. From the point of view of the mighty spiritual struggle between God and Satan, whether a man lives or dies is not of ultimate importance. The all-important issue is whether he worships Christ or Antichrist. So even though Satan through the Antichrist is allowed to wage terrible tribulation against the saints, God will bring them safely and victoriously through into the Kingdom of God.

Verse 9. The setting of this vision is not explicitly stated, but the language of vss. 15-17 suggests that it is in the consummated Kingdom of God after the **throne** of God has descended from heaven to dwell with men (22:3). Here we find the first proleptic vision in the Revelation when John looks forward to picture some situation that will not come actually into being until some later time. **White robes** and **palm branches** are symbols of victory.

Verse 10. Their song is not primarily one of gratitude for their own deliverance but one of praise to God for the greatness of the salvation he has wrought.

Verses 11-12. The **angels** join the redeemed in praise to God. It is to be noticed that the twenty-four **elders** are here grouped with the angels and the cherubim, in distinction to the redeemed. This supports the view that they are angelic powers.

Verse 13. The great multitude is identified by a dramatic question addressed to John by one of the elders.

Verse 14. John's answer, using the address **Sir,** is suitable if the elders are angels but not if the elders represent the redeemed. This is a form of speech used elsewhere of super-human persons. See Dan. 10:16; Zech. 4:5, 13.

If this great company **has come out of the great tribulation,** the assumption is that they have suffered martyrdom. However, they have not surrendered their faith in Christ nor permitted themselves to be stained by unbelief or by worship of any false gods; **they have washed their robes and made them white in the blood of the Lamb;** they have remained steadfast in their faith in Christ.

Verse 15. **Therefore they are before the throne of God:** they have entered into perfected fellowship with God. **They serve him day and night within his temple:** they have direct access into the immediate presence of God.

Verses 16-17. In their present context, these words could refer to the blessing of the intermediate state, with the throne of God and his temple conceived of as in heaven. But the blessings they enjoy — no more **hunger** or **thirst,** no **scorching heat,** the shepherding of the Lamb, **the springs of living water,** the wiping away of **every tear from their eyes,** and especially the statement, "he will shelter them with his presence" (vs. 15) — sound more like the blessings of the consummated Kingdom (Rev. 22:1-5) when the throne of God comes down from heaven to dwell with men. There is a difficulty in the fact that we are told that in this new order there will be no temple (21:22). However, this only reflects the fluidity of apocalyptic language. In 7:15, the temple is the dwelling place of God and represents the actual presence of God. In 21:22, the temple represents mediation into the presence of God, which will no longer be necessary in the new order, for "they shall see his face" (22:4).

CHAPTER EIGHT

THE SEVENTH SEAL AND
THE SIX TRUMPETS

(4) The Seventh Seal (8:1).

Chapter seven consisted of an interlude which interrupted the continuity of the breaking of the seven seals. The first six seals, which were broken in chapter six, represent the character of the age and the course of the gospel in the world down to the end of the age. The end was announced in the sixth seal. Then before further details were given about the events of the end, particularly the time of great tribulation, chapter seven pictured the fate of the church in this fearful period. Chapters eight and nine relate the breaking of the seventh seal and the sounding of seven trumpets.

Before this is discussed in detail, a significant parallelism between the seven seals and the seven trumpets must be pointed out. It is noteworthy that both the seals and the trumpets bring us to the end. The sixth seal, as we have seen, related cosmic catastrophes which signal the coming of the day of the Lord (6:17). Similarly, the seventh trumpet announced the coming of the end. When the seventh angel sounded, heavenly voices were heard saying, "The kingdom of the world has become the kingdom of our Lord and of his Christ, and he shall reign for ever and ever" (11:15). This requires us to recognize some measure of recapitulation, when the narrative backs up and recovers some of the same ground. The question is: Do the seven seals and the seven trumpets cover the same period; i.e., do they overlap in their entirety; or do they overlap only in part?

A clue to the answer may be found in the fact that the seventh seal, unlike the first six, contains no plague or judgmental content. On the contrary, when the seventh seal was broken, the seven angels prepared to sound their trumpets. This suggests that the seven trumpets in fact constitute the contents of the seventh seal; there is only a partial recapitulation. The six seals relate the forces leading up to the end while the seven trumpets relate the beginning of the events of the end itself, particularly the time of the great tribulation which will introduce the end.

Another similarity in structure is found in the fact that both the seals and the trumpets are interrupted by interludes. Between the sixth and the seventh seal is inserted the vision of the two multitudes, which pictures the fate of the church in the time of tribulation. Between the sixth and the seventh trumpets is inserted the visions of the angel and the little book and the measuring of the temple (chapters 10-11).

Another parallelism between the seals and the trumpets is found in the fact that neither the seventh seal nor the seventh trumpet represents a plague or a woe as do the other six seals and trumpets. The seventh seal has no content; we have been led to the conclusion that the seven trumpets constitute the content of the seventh seal. In a similar way, the seventh trumpet has no plague or woe like the preceding six, but has only an announcement of the end and is followed by the seven bowls. This suggests the possibility that the content of the seventh trumpet is in fact the seven bowls. If so, we see in the seven trumpets and the seven bowls an intensification of the woes poured out upon mankind before they are overtaken in the final judgment and it is too late.

Verse 1. **When the Lamb opened the seventh seal, there was silence in heaven for about half an hour.** It is possible that this silence is itself the content of the seventh seal and is meant to suggest the beginning of the eternal rest of the saints. This, however, is unlikely, for it is completely out of character with the first six seals. Others have suggested that silence prevailed in order that the prayers of the saints might be heard (vs. 3). The best suggestion is that the silence represents an attitude of trembling suspense on the part of the heavenly hosts in view of the judgments of God which are about to fall upon the world. It is the silence of dreadful anticipation of the events that are about to ensue, now that the time of the end has come.

3. THE SEVEN TRUMPETS (8:2 — 14:20).

Now that the seven seals have been broken, we would expect to read about the opening of the scroll and the disclosure of its contents. However, nothing of the sort occurs; the scroll simply drops out of sight. This is probably due to the fluidity of apocalyptic symbolism and to the highly imaginative character of its language. It is proper to assume, however, that what follows the breaking of the seven seals is in fact the content of the scroll.

(1) The Six Trumpets (8:2 — 9:21).

The sixth seal brought us to the time of the end, and the seven trumpets and the seven bowls (chs. 15-16) constitute one of the most important aspects of the short but terrible time of the end. With each trumpet and each bowl, a plague is poured out upon the world. These plagues embody expressions of the wrath of a holy God upon a civilization which has chosen to give its allegiance to Antichrist rather than to God's Messiah, the lamblike Lion. This is clearly stated in the introduction to the seven bowls; they are "seven plagues, which are the last, for with them the wrath of God is ended" (15:1). This wrath is not directed against mankind in general but against "the men who bore the mark of the beast and worshiped its image" (16:2). It is explicitly stated that these plagues were directed only upon "those of mankind who have not the seal of God upon their foreheads" (9:4). Those who worship the Lamb have been sealed so that they are sheltered from God's wrath.

In other words, John sees a day when the forces of righteousness and of evil will be so open and clear that every man must declare himself: either for Christ or for Antichrist. The struggle that is implicit in the mission of the gospel in the world for the souls of men will become so explicit that there will no longer be any middle ground. The powers of unbelief and of hostility to God will break into the open in the person of Antichrist, and every man's loyalty will become plain.

123

Yet the wrath of God is not merely judicial; it also embodies a merciful purpose. It is designed to drive men to their knees by harsh experiences while the time for decision remains, before it is too late. This is hinted at in several passages. After the sixth trumpet, we read, "The rest of mankind, who were not killed by these plagues, did not repent of the works of their hands nor give up worshiping demons and idols" (9:20). It is implied that when men are confronted by the evident wrath of God in judgment, they should be humbled in repentance and turn from their wickedness to worship the God of heaven. The same note resounds in connection with the bowls of wrath. After the fifth bowl, we read that men "cursed the God of heaven for their pain and sores and did not repent of their deeds" (16:10). If it were possible to drive men to repentance, the plagues of the trumpets and bowls would do so.

a. Preparation (8:2-6).

Verse 2. At the beginning of the interlude in chapter seven, we read of the restraining of the four angels who stood at the four corners of the earth that they should not hurt the earth until God's servants had been sealed. Now we would expect to meet again these four angels; but, instead, we read of **the seven angels who stand before God** to whom are given **seven trumpets.** Such, however, is the characteristic fluidity of apocalyptic language and vision; it is surrealistic rather than rational and logically consistent.

The language suggests seven well-known angels. Seven angels who stand before God do not appear in biblical literature; but *Enoch* 20:7 gives the names of seven holy angels, and *Tobit* 12:15 speaks of Raphael, "one of the seven holy angels who present the prayers of the saints." Luke 1:19 speaks of Gabriel, who stands in the presence of God.

Verse 3. Before the sounding of the seven trumpets John saw in vision a brief episode whose basic meaning is clear but whose details are difficult. The vision of the angel casting a censer on the altar conveys the simple truth, already expressed in the prayer of the souls of the martyrs under the altar (6:9-11), that God's judgments will come upon the world in answer to the prayers of the saints.

124

John saw **another angel**. Many commentators feel that this angel must be Christ himself, for the Bible does not teach the mediatorial role of angels in the prayers of God's people. However, in Dan. 9:20ff. and 10:10ff., the angel Gabriel plays a mediatorial role in bringing Daniel the answer to his prayers. Heb. 1:14 tells us that angels perform some kind of ministry for the saints. It is not quite a role of mediation, for the saints are priests unto God (Rev. 1:6; 5:10), i.e., they have direct access to God. But in some way unknown to us, angels may be thought of as assisting the prayers of the saints.

The angel **stood at the altar** like a priest about to offer incense (Exod. 40:5; Lev. 4:7; Heb. 9:4). It is possible that this passage refers to two altars; the picture is not clear. Possibly the vision represents the angel going first to the altar of burnt offering to secure glowing coals (vs. 3a), then going to the altar of incense, which is designated as **the golden altar before the throne** where he casts the coals taken from the altar of burnt offering (vs. 3b), and finally returning to the altar of burnt offering to take fire to cast upon the earth (vs. 5). However, the entire subject of the identity of the altar and its relationship to the throne is difficult and may be deliberately inexact because of the nature of apocalyptic thought.

The angel **was given much incense to mingle with the prayers of all the saints.** This concept is rather difficult. It suggests that the prayers of the saints were lying on the altar and the angel came with incense to cense the holy things. It is notable that the vision refers to the prayers of *all* the saints, not merely to those of the martyrs. This is further evidence that the Revelation is concerned with the fate of all of the church on earth.

Verse 4. **The smoke of the incense** is *not* said to enable **the prayers of the saints** to rise to God; this would contradict the fact that believers are themselves priests to God. The smoke of the incense rose with the prayers of the saints, adding fragrance to them. We may assume that the object of the prayers of the saints is for the coming of God's Kingdom and the manifestation of God's judgment against the demonic powers of evil which have oppressed those who have faithfully confessed the name of Jesus (see 6:10).

Verse 5. This verse dramatically pictures the fact that it is in answer to the prayers of the saints that God's judgments will fall upon the earth. It conveys the assurance that the prayers of the saints have been heard and will be answered. Similar assurances of God's faithfulness are given at the sounding of the seventh trumpet (11:19) and the emptying of the seventh bowl (16:17). Background for the vision is Ezek. 10:2, where coals of fire from between the cherubim are scattered over Jerusalem as a token of God's judgment.

The **peals of thunder, loud voices, flashes of lightning and an earthquake** which follow the casting of fire upon the earth are premonitory signs of God's judgments which are about to fall.

Verse 6. Now in answer to the prayers of all the saints, **the seven angels who had the seven trumpets made ready to blow them.** The plagues of the trumpets are in two groups: the first four involve natural catastrophes; the last three plagues fall directly upon men. A similar division is found in Matt. 24:4-8 and 24:13-22. The first four plagues are all partial in their effect, affecting only a third of nature. These preliminary judgments are designed to bring men to repentance (9:20). The first four judgments have many details in common with the plagues in Egypt.

b. The First Trumpet (8:7).

Verse 7. The first plague destroys a third of the earth, its foliage, and green vegetation. The destruction falls on a third part of the earth. There is no reason to follow those interpreters who find this plague a picture of civil disorder and anarchy resulting from man's rejection of God. Trees do not mean men of high rank and grass men of common standing. This pictures an actual catastrophe falling upon the physical world. Possibly the **fire** means an electrical display in a fierce thunderstorm.

c. The Second Trumpet (8:8-9).

Verse 8. Upon the sounding of the second trumpet, a burning mass fell from heaven into the sea. It is futile to try to limit this to a volcanic eruption. Volcanos hurl forth rocks and lava but are themselves not flung bodily into the sea. How we are to conceive of the actual event we cannot say.

Verse 9. That **a third of the sea became blood** reminds us of Exod. 7:20 when the Nile was turned to blood. The death of a third of the fishes reminds us of the similar plague in Exod. 7:21. **A third of the ships were destroyed,** apparently by the fire from the burning mountain. This is a severe plague, but as yet it is only partial in its effects.

d. The Third Trumpet (8:10-11).

Verse 10. The sounding of the third trumpet sees a great blazing meteor fall from heaven poisoning a third of the rivers and fountains of waters. We are reminded of the first Egyptian plague, which fell upon the Nile River.

Verse 11. The word translated "wormwood" is a rare word, occurring nowhere else in the Greek Bible, although the Greek translation of Aquila uses it several times. Wormwood mixed with water was not a deadly poison; but in the present case, **the waters became wormwood,** and **many men died** of the bitter water. In Jer. 9:15, wormwood is a symbol of divine judgment: "Therefore thus says the Lord ... Behold I will feed this people with wormwood, and give them poisonous water to drink." In Jer. 23:15, the same judgment is to fall upon the prophets for their ungodliness.

e. The Fourth Trumpet (8:12-13).

Verse 12. The fourth plague falls upon the heavenly bodies — the sun, moon and stars. This is similar to the ninth plague in Egypt, when the land was enveloped in darkness (Exod. 10:21). We are not told what happened to the heavenly bodies, only that they were darkened. The darkness is not complete; the plague affects only a third of the heavenly bodies.

The independence of the picturesque apocalyptic way of thinking is shown by the nature of this plague, which is logically impossible. If a third of the sun, moon and stars were darkened, then their light would be diminished throughout the entire period of their shining by a proportionate amount. Furthermore, the darkening of the moon when it is in its first phase as a tiny sliver of light is hard to conceive. But such considerations do not bother apocalyptic thought. A third of the heavenly bodies is darkened, and the result is that a third of the day and a third of the night were darkened.

127

Verse 13. The first series of trumpets and the accompanying plagues is now complete. The forces of nature have fallen under divine judgment as a warning to sinful men; and now sounds forth a warning of worse things to come. The fifth and sixth trumpets are plagues which fall directly upon the persons of men.

An **eagle** announces the impending woes. An eagle is chosen because of its strength of wing (12:14), which gives it a wide perspective. The eagle flies at the meridian or zenith of the sky where the sun stands at midday where it can be seen by all. The threefold **woe, woe, woe** announce the last three trumpets and the plagues that will accompany them. **Those who dwell on the earth** is a repeated expression in the Revelation designating the pagan world in its hostility to God (3:10; 6:10; 11:10; 13:8; 17:2). Here, again, it is implied that the plagues of divine wrath fall upon the rebellious, evil society, but that the church, which has been sealed with the protective seal of God, is somehow spared from the suffering of these plagues. This is explicitly stated after the fifth angel sounds his trumpet in 9:4.

CHAPTER NINE

THE SIX TRUMPETS
(continued)

f. The Fifth Trumpet (9:1-12).

The fifth plague is that of a host of demonic locusts who attack the bodies of men but do not kill them. Background for this is a plague of locusts in Joel 2:4-10 which is to precede the coming of the day of the Lord. The appearance of the locusts in Joel was like horses who run with the rumbling of chariots, who charge like mighty men of war, who darken the heavens with their hosts. The difference is that in Joel a plague of actual locusts is envisioned, while in the Revelation, the locusts are symbolic of demonic hosts.

Verse 1. When the fifth angel sounded his trumpet, John **saw a star fallen from heaven to earth.** It is questionable whether any emphasis is to be placed in the word "fallen." Some commentators refer to Isa. 14:12: "How you are fallen from heaven, O Day Star, son of Dawn!" and find in these words a fall of Satan from his place of exaltation. Our Lord also speaks of a fall of Satan: "I saw Satan fall like lightning from heaven" (Luke 10:17). However, there is no reason in Revelation to identify the star with Satan or any evil power. The star represents some angelic figure divinely commissioned to carry out God's purposes. "Fallen" is used because this is the way stars come from the sky to earth, but it signifies no more than that an angelic being has descended from heaven to earth.

The language of the passage immediately changes from the

star to the one symbolized by the star. To him **was given the key of the shaft of the bottomless pit.** There is no single consistent cosmology in biblical literature, but it is true that we often meet the concept of three levels of existence: the earth, heaven above, and the underworld beneath. We have already discovered in John's extensive description of heaven that he does not intend his language to be taken literally but describes heaven with symbolic language. In the same way he now refers to the underworld, which is conceived as a great hollow space in the depths of the earth which is connected with the world by a shaft.

The Greek word translated "bottomless pit" is *abyssos,* from which we get our word abyss. There cannot, of course, really be such a thing as a bottomless pit; one need only ask the question, How deep is the bottomless pit? The word *abyssos* is used in the Greek Old Testament of the deep waters (Gen. 1:2; 7:11; Ps. 107:26). It is also used of the depth of the earth (Ps. 71:20) and came to designate the realm of the dead. So Paul asks, "Who will descend into the abyss? (that is, to bring Christ up from the dead)" (Rom. 10:7). It is the abode of the beast or Antichrist before he appears on earth (Rev. 11:7) and will be the temporary prison of Satan during the millennial reign of Christ (Rev. 20:3). It is also sometimes represented as the home or else the place of imprisonment of demons (Luke 8:31).

In the present instance, it is the abode of hosts of demons who fly forth, scorpionlike, to plague men. That this conceptualization is not meant to be taken literally is suggested by Paul's different thought that Satan is "the prince of the power of the air" (Eph. 2:2) and demons are "spiritual hosts of wickedness in heavenly places" (Eph. 6:12). Furthermore, the Revelation does not uniformly represent Satan as having his abode in the underworld. In chapter 12, Satan is represented as a fiery red dragon who engages in a fearful conflict with the angel Michael. As a result, Satan was thrown down from heaven to the earth along with his angels. This reflects the same idea found in Eph. 2:2, that Satan is the prince of the power of the air. Obviously this is meant to be picturesque, symbolic language to describe realities in the spiritual world.

The shaft, which is the entrance and exit to the abyss, is pictured as being kept under lock and key under the sovereignty of God. Thus, Satan will be locked up in the pit for a thousand years (Rev. 20:3). In the present instance, the key is given to the angelic emissary who has descended from heaven.

Verse 2. **He opened the shaft of the bottomless pit** (with the key he had been given), **and from the shaft rose smoke like the smoke of a great furnace, and the sun and the air were darkened with the smoke from the shaft.** Many interpreters think that this cloud of smoke represents the fires of hell, but there is nothing in the text to suggest it, and in the Old Testament, Sheol — Hades — is a dark and gloomy place. However, the idea of an underworld where fires of torment burn is reflected in the parable of the rich man and Lazarus, which at the least reflects contemporary Jewish ideas employed by our Lord to convey his message to the people of his day (Luke 16:23, 24). The final place of punishment — Gehenna, or Hell — is likened to a lake of fire (Rev. 20:10, 14-15), but it is not located in the heart of the earth; in fact, it is given no location in the biblical writings.

Verse 3. **Then from the smoke came locusts on the earth.** It is tempting to view the cloud of dense smoke itself as the cloud of locusts which, in Palestine, can actually be so thick as to darken the sun (Joel 2:10). However, the text seems clearly to distinguish between the locusts and the cloud of smoke; the locusts came out of the smoke. This is John's vivid way of describing the ascent of demonic hosts. Locusts in the Old Testament are a symbol of God's anger (Exod. 10:13; Joel 1:4). However, in the present instance, they are not actual locusts but creatures symbolic of demonic powers.

They were given power like the power of scorpions of the earth. The scorpion, like the snake, was a creature hostile to man and so became a symbol of the forces of spiritual evil (Luke 10:19; *Sirach* 39:29). Their poisonous sting was proverbial (Ezek. 2:6; cf. Luke 11:12).

Verse 4. **They were told not to harm the grass of the earth or any green growth or any tree.** These locusts out of the abyss have an unusual mission. Ordinarily they consume the green foliage (Exod. 10:15), but this is here explicitly forbidden.

The objects of the scorpions' attack are men, but **only those of mankind who have not the seal of God upon their foreheads.** This takes us back to the seventh chapter where John

131

sees the sealing of the people of God before the last terrible period of tribulation, and this verse gives the purpose of the sealing. The tribulation will be a time of the beginning of the wrath of God upon a rebellious society, a time of fearful persecution of the church by the beast, and, as this trumpet shows, a time of demonic activity. God's wrath will fall only on the worshipers of the beast (16:2), and God's people will be sheltered by a divine protection from demonic activity. But the church in the tribulation will be the victim of persecution and martyrdom as she has been throughout her entire history.

Verse 5. **They were allowed to torture them for five months.** The significance of the five months' period of torture is not clear. It may merely designate a relatively short period in which men will suffer this plague, or it may be derived from actual plagues of locusts which can attack trees and crops at any time during the five months of the warm dry season in Palestine. However, actual attacks of locusts can occur at any time during the five months; here, they attack men continuously throughout the five-month period.

But not to kill them. When scorpions sting men, the result is seldom fatal but causes excruciating pain. This plague is caused by almost indescribable monsters which fly like locusts but sting like scorpions.

Verse 6. The plague of locusts brings suffering which will make men **long to die** in order to be relieved of their agonies; but the sting of the scorpions will not be fatal.

Verse 7. **In appearance the locusts were like horses arrayed for battle.** This descriptive feature is taken directly from Joel 2:4 where an invasion of locusts is described. They looked like war horses. A resemblance has often been imagined to exist between the head of the locust and the head of a horse. An old Arab proverb is often quoted which says that the locust has a head like a horse, a breast like a lion, feet like a camel, a body like a serpent, and antennae like the hair of a maiden.

The locust-scorpions are not said to be wearing crowns; rather, **on their heads were what looked like crowns of gold.** There is no natural feature of locusts which looks like crowns; this is a purely symbolic element used probably to suggest the success of the locusts in their mission.

Their faces were like human faces. This again is not a feature analogous to real locusts. Possibly it is designed to indicate the intelligence of these demonic monsters, or it may be only a feature to add to the terrifying appearance of these hellish locusts.

Verse 8. **Their hair like women's hair.** Ancient commentators often interpreted this as representing the abuse of sexual relations. Some modern commentators see here a reference to the Parthian hosts who dwelt just outside the limits of the Roman Empire to the east who were a constant threat to the Roman peace. The Parthians were known for wearing long hair. The most probable interpretation, in view of the Arab proverb quoted above, is that this is an allusion to the long antennae of locusts.

Their teeth like lions' teeth. This feature is taken from Joel 1:6, where a hostile nation is likened to the threat of a plague of locusts who are described as having teeth like a lion's teeth and fangs of a lioness. This is designed to heighten the intensity of the fierceness of this demonic plague by describing the voracity with which locusts devour the vegetation.

Verse 9. **They had scales like iron breastplates.** The scaly bodies of locusts can be likened to iron breastplates. Iron suggests the powerlessness of men to destroy their demonic foes.

The noise of their wings was like the noise of many chariots with horses rushing into battle. This is again an allusion to Joel's prophecy, where the plague of locusts is described as being "like the appearance of horses, and like war horses they run. As with the rumbling of chariots, they leap in the tops of the mountains" (Joel 2:4-5). An actual invasion of locusts is accompanied by a loud rushing sound made by the beating of millions of wings; the Seer likens the sound to a host of chariots rushing into battle.

Verse 10. **They have tails like scorpions, and stings.** Verse 5 has told us that these demonic locusts have power to torture men for five months as a scorpion stings a man. The present verse describes the way in which this torture is inflicted. These monsters are part locust, part scorpion, having scorpion tails by which they inflict their torture. This obviously is a symbolic representation of demonic powers.

Verse 11. **They have as king over them the angel of the bottomless pit.** Since these scorpionlike locusts ascend from the underworld, we might expect that Satan would be their king. In fact, it is surprising to find that they have a king at all in view of Prov. 30:27: "The locusts have no king, yet all of them march in rank." Their king is **the angel of the bottomless pit,** a figure who appears nowhere else in biblical or Jewish literature. Perhaps he is to be identified with the angelic figure represented in vs. 1 as a fallen star, who has the key to the shaft of the bottomless pit.

His name in Hebrew is Abaddon, and in Greek he is called Apollyon. *Abaddon* is a Hebrew word meaning "destruction," and is always translated in the Greek Old Testament by the word *apoleia,* "destruction," with the single exception of Job 31:12. The word is used to designate the place of destruction synonymously with Sheol or the underworld of the dead in Job 26:6; 28:22; Prov. 15:11; 27:20, and is used by itself of the underworld in such passages as Job 31:12; Ps. 88:11. John renders the word into Greek not by its usual equivalent, *apoleia,* "destruction," but by a participle, *apollyon,* meaning "the destroyer." Some commentators see here a reference to the Greek god Apollo, one of whose symbols was the locust and who sometimes was thought to visit men with plagues and destruction. There is, however, no persuasive reason for this interpretation. John merely gives a symbolic name to the angel of the abyss, "the destroyer," in both its Hebrew and Greek equivalents.

Verse 12. **The first woe has passed; behold, two woes are still to come.** The last three of the seven trumpets are looked upon as three woes because of their terrible destructive power. Before the sounding of the fifth trumpet, an eagle had announced the coming of these three woes (8:13). The second woe is the plague of the sixth trumpet (9:13-21) and the third woe is the seventh trumpet (11:14). The passing of the first woe is not to be taken from the point of view of John in history, but from his future eschatological perspective.

g. The Sixth Trumpet (9:13-21).

The plague of the sixth trumpet is similar to that of the fifth, in that both involve judgments upon the pagan world by demonic hosts. The main difference is that the plague of the fifth trumpet inflicted only torture and suffering while the plague of the sixth trumpet inflicts death.

This is a plague of demonic horses with lionlike heads and serpentlike tails with which they are able to kill men. These demonic hosts come from the East — from the borders of the Roman Empire. It is a historical fact that in the first century the Parthian armies from beyond the Euphrates were a constant threat to the Roman peace, and Jewish apocalyptic anticipated an eschatological invasion from these heathen forces (*Enoch* 56:5-8). These Parthians were famous horsemen and were feared because of their skilled use of the bow and arrow. Some commentators see in John's vision an expectation of such a Parthian invasion; but this is highly unlikely. In the vision the riders of the horses play practically no role; the scourge is inflicted by the horses themselves which represent demonic powers.

Some background for the idea of an eschatological invasion of horses is found in the Old Testament. Ezekiel saw an invasion of horses pouring in from the North (Ezek. 38:14ff.) and such an invasion is often mentioned in other prophets (Isa. 5:26-30; Jer. 6:22-26), usually coming from the North. John has transformed these actual military expectations into an invasion of demonic hordes.

One important new emphasis distinguishes John's vision from the similar expectations of the prophets and apocalyptists. The latter always envision the foreign invasion as an attack against the people of God by pagan hosts while John sees it as a divine judgment upon a corrupt civilization.

Verse 13. After the sounding of the sixth trumpet, John hears **a voice from the four horns of the golden altar before God.** This altar has already been seen in the apocalyptist's vision in the opening of the seventh seal, which brought us to the threshold of the end (8:3). It is the altar of incense which symbolizes the prayers of the saints who constantly cry out to God for deliverance, for vindication of the divine justice, and for the establishing of the divine rule upon the earth. This symbolically portrays the fact that the divine judgment of evil will occur in answer to the prayers of God's people. In the vision it is the altar itself which speaks through its four horns; but this is only a symbolic way of expressing the same idea found in 6:9-10 where the voices of the martyrs are heard coming from under the altar.

Verse 14. The voice from the four horns spoke to the sixth

angel who had sounded the trumpet, saying, **Release the four angels who are bound at the great river Euphrates.** The use of the definite article indicates that a definite group of four angels is indicated. They cannot be the same four angels appearing in 7:1, for those stood at the four corners of the earth. These angels are bound at the river Euphrates. This group of four angels is not known in either prophetic or apocalyptic literature, nor can we say why there are four of them. The fact, however, that they were bound indicates that they were evil angels who could not carry out their desires until they were released. Since they share the same mission as that of the demonic horses, viz., "to kill a third of mankind" (vs. 15), we may assume that they are the supernatural leaders of these demonic hosts.

The Euphrates was the ideal limit of the promised land to the East (Gen. 15:18); and in the Old Testament, it was called the great river (Gen. 15:18; Deut. 1:7; Josh. 1:4). Beyond the Euphrates were the hordes of the heathen kingdoms, particularly Assyria, and thus the river became symbolic of the enemies of Israel and of God (Isa. 7:20; 8:7; Jer. 46:10). An invasion by these forces could be described as an overflow of the river (Isa. 8:7). So the angels are bound on the banks of the Euphrates until the time of judgment when they will be loosed and a flood of demonic powers burst forth upon the civilized world. Undoubtedly first-century readers of the Revelation would have thought of the Parthian hosts, but this does not seem to be John's primary thought.

Verse 15. **So the four angels were released, who had been held ready for the hour, the day, the month, and the year, to kill a third of mankind.** This verse contains an unusual way of designating time, pinpointing this plague to the exact hour. The idea intended is that these evil angels are under God's control; they have no freedom to act until the very hour God designates. They are thus instruments of the divine judgments, all of which are carried out as part of the unfolding of the divine plan for the rebellious world.

Apocalyptic writings often reflect a sense of determinism, i.e., that the events and the time of the end are predetermined. Sometimes, such emphasis is placed upon the necessary unfolding of the times that God himself seems almost subject to the times he has decreed. "For he has weighed the age in the balance, and measured the times by measure, and numbered the times by number; and he will not move nor arouse them until that measure is fulfilled" (*IV Ezra* 4:36-37. See also *Enoch* 81:2). Such a rigid determinism is not found in the Revelation. The times are under God's control; he is the "King of the ages" (15:3). The time of the end and the whole complex of final events unfold according to the divine purpose.

When the angels were released, they went forth to kill a third of mankind. How they accomplished this is not indicated; we may assume that they did so as leaders of the demonic horses. A third of mankind designates a large but not the greater part of mankind. Their mission was not the destruction of the race but, as agents of divine judgment, to warn men of the terrible judgment which awaits those who reject God's love and mercy. Again, it is important to note that this is a judgment which falls upon the people of a rebellious civilization, not upon the people of God (9:4, 20). The fifth trumpet had brought torture; this one brings death.

Verse 16. The size of this demonic host is inconceivable: 200,000,000. They could not be counted; John **heard their number;** i.e., he had to be told. This vast number rests upon Psalm 68:18: "With mighty chariotry, twice ten thousand, thousands upon thousands, the Lord came from Sinai into the holy place." Here, it is not chariots but horses — cavalry. The four destroying angels have dropped out of sight and the demonic horses fill the scene. It is difficult to believe that a literal number is intended; the demonic hosts are simply innumerable.

Verse 17. John now gives us a description of the demonic horses and their riders. By the words, **I saw . . . in my vision,** he reminds us that these are no natural horses and riders but demonic creatures which he has seen in his ecstatic state. This is the only thing that is said about the riders: they wore cuirasses whose color was fiery red, smoky blue, and sulphurous yellow. The grammar of the passage allows the interpretation that both the riders and the horses wore these bright-colored cuirasses, but it is easier to see here a description of the armor of the riders, which corresponds in color to the fire and smoke and brimstone which proceed from the horses' mouths. It is not clear whether all of the armor was tricolored, or whether different riders wore different colors. It is interesting that no offensive weapons of the riders are described, only their protective armor. The center of attention is the demonic horses.

The horses were like nothing ever seen on earth — their **heads . . . were like lions' heads, and fire and smoke and sulphur issued from their mouths.** The emphasis here is certainly upon their ferocity and destructiveness, not upon their regal bearing. Their terror-inspiring appearance is emphasized by the sulphurous, fiery smoke that poured from the mouths' of these beasts. Fire and brimstone (sulphur) indicate their hellish nature (14:10; 19:20; 21:8).

Verse 18. The fire, smoke, and sulphurous brimstone issuing from their mouths are regarded as three separate plagues which bring death to a substantial portion of mankind. The rendering of the AV, "by these three," does not make this as clear as the RSV: **by these three plagues.** The repetition of the words **issuing from their mouths** reminds us of the demonic quality of these plagues.

Verse 19. **For the power of the horses is in their mouths.** The torment of death is inflicted upon a great portion of mankind by the three plagues of fire, smoke, and brimstone which issue from their mouths. Just how these plagues inflict death we are not told.

These demonic horses have another weapon by which they **wound** men: **their tails are like serpents** with which they sting men and cause them to suffer. This feature connects this plague with the demonic locusts of the fifth trumpet which looked like horses and which had tails like scorpions, and stings (9:10). The fifth plague caused only torture; the sixth plague causes both torture and then death. Men are tortured by the snakelike tails of the demonic horses and killed by the **power . . . in their mouths.**

Verse 20. **The rest of mankind, who were not killed by these plagues, did not repent.** The demonic plagues of suffering and death, terrible as they seem, embody a merciful purpose; they are designed to turn men to repentance before it is too late. Throughout the course of the age, men have been able to pursue a path of sin and to defy God with impunity and apparent safety. As the end approaches and the time of judgment draws near, God pours out on men a taste of his judgment and wrath; but this is not because he takes pleasure in wrath but in order to warn men that the way of sin and defiance of God can lead only to disaster.

One would think that the rest of mankind, who were not killed by these plagues, would learn a lesson from the one-third who were killed and would cast themselves in fear and trembling upon God. But not so; they continued in their defiant path of worshiping demons and idols. Idols can be viewed from two different perspectives. In and of itself, "an idol has no real existence" (I Cor. 8:4). This viewpoint is reflected in John's description of idols as **idols of gold and silver and bronze and stone and wood, which cannot either see or hear or walk.** This motif that idols are lifeless wood or stone or metal occurs in the Old Testament (Pss. 115:4-8; 135:15-18; Dan. 5:23) and is frequently found in Jewish apologetic literature (see *Bel and the Dragon*). From another perspective, demons are seen to stand behind idol worship; and while meats offered to idols are not rendered unclean since an idol has no real existence, nevertheless "what pagans sacrifice they offer to demons and not to God" (I Cor. 10:20). Therefore, sacrifice to idols involves one in partnership with demons. This same tension between idols as lifeless wood and stone and yet symbolic of demons appears in the present passage.

Verse 21. The defiance of the rest of mankind is reflected not only in their idolatry but also in their immorality. They did not **repent of their murders or their sorceries or their immorality or their thefts.** Here is the same theology expounded by Paul in Rom. 1:18ff.: ungodliness issues in all kinds of unrighteousness and wickedness. The word translated "sorceries" can mean "poison," but here it designates the use of magic potions and charms in incantations and degraded religious practices. The word for "immorality" designates sexual sin in general.

CHAPTER TEN

THE ANGEL AND THE LITTLE BOOK

John has just finished the account of the sounding of the first six of the seven trumpets, together with the plagues or woes which accompanied them. We would expect him now to relate the sounding of the seventh trumpet; but instead of doing so, John inserts the account of a vision of a great angel who comes down from heaven with a little book in his hand, which John is required to eat (10:1-11). To this he adds the account of the measuring of the temple and the ministry, death, and ascension of two witnesses. After this interlude, John continues the interrupted narrative and records the sounding of the seventh trumpet in 11:14-19.

This is consistent with John's style elsewhere and is an essential factor in the artistic structure of the book. Between the sixth and seventh seals, John inserted the interlude of the two multitudes (7:1-17). Between the seven trumpets and the seven bowls, John inserts the interlude of the dragon and the woman (12:1-17), the vision of the two great beasts (13:1-18), and the vision of the Lamb on Mount Zion (14:1-20).

In the present instance, the interlude is directly preparatory for the continuation of the trumpet visions, for one of the purposes of the interlude is to announce that "in the days of the trumpet call to be sounded by the seventh angel, the mystery of God, as he announced to his servants the prophets, should be fulfilled" (10:7). Then John the prophet is prepared by a renewed commission for his mission in communicating to men the consummation of God's redemptive purpose.

140

(2) Interlude (10:1 — 11:13).

a. The Angel and the Little Book (10:1-11).

Verse 1. **Then I saw another mighty angel.** Angels play a large role in apocalyptic literature; this angel is called "another," possibly to distinguish it from the angel of 8:3, but more likely to distinguish it from the angels of the seven trumpets. The fact that he is a strong angel may identify him with the strong angel of 5:2. But see 18:21 for similar language.

Coming down from heaven. In 4:1, John was caught up into heaven in an ecstatic state, and the visions related in 4:9 were seen in heaven. But suddenly, without explanation, John represents himself as being on earth, for the angel comes down from heaven, takes his stand on the earth and on the sea, and John goes to him to receive the little book from his hand (10:9). This illustrates the fluidity of apocalyptic thought; one can move from heaven to earth in vision without explanation.

Wrapped in a cloud, with a rainbow over his head, and his face was like the sun, and his legs like pillars of fire. All of these items are similar to descriptions of the glorified Christ, and many commentators have identified this figure with Christ. However, in the Apocalypse, angels are always angels; Christ is never called an angel. The fact that the angel "swore by him who lives for ever and ever" (10:6) is meaningful of an angel but very difficult if applied to Christ. Furthermore, this angel plays the role solely of messenger; he is not given the rank of deity, nor is he worshiped.

Clouds were conceived of as the vehicle by which heavenly beings ascend and descend (Ps. 104:3; Dan. 7:13; Acts 1:9); but in the present instance, a cloud provides the angel's garb. This, like the other details, seems designed to enhance the glory of the angel's appearance. The rainbow over his head (or *upon* his head) may be taken as a kind of glorious headdress; some understand it to result from the brilliance of his countenance shining on the clouds. "His face . . . like the sun" recalls the glorified Christ (1:16; but see Dan. 12:3; Matt. 13:43) as do the "legs like pillars of fire" (1:15), but these features do not provide ground for identifying the angel with Christ. They are used to depict the heavenly glory of this strong angel.

Verse 2. **He had a little scroll open in his hand.** The Greek word is different from the word for a book-scroll used in 5:1.

A modern equivalent would be "a little booklet"; but this would not convey the idea of a scroll type of book. The word occurs nowhere else in earlier Greek and appears to be of Johannine coinage. The fact that the book was open suggests that its contents were not hidden but disclosed to those for whom it was intended. Since the angel later lifts his right hand to heaven (10:5), we must conclude that the book rested in his left hand.

The text does not identify the book, and we can only make inferences from the context. Some have placed great emphasis upon the fact that it is a *little* book and have contrasted it with the larger scroll-book of 5:1. If the latter contains the revelation of the unfolding of the divine redemptive and judicial purpose in human history, the little book must contain a fragment of the divine purpose. Many have identified the larger book with Rev. 1-11 and the little book with chapters 12-22. This, however, would make them of approximately equal size. Some see the little book as the word of God, which must be preached in all the world before the end comes.

However, we have a biblical analogy in the experience of Ezekiel. John was commanded to take the book and eat it (10:9) and therefore continue his prophetic ministry; and Ezekiel had a similar experience. He was shown a scroll, written on both sides, containing words of lamentation and mourning and woe. He was told to eat the scroll, which tasted as sweet as honey in his mouth (Ezek. 2:9; 3:3; see also Jer. 15:16-17). This is obviously a symbolic representation of Ezekiel's prophetic commission by which he received the word of God and was commissioned to proclaim God's word of judgment and woe to a rebellious people. This interpretation fits the context of the Revelation. God's judgments are about to reach their terrible climax, and on the threshold of the consummation, John's prophetic call is renewed and reinforced.

And he set his right foot on the sea, and his left foot on the land. The angel brings both a renewal of John's prophetic ministry and also new revelations of divine judgment. The angel's all-encompassing stance suggests not only his gigantic size but intimates that his message involves the whole world.

Verse 3. **And called out with a loud voice, like a lion roaring.** The verb in this sentence is used of the bellowing and lowing of cattle, but it may also indicate the roaring of a lion. The emphasis here is upon the volume of the angel's voice, not upon any animal-like quality. There is no reason to conclude that the angel uttered only inarticulate sounds like a lion. God's voice is also likened to the roaring of a lion in Amos 3:8 and Hosea 11:10.

When he called out, the seven thunders sounded. This phrase is difficult because the use of the definite article in Greek ("*the* seven thunders") usually designates something that is familiar or known. We might expect that John had already referred to the seven thunders, but such is not the case. We may surmise that John refers to something familiar to his readers, but this is only surmise; we do not know. In Psalm 29:3, the voice of the Lord is likened to thunder.

Verse 4. John understood the message uttered by the seven thunders, and he was about to write down what he had heard; but a **voice** commanded him, **Seal up what the seven thunders have said, and do not write it down.** The voice is probably that of either Christ or God. This command is an emphatic way of telling John not to record what the thunders uttered. Technically, of course, it is impossible to seal up a book which has not been written. In apocalyptic writings, the idea of sealing a book means to conceal its contents (Dan. 12:4; Rev. 5:1).

The only hint we have as to the message of the seven thunders is to be found in the fact that in all other passages in the Revelation where thunders occur, they form a premonition of coming judgments of divine wrath (8:5; 11:19; 16:18). This fits the present context, for the angel announces that the consummation of the divine judgments is about to take place. However, John is forbidden from including in his written record the revelations uttered by the seven thunders. The reason for this prohibition is not suggested. Paul had experienced ecstasies in which he heard words which he could not relate (II Cor. 12:4); John is allowed to hear words of judgment which he may not communicate to the churches.

Verse 5. The strong angel who held the book in his left hand **lifted up his right hand to heaven** in the familiar gesture of an oath (Deut. 32:40; Dan. 12:7).

Verse 6. The oath taken by the angel is a very solemn one, in the name of **him who lives for ever and ever, who created heaven and what is in it, and the earth and what is in it, and the sea and what is in it.** This is no mere proliferation of words. The angel announces the imminence of the end in the name of the eternal God, who is also creator and Lord of all creation. In other words, the imminent end will occur because God is the eternal and sovereign one who ultimately rules and overrules all things in his universe.

The content of the oath is **that there should be no more delay.** The translation of this phrase in the AV is very misleading: "that there should be time no longer." We sing in the stirring hymn,

> When the trumpet of the Lord shall sound,
> and time shall be no more. . . .

This rendering suggests that the angel announced the end of time and the beginning of eternity, as though eternity were somehow qualitatively different from time as we know it. However, Oscar Cullmann has made it clear that such a contrast between time and some sort of timeless eternity is a philosophical notion finding little support in biblical theology.[1] To be sure, the Jewish apocalypse *The Secrets of Enoch* describes the age of the consummation as one "where there is no computation, and no end; neither years, nor months, nor days, nor hours" (33:2; see also 65:7). However, this may well be a very late book and does not express a typical Jewish idea. In both the New Testament and Judaism, as Cullmann has shown, the present is viewed as "this age" and the future as the "age to come" (Mark 10:30; Luke 20:34, 35; Eph. 1:21), and the age to come is viewed as unending time. What the angel announces is that there will be no more time intervening before the coming of the end. The consummation will be no longer delayed; the prayers of the saints are about to be answered. This contrasts sharply with the exhortation given to the souls under the altar who cry out for vindication, and who are told "to rest a little longer" until the divine purpose has come to completion.

Verse 7. The affirmation of the strong angel is enlarged in the present verse: **but that in the days of the trumpet call to be sounded by the seventh angel, the mystery of God, as he announced to his servants the prophets, should be fulfilled.** The words are introduced by a strong adversative, "but." Instead of further delay, the end is about to come. This will occur

[1]Oscar Cullmann, *Christ and Time* (Philadelphia: Westminster Press, 1962).

not when the seventh angel sounds, but "in the days" of the sounding of the seventh trumpet. The AV renders the passage "when he shall begin to sound," but this is the less likely translation. The Greek expression is indeed capable of two renditions. The word which John used ordinarily means "to be about to do something" or "to be about to happen" (3:2; 8:13; 10:4), and many commentators accept this translation. However, this is difficult. If this is correct, the verse asserts that the end will come just before the seventh angel sounds; but this is impossible. However, the Greek word can express simple futurity (3:16), and this is the meaning which fits the present passage, and is so rendered by the RSV.

The verse does not say, "when the trumpet sounds," but "in the days of the trumpet call." This suggests clearly that the sounding of the seventh trumpet is not to be thought of as a simple act; it embodies a period of time. We shall see that the period of the seventh trumpet includes the seven bowls (16:1-20) which lead directly to the final judgment of Babylon, the rebellious civilization, and the consummation itself.

"Mystery" is an important biblical word whose primary meaning is not something secret or mysterious but a divine purpose revealed to men. It is used this way in the Greek translation of Daniel 2:29-30, where it designates the eschatological purpose of God revealed first to the king and then to Daniel. In the Qumran literature, we read that, to the Teacher of Righteousness, the leader of the sect, "God made known all the mysteries of the words of his servants, the prophets" (*Commentary on Habakkuk* 7:4-5). That is, God has revealed to the Teacher his divine purpose hidden in the prophetic writings. The classic passage in the New Testament is Rom. 16:25-26, where "mystery" clearly refers to God's redemptive plan, at first hidden in the mind of God, but then revealed and made public to all who will listen to the prophetic word. This is the meaning in the present passage. The "mystery of God" is his total redemptive purpose, which includes the judgment of evil and the eschatological salvation of his people.

The verb translated "announced" is the usual word for preaching the gospel. It might be more closely (if a bit awkwardly) rendered, "as he announced the good news to ... the prophets." *Prophets* were those men, both in the Old Testament and the New, through whom God spoke to his people,

145

giving them the divinely authorized meaning of his redemptive work (see Eph. 3:4-5). While the prophets, particularly those of the Old Testament and the New Testament prophet John, devote much of their God-given message to judgment, both of God's people and of a rebellious world, this is nevertheless good news. God's people can never enjoy in their fullness the blessings of salvation and of fellowship with God until all that disrupts that fellowship and brings pain, oppression, suffering, and death to God's people is purged from the universe.

Verse 8. The voice that John had heard prohibiting him from writing the words of the seven thunders now bids him to go to the great angel and take the little book out of his left hand. This suggests, as we have already noted, that John pictures himself as having been moved in vision from heaven back to earth. The fact that for the third time the angel is described as the one who stands on both land and sea (vss. 2, 5) suggests that this is no unimportant detail. The message of the angel is primarily directed to the prophet John, but it is intended for the whole world.

Verse 9. **So I went to the angel and told him to give me the little scroll; and he said to me, "Take it and eat, it will be bitter to your stomach, but sweet as honey in your mouth."** As we have indicated above (see on vs. 2), this experience of John is analogous to that of the prophet Ezekiel (Ezek. 2:9; 3:3), and represents the reaffirmation of his prophetic commission in view of the impending end, and particularly in view of the judgments of God's wrath which are about to fall. The symbol of eating the scroll is a natural one suggesting the complete assimilation of the prophetic message. The prophet is no mere automaton in the hand of God — an unfeeling herald of events which do not involve him. The word of God — the message of both salvation and judgment — must be ingested and personally assimilated by the prophet, as it must be by every servant of God who proclaims his word. In the same way, Ezekiel was told to eat the scroll of God's word and fill his stomach with it (Ezek. 3:3); and Jeremiah ate God's words, and they became to him a joy and the delight in his heart (Jer. 15:16). This is an important insight, for although Jeremiah's message was largely one of judgment, so that he is popularly known as the weeping prophet, the word of God was his delight.

146

The sweetness and bitterness do not refer to different parts of the scroll or different aspects of the prophet's message which, for the church, is partly a message of salvation and partly a message of persecution, suffering, and martyrdom. Rather, the sweetness and bitterness refer to the twofold reaction on the part of the prophet as he digests his message and understands it. It is a sweet thing to be close to God, to be the recipient of his word. This is true of all believers. The word of God is "sweeter also than honey and drippings from the honeycomb" (Ps. 19:10). Every Christian can say, "How sweet are thy words to my taste, sweeter than honey to my mouth" (Ps. 119:103). This is particularly true of the prophetic commission. The scroll eaten by Ezekiel was sweet as honey in his mouth (Ezek. 3:3) even though he was to proclaim his God-given message to an unresponsive, stubborn, and rebellious people (Ezek. 3:7-9); and God's word was a delight to Jeremiah's heart even though his was a message of doom (Jer. 15:16). In the same way John found God's word to be sweet as honey in his mouth. But as he digested his message and pondered its implications, it became bitter in his stomach. This is a new feature in the Revelation which goes beyond the accounts in Ezekiel and Jeremiah. We are reminded of Jesus' weeping bitter tears over Jerusalem because the people had rejected him and his message and so brought upon themselves the wrath and judgment of God (Luke 19:41; see Matt. 23:37-38).

Here is an important truth for all who proclaim the word of God. The full counsel of God contains a word of judgment as well as mercy, and the messenger of the gospel must be faithful to both aspects of his message. But the man who knows the love of God and the compassion of Christ can never take delight in preaching the wrath of God or find satisfaction of spirit in proclaiming divine judgments. He must always do this with a broken heart, with a bitter spirit, following the example of his Lord who wept over those upon whom God's judgment was to fall.

Verse 11. **And I was told, "You must again prophesy about many people and nations and tongues and kings."** This verse determines the meaning of the little scroll: it is a reaffirmation of John's prophetic ministry. The end is not yet, but it is soon to come. The final era — the days of the seventh trumpet — are about to begin. But this will be a period of the outpouring of

God's wrath to a degree not previously experienced, and in the face of it, John's prophetic commission is reaffirmed.

This verse contains one small word whose exact meaning is very difficult to determine: the Greek preposition *epi,* which has a host of nuances and meanings. The three most important possibilities in the present context are "before" (Matt. 28:14; Acts 25:12), "against" (Luke 12:52; Acts 11:19), and "about" (John 12:16; Heb. 11:4). The translation, "You must prophesy again before many peoples and nations ..." (AV) makes good sense; but this meaning requires the genitive case, whereas the object in the text is in the dative case. This leaves us with the choice of prophesying against many peoples, or prophesying about many peoples. The balance of probability must be determined by the fact that this idiom occurs not infrequently in the Greek Bible to render a Hebrew idiom meaning "to prophesy in regard to." Thus, we conclude that the RSV, to "prophesy about many peoples ..." (see NEB, to "utter prophecies over many peoples") is probably correct (see the similar usage in Rev. 22:16). John's prophetic message of coming judgment does not concern one people or nation but many, i.e., the entire civilized world. In the immediate foreground are the people of the Roman Empire who were willingly subservient to Rome; but the ultimate view includes an apostate civilization willingly subservient to Antichrist.

"You must *again* prophesy," John is told. John has already prophesied about the seven seals and six of the seven trumpets. Now with the coming of the period of the last trumpet he must prophesy again, and this prophecy will include the consummation itself and the coming of God's Kingdom.

CHAPTER ELEVEN

THE MEASURING OF THE TEMPLE
AND THE TWO WITNESSES

The interlude between the sounding of the sixth and seventh trumpets is contained in this chapter, most of which is devoted to the measuring of the temple and the mission of two witnesses. At 11:14, the trumpet series is resumed and the seventh trumpet is sounded. We must remember that chapter and verse divisions are a relatively modern invention and do not always represent units of thought in the text.

It will be helpful first to summarize the chapter. John is told to measure the temple of God and its worshipers, but to exclude from the measurement the outer court, which is to be trampled down by the nations for forty-two months. God sends two witnesses to Jerusalem to testify against the nations, but the beast kills them and all the people rejoice at this martyrdom. After three and a half days, they are revived and caught up to heaven. Then a great earthquake destroys a tenth of the city, seven thousand people are killed, but the rest give glory to the God of heaven.

There are four plausible interpretations of this chapter. Many commentators understand it to be a piece of earlier Jewish apocalyptic, written before A.D. 70 while the temple was still standing and thus to be taken literally and historically in its intent. In this view, the temple is the actual historical temple in Jerusalem and the passage predicts that when the temple was besieged by Roman armies, the inner shrine would be preserved from the destruction that befell the temple as a whole. Such an alleged prophecy, of course, was not fulfilled.

It is highly unlikely that John would have included such a prophecy, which would have been meaningless both to him and to his readers.

Dispensationalists interpret the main features in the passage with stark literalism and see a prophecy of the restoration of the Jewish temple in Jerusalem at the end of the age and of the struggle between the restored Jews and the Antichrist (the Beast). The difficulty with this is that there are elements in the chapter which demand symbolic interpretation, which even dispensationalists admit. The most recent dispensational interpreter has recognized that this is a symbolic picture;[1] and if this is admitted, there is no logical or compelling reason for not taking the Holy City and the temple as symbolical either of the church or the Jewish people.

A third interpretation finds a prophecy of the church and its fate in a hostile world. While the church outwardly will suffer persecution and martyrdom, God will preserve his people and assure their ultimate triumph.[2]

A fourth interpretation sees here a prophecy of the preservation and ultimate salvation of the Jewish people. In the day when John wrote, Jerusalem had been long destroyed and the temple laid waste. Just before the conflagration of A.D. 66-70, the Jewish Christian community had fled from Jerusalem to the city of Pella in Transjordan. This had augmented the hostility of the Jews toward the Jewish Christian community and hastened the complete break between the synagogue and church. The burning question among Jewish Christians was, "Has God rejected his people?" (Rom. 11:1). Paul devoted three whole chapters to this problem and concluded that finally the natural branches (Jews) which had been broken off the olive tree (the people of God) would be grafted back onto the tree; "and so all Israel will be saved" (Rom. 11:26). It is difficult to interpret these three chapters symbolically of the church — the spiritual Israel. They teach that literal Israel is yet to be included in spiritual Israel.

Our Lord himself had anticipated this. After his lament over Jerusalem, he asserted, "For I tell you, you will not see me

[1]John Walvoord, *The Revelation of Jesus Christ* (Chicago: Moody Press, 1966), p. 176.

[2]See the commentaries by Henry Alford, H. B. Swete, G. B. Caird, Leon Morris.

again, until you say, 'Blessed be he who comes in the name of the Lord'" (Matt. 23:39). Again, he implied the salvation of Israel when he said, "Jerusalem will be trodden down by the Gentiles *until* the times of the Gentiles are fulfilled" (Luke 21:24). We believe with such scholars as I. T. Beckwith, W. H. Simcox, and Theodor Zahn that the prophecy in Revelation 11 is John's way of predicting the preservation of the Jewish people and their final salvation.[3]

b. The Measuring of the Temple and the Two Witnesses (11:1-13).

Verse 1. **Then I was given a measuring rod like a staff, and I was told: "Rise and measure the temple of God and the altar and those who worship there."** The Greek word translated "temple" designates the temple building proper in distinction to the outer court. This is important in the interpretation of the passage. The temple area as a whole consisted of a complex, at the center of which stood a building or shrine within which were the Holy Place and the Holy of Holies. This was surrounded or bordered by three courts: the court of the priests containing the altar of burnt offering, into which only priests were admitted, and two adjoining courts: the court of Israel and the court of the women. As the terms suggest, these were the courts where the Jewish people might assemble to worship. These inner courts were surrounded by a vast outer court — the court of the gentiles, to which all interested men were given access.

In the present vision, the temple proper, the courts of the priests, of Israel, and of the women, together with those who worship there, were measured off and separated from the outer court of the gentiles. The metaphor of measuring a city has nothing to do with determining its dimensions. It is a symbol of setting a city aside either for preservation or for destruction. Zechariah saw a man measuring Jerusalem, which was symbolic of her divine protection (Zech. 2:1-5). Ezekiel had an elaborate vision of the measuring of Jerusalem — a symbol of the fact that Jerusalem would yet become the true city of God (Ezek. 40-43). In other places, measuring is a symbolic act indicating destruction rather than preservation (II Kings 21:13; Isa.

[3]For a further discussion of Israel and the church, see notes on 7:4-8.

34:11; Lam. 2:8). In John's vision, the measuring of the temple, its inner courts, and those who worship there is a symbol of preservation and protection.

It is interesting, although not particularly important, to note that John has become an actor in his vision. He was given a reed and was told to "rise and measure the temple of God." However, once this action was completed, he became again an observer.

Verse 2. **But do not measure the court outside the temple; leave that out, for it is given over to the nations, and they will trample over the holy city for forty-two months.** The temple and the inner courts are separated from the outer court — the court of the gentiles — which is not protected but, together with the holy city, Jerusalem as a whole, is to be trampled by the nations.

It is true that the Greek word used for "temple," *naos,* is used in the New Testament of the church as the true dwelling place of God in contrast to the obsolete Jewish temple (I Cor. 3:16; II Cor. 6:16; Eph. 2:21). In principle, there is no reason why the measuring of the temple might not represent symbolically the preservation of the church. However, here the temple is not represented primarily as the dwelling place of God but as the Jewish temple in Jerusalem. Furthermore, something specific seems to be intended in the contrast between the preservation of the temple proper and its courts, and the nonpreservation of the outer court and Jerusalem as a whole. It is difficult to recognize here, as some do, a contrast between spiritual preservation in the midst of physical persecution and martyrdom.

The key to our understanding of the passage is found in the fact that the outer court and the entire city of Jerusalem are both trampled by the gentiles. The most natural meaning of Jerusalem is that it stands for the Jewish people. When Jesus spoke of the trampling of Jerusalem by the gentiles (Luke 21:24), he meant to designate the city as representative of the entire people. When in contrast to the city as a whole, the temple proper and its worshipers are preserved, the contrast seems to be between the Jewish people as a whole and a remnant who are true worshipers of God. Historically, all Jews had access to the inner court of Israel to engage in the worship of God. Yet it is obvious that here the temple and its wor-

shipers cannot represent all Israel, for they stand in contrast
to the outer court and to the city of Jerusalem as a whole
which represent the nation. This suggests a contrast between
a faithful remnant of believing Israelites who, in contrast to
the city as a whole (the holy city), are true worshipers of God.
Israel as a whole will be trodden down by the nations; i.e., they
will fall under the divine judgment because they have become
spiritually apostate. This is supported by verse 8 where Jerusalem is "allegorically called Sodom and Egypt, where their
Lord was crucified." Elsewhere in Scripture, Jerusalem stands
for the nation (Ps. 137:5-6; Isa. 40:1-2; Matt. 23:37).

The figure "forty-two months" harks back to the prophecy
in Daniel 9, where the forecast of time down to the confirming
of the covenant is said to be "seventy weeks of years" (Dan.
9:24). This cannot be interpreted by anyone's calculation as an
exact prognosis of time.[4]

Three and a half years is the time of the domination of evil
before the end. The little horn which arises out of the ten
horns of the fourth beast in Daniel 7 will oppress the saints
of the Most High for "a time, two times, and half a time"
(Dan. 7:25; see also 12:7). In the Revelation, this figure is the
time of the oppression of the holy city (Rev. 11:2), of the
mission of the two witnesses (11:3), the time of the preservation
of the heavenly woman (the church) in the wilderness (12:6,
14), and the time during which the beast is allowed to exercise
his authority (13:5). We must recall that John wrote the
Revelation probably some sixty years after the ministry of our
Lord, which makes it obvious that this interval cannot stand in
John's mind in any kind of direct continuity with the seventy
weeks of Daniel. We must conclude that the forty-two months
(1,260 days) represent the period of the satanic power in the
world, with particular reference to the final days of the Antichrist. All that God's people are to suffer at the hands of satanic
evil throughout the course of the age is but a preview of the
final convulsive oppression by Antichrist in the time of the
end. In this sense, the entire course of the age may be viewed
as the time of the end.[5]

[4]For interpretation of the passage, see E. J. Young, *The Prophecy of
Daniel* (Grand Rapids: Eerdmans, 1949), pp. 201-221.

[5]The eschatological expression "the last days" is used in the New Testament of the age of the gospel of Christ (Heb. 1:2), the age of the Holy
Spirit (Acts 2:17), as well as the last days of evil (II Tim. 3:1).

Verse 3. **And I will grant my two witnesses power to prophesy for one thousand two hundred and sixty days.** Although the holy city is to be trodden by the nations for forty-two months, God will not abandon his people. He will send to them two witnesses to prophesy the word of God to an afflicted people. It is difficult to decide whether John thought of these two witnesses as actual historical persons or whether they are representative of the church in its witness to Israel. In favor of the latter conclusion is the fact that the two preceding verses, which speak of the measuring of the temple and the inner courts and of the trampling of the outer court, are clearly symbolic. However, the description of the two witnesses and the character of their ministry is given in such detail that it seems more likely that John conceived of these two witnesses as two actual historical eschatological personages who will be sent to Israel to bring about her conversion. Possibly there is a blending of the symbolic and the specific. Even as the three and a half years appear to represent the entire period of the domination of evil but with special reference to the last days of this age, so the two prophets may represent the witness of the church to Israel throughout the age, which witness will be consummated in the appearance of two prophets in the time of the end. The flexibility of apocalyptic symbolism must allow for such possibilities.

Clothed in sackcloth indicates the usual garb of prophets (II Kings 1:8; Isa. 20:2; Zech. 13:4).

Verse 4. **These are the two olive trees and the two lampstands which stand before the Lord of the earth.** This is a definite allusion to a vision of Zechariah, in which he saw a golden lampstand with seven lamps, flanked by two olive trees (Zech. 4:1-3) from which they drew their supply of oil (Zech. 4:12). In Zechariah, these two represent the two anointed "who stand by the Lord of the whole earth" (Zech. 4:14), his two witnesses, Joshua the priest (Zech. 3:1) and Zerubbabel the governor (Zech. 4:6-7). The symbolism of Zechariah is used by John to affirm the divine authorization of the two witnesses and the source of their prophetic utterances. It seems quite clear that we are to think of them as Christian prophets because of the phrase "where their Lord was crucified" in verse 8. The great sin of Israel was the rejection of Jesus as their Messiah and Lord. The two prophets bear the witness of the law and

154

the prophets to the lordship of Jesus as Messiah and therefore to the sin of Israel in rejecting him.

Verse 5. No one can harm the two witnesses so long as their mission is incomplete. If anyone tries to harm them, **fire pours from their mouth and consumes their foes.** Any effort to destroy the two prophets leads to self-destruction. Here is an allusion to the story of Elijah whose prophetic call was certified by fire from heaven (II Kings 1:11-12), but more clearly to Jeremiah, the words in whose mouth were a fire devouring a rebellious people (Jer. 5:14). These two prophets bring destruction upon their enemies by the words they utter.

Verse 6. This verse suggests the identity of the two witnesses. It was Elijah who had **power to shut the sky, that no rain may fall** and Moses who had **power over the waters to turn them into blood, and to smite the earth with every plague.** Moses and Elijah appeared on the Mount of Transfiguration talking with Jesus (Mark 8:4). However, these two prophets need not be thought of as the historical prophets Moses and Elijah returning to earth, but as two eschatological prophets who will be the embodiment of these two great prophets, even as John the Baptist was the embodiment of Elijah (Matt. 11:14; 17:10-13).

Verse 7. **And when they have finished their testimony, the beast that ascends from the bottomless pit will make war upon them and conquer them and kill them.** Until their mission is completed, the person of the two witnesses is inviolate; but when they have accomplished their task, they fall prey to the wrath of the beast.

Here is the first mention of the beast, and he is referred to almost casually, as though he were a familiar figure. Some commentators see here a proleptic reference to the beast of chapter 13, and this is obviously true in part. However, the beast or Antichrist was a familiar concept in Jewish-Christian thought and did not require detailed description. The idea goes back to Daniel 7 where a succession of great world empires is symbolized by the appearance of four fierce beasts. The fourth beast had ten horns, out of which grew another horn which was greater than its fellows (Dan. 7:20) and which "made war with the saints, and prevailed against them." This "little horn" (Dan. 7:8) "shall speak words against the Most High and shall wear out the saints of the Most High . . . , and they shall be given into his hand for a time, two times, and half a time" (Dan. 7:25). This little horn had an initial fulfillment in Antiochus Epiphanes, the Seleucid king who tried to turn the entire Jewish nation away from the worship of her God (see the account in *I Maccabees*), but it refers ultimately to the eschatological Antichrist.

In his Olivet Discourse, Jesus foretold the coming of an eschatological figure called the "desolating sacrilege" (Mark 13:14; Matt. 24:15), who will inflict upon God's people the most fearful time of trouble and persecution ever known. So devastating will it be that "if the Lord had not shortened the days, no human being would be saved" (Mark 13:20). This fearful personage was prefigured in the terrible event in A.D. 66-70 when Jerusalem was surrounded by armies and the temple desolated by the Roman hosts under Titus (Luke 21:20). Here is a fundamental clue to the understanding of biblical prophecy: eschatological events are foreshadowed in historical events.

Paul also was familiar with this figure, whom he called the man of lawlessness because he defied the laws of God and man and claimed absolute sovereignty for himself (II Thess. 2:3-4). He will oppose and exalt himself against every so-called god or object of worship and even seek to dethrone God that he might himself be the absolute sovereign. Paul added a feature which reappears in the Revelation: this eschatological figure will be satanically inspired, and will have as his chief end the turning of men from Christ that they might perish (II Thess. 2:9-10).[6]

The beast (or Antichrist) is a central figure in the Revelation. He is primarily an eschatological figure in whom will be concentrated the centuries-long hostility to God manifested in the history of godless nations; but this hostility is also foreshadowed in Rome and its emperor as it was in Antiochus Epiphanes. In the present passage, the beast represents both every hostile evil power that oppresses and persecutes God's people, but primarily the eschatological figure at the end of the age.

The abyss or "bottomless pit" from which the beast ascends was the source of the demonic plagues of the fifth and sixth

[6]The Antichrist expectation is found in Jewish apocalyptic in such passages as *Psalms of Solomon* 2:29; 17:3; *Apocalypse of Baruch* 40:1-3; *Ascension of Isaiah* 4:2-8; *Sibylline Oracles* 3:63-74.

trumpets. The beast too is of satanic origin and power, and derives his authority from the demonic realm.

When the two witnesses have fulfilled their divinely appointed mission, the beast is allowed to make war on them and to kill them. Too much should not be made of the metaphor of war; in chapter 12, war occurs in heaven between Michael and his angels and the dragon (Satan) (12:7-8), where it is obvious that "war" means a spiritual conflict. In the present passage, war is simply conquest by whatever means, not necessarily by military weapons.

Verse 8. **Their dead bodies will lie in the street of the great city which is allegorically called Sodom and Egypt, where their Lord was crucified.** To leave dead bodies lying exposed and unburied was the extreme indignity in the ancient world (I Kings 21:24; Jer. 8:1-2; 14:16). It is obvious that the city of Jerusalem is intended. In vs. 2, we have found reason to believe that "the holy city" was used synonymously with the outer court of the temple in contrast to the temple building and the inner courts and demanded a symbolical interpretation, referring to the Jewish people as a whole. The symbolic interpretation is more difficult in the present passage. The fact that the city is the place where the Lord was crucified seems to point to the literal city. In chapter 13, the sphere of the beast's power is Rome, both historical and eschatological. Here we must conclude that John envisaged the rule of the beast as extending to Jerusalem. This prophecy could have no relevance for John's own day; for in the Jewish war of A.D. 66-70, the city had been utterly razed, the temple destroyed, and Jerusalem had ceased to be a Jewish center. We can only agree with Hanns Lilje, "Thus here Jerusalem is not merely mentioned as an empty theoretical metaphor. In some way or another the earthly, geohistorical Jerusalem will have its place in the history of the last days."[7] The beast has established his sovereignty in the capital city of his empire, and it extends even to Jerusalem, which is here pictured as rebuilt and inhabited by Jews.

"Sodom and Egypt" are symbolic of hostility to God and God's people, Sodom for the way its inhabitants tried to treat Lot's angelic visitors (Gen. 19:1-11), and Egypt because she had enslaved God's people. "Sodom" became a symbol of wick-

[7]Hanns Lilje, *The Last Book of the Bible* (Philadelphia: Muhlenberg Press, 1955), p. 161.

edness and is applied to Judah in the days of her apostasy (Deut. 32:32; Isa. 1:9; Ezek. 16:46, 49, 55; Jer. 23:14). "Egypt" was never applied to God's people in the Old Testament. The particular nature of Jerusalem's sinfulness consisted in the fact that she was the city "where their Lord was crucified." It is also the city which has thus far rejected the witness of the two prophets sent by God to turn Israel to her Messiah.

Verse 9. Not only the inhabitants of Jerusalem treat the dead bodies of the prophets with great indignity; **men from the peoples and tribes and tongues and nations,** i.e., gentile people **gaze at their dead bodies and refuse to let them be placed in a tomb.** This statement leads to the assumption that the Jews of Jerusalem have entered into sympathetic alliance with the nations round about them, and both Jew and gentile join in their despite of the two prophets.

For three days and a half is a symbolic number designating a time of calamity or of evil. This usage reinforces our conclusion that the number three years and a half (see vs. 2) is not meant to be taken with strict literalness but is symbolic of the time of trouble.

Verse 10. **Those who dwell on the earth** is a frequent idiom in the Revelation designating the pagan world (3:10; 6:10; 8:13; 13:8, 14; 17:8). While the witness of the two prophets had been addressed primarily to the Jews, their message had included a rebuke to the pagan world and a denunciation of their wicked ways. Therefore the pagans rejoiced at the death of the two preachers and sent presents to one another as an expression of their delight.

Verse 11. **But after the three and a half days a breath of life from God entered them, and they stood up on their feet, and great fear fell on those who saw them.** It is difficult to think that John intends by these words anything less than a literal statement. The conversion of Israel is to be accomplished by a miracle of resurrection. The "three and a half days" is no reference to the three days of Jesus' entombment, but refers simply to the period when their bodies lay unburied in the streets of the city (vs. 9). "Breath of life" is a good Old Testament phrase (Gen. 2:7; 6:17; 7:15, 22). The resurrection of the two prophets reminds us of the prophecy of the revival of Israel in Ezek. 37:10. Some commentators understand John to be speaking symbolically of the perseverance of the church through times of persecution and martyrdom, of her triumphal vindication in the face of her enemies, or even of the rapture of the church (I Thess. 4:17), but this seems doubtful. The resurrection of the martyrs is a public event designed to bring "great fear . . . on those who saw them."

Verse 12. The resurrection of the two martyrs is followed by their ascension to heaven. The people who beheld their resurrection **heard a loud voice from heaven saying to them, "Come up hither!" And in the sight of their foes they went up to heaven in a cloud.** The words are nearly the same as those addressed to John in 4:1, but the meaning is different. John was caught up to heaven in spirit, in ecstasy, while the two witnesses were translated to heaven bodily in the sight of those who had so recently rejoiced over their death. Here, the two witnesses are openly caught up to heaven as a sign to those to whom they had been witnesses that they were truly prophets empowered by God.

Verse 13. **And at that hour there was a great earthquake, and a tenth of the city fell; seven thousand people were killed in the earthquake, and the rest were terrified.** An earthquake is one of the usual convulsive events that presage the end (see 6:12 and Ezek. 38:19, 20). The death and ascension of the two witnesses was accompanied by a great physical catastrophe which killed seven thousand of the residents of Jerusalem. This figure represents about one tenth of the population of the city. The population of the city is thought to be about 100,000. This indicates a limited catastrophe.

The result of the resurrection and ascension of the two martyrs and of the following earthquake was the conversion of the rest of the city. This appears to be a symbolic way of describing the final conversion of the Jewish people as a whole. "The rest" suggests the other inhabitants of Jerusalem; there is no reason to apply the term to the gentiles who are constantly represented in the Revelation as unrepentant dedicated worshipers of the beast (9:21; 16:9).

The statement that they **gave glory to the God of heaven** suggests repentance, not merely remorse. Some interpreters understand the phrase to mean that they glorified God in fear and terror but did not really repent. However, the phrase as it is used elsewhere suggests repentance (Josh. 7:19; Isa. 42:12; Jer. 13:16; I Pet. 2:12; Rev. 14:7; 15:4; 16:9; 19:7; 21:24). Be-

159

cause of these mighty acts of God in the end time, the Jewish people will repent of their sins and give glory to the true God. Previously they have not glorified God; they had crucified his Messiah and rejected his prophets. But now they repent of their disobedience and glorify God.

(3) The Seventh Trumpet (11:14-19).

John has now concluded his interlude about the angel and the little book and the measuring of the temple, and he resumes the series of the sounding of the seven trumpets which he had interrupted. The time of the seventh trumpet will be the time of the end (10:6), but before the end, John has been given a reassurance of his prophetic commission and has been assured that not only will the church be preserved during this terrible period (7:1-17), but that Israel, God's covenant people, would be saved. We must be reminded that the sounding of the seventh trumpet is not said itself to introduce the end, but to introduce the period of the end (9:7). As we shall see, this is a somewhat extended period and includes the period of the seven bowls.

Verse 14. **The second woe has passed; behold, the third woe is soon to come.** John introduces the seventh trumpet as though there had been no interruption. The plagues of the last three trumpets constitute these three woes (9:12). The first two woes, which consisted of the plagues of the fifth and sixth trumpets, are past; the third woe — the seventh trumpet — is about to occur.

Verse 15. When the seventh angel sounded his trumpet, no woe immediately fell upon men. The woe involved in the seventh trumpet really consists of the seven bowls of 16:1-21. We must again be reminded of the literary parallelism in the structure of the Apocalypse. Each of the six seals (6:1-17) has a specific content; these are followed by an interlude affirming the security of God's people in the last days. The seventh seal (8:1) has of itself no specific content; instead, John describes the sounding of the seven trumpets (8:1 — 9:20). We have been forced to conclude that the seven trumpets themselves constituted the seventh seal. In the same way, the seventh trumpet, which is the third woe, contains no plague or woe; we must conclude that the seven bowls constitute the woe of the seventh trumpet.

Instead of a woe or plague, loud voices in heaven announce
the coming of the end. **The kingdom of the world has become
the kingdom of our Lord and of his Christ, and he shall reign
for ever and ever.** These heavenly voices announce that the
time of the end has come, but the end itself is not yet described. The AV renders the passage, "the kingdoms of this
world," but the correct form is the singular, as RSV. The idea
is that behind the many diverse kingdoms which have ruled
men in human history, there lies a single source of authority.
This will be manifested in concentrated form in the Antichrist
in the last days. Here is a profound bit of theology: the evil,
demonic powers which the church must face in the eschatological consummation are in principle no different from the auto-
cratic power which the church has had to face in secular states
throughout her history.

The verb is in the past tense — "The kingdom of this world
has become the kingdom of our Lord and of his Christ" — but
the past tense can be used proleptically of a certain event in the
near future. Referring to his impending conflict with the
powers of evil involved in his death, Jesus said, "Now *is* the
judgment of this world, now *shall* the ruler of this world be
cast out" (John 12:31).

This is the central theme of the book of Revelation: the
establishment of the Kingdom of God on the earth. This involves the wresting of authority from all hostile powers, including the godless nations of earth, and the exercise of all
authority by the *Lord and his Christ.* Usually in the New Testament *Lord* is a name for the exalted Christ; here it designates
the Lord God. *Christ* is the Greek word for Messiah, God's
anointed king.

The perspective here employed in the establishment of
God's Kingdom does not distinguish between the millennial
reign of Christ and God's reign in the age to come. Paul seems
to anticipate two periods in the establishment of God's Kingdom: the messianic reign of the exalted Lord between his
resurrection-ascension and the end *(telos),* and the consummation when he turns the Kingdom over to God the Father (I
Cor. 15:24-28).[8] But even if the immediate agent is the Messiah,

[8]See Oscar Cullmann, *The Early Church,* A. J. B. Higgins, ed. (Philadelphia: Westminster, 1956), pp. 111-112.

the Kingdom is still God's rule; and the subject of "he shall reign for ever and ever" is God.

This same proleptic announcement of the establishing of God's reign occurs again in 12:10; 19:6, 16.

Verses 16-17. At the proclamation of these voices, **the twenty-four elders who sit on their thrones before God fell on their faces and worshiped God, saying, "We give thanks to thee, Lord God Almighty, who art and who wast, that thou hast taken thy great power and begun to reign."** The twenty-four elders repeat the proleptic announcement in different words. All authority and power belongs to God, but he in his sovereign wisdom has permitted satanic powers to exercise great authority in the world, and he has allowed godless nations to defy the divine sovereignty with apparent impunity. Now, at the consummation of his redemptive work, God, the eternal one, has wrested this authority from both demonic and human hosts and is about to enter upon his triumphant reign. The reference must be to the eschatological consummation. It is true that the exalted Jesus since his resurrection-ascension has been enthroned at the right hand of God as Lord and Messiah (Acts 2:34-36; Heb. 1:3; Rev. 3:21). It is not this intermediary reign which is here celebrated; this is hidden from the world and visible only to the eye of faith. The twenty-four elders here celebrate the visible establishment of God's reign over all hostile powers; but this in turn is only possible because of the present heavenly reign of Christ.

What the RSV translates "begun to reign," the AV renders as a past tense: "hast reigned." The Greek tense is indeed a past tense, but Greek has what is called an ingressive use of the aorist (past) tense which places the emphasis upon the inception of an action with little emphasis upon the time of the act. This explains the translation of RSV.

Verse 18. **The nations raged.** John looked for no universal salvation. A feature which has characterized the entire course of human history — the anger of nations which defy God (Ps. 2:1) — will come to its consummation in a final expression of rage.

Thy wrath came. God's Kingdom can never be established so long as hostile nations are allowed to defy his rule and to oppress his people. The visitation of God's wrath is absolutely essential to the establishing of his gracious rule in the world.

And the time for the dead to be judged. The coming of God's Kingdom will concern not only those who are living in the last day; it will concern also the entire human family when the dead will be raised and judgment held to determine who will enter God's eternal Kingdom and who will be excluded.

The day of judgment will include a **rewarding** of those who have served God, particularly **the prophets and saints.** "Saints" designates God's people in general of every era.

And those who fear thy name, both small and great is probably an "epexegetic" clause enlarging upon "the prophets and saints." The Greek word usually translated "and" can be a connective meaning "even."

And for destroying the destroyers of the earth. God's judgment will not be arbitrary but will be suited to the conduct of those who fall under his wrath.

Verse 19. **Then God's temple in heaven was opened.** Here again we find symbolic language which suggests the coming of the Kingdom of God. At the death of our Lord, the curtain which separated men from the presence of God was rent in two (Matt. 27:51), signifying that now because of the fulfillment of the Old Testament sacrificial rites in the death of Jesus, the presence of God was no longer limited to Israel but is open to all men (see Heb. 9:8; 10:20). This, however, was only a spiritual fact, not yet a visible reality. All men now have access in spirit to God through Christ. They remain in their mortal bodies on earth, while God's temple is located in heaven. God has revealed himself to men through Jesus of Nazareth, but his own dwelling remains in heaven (3:12; 7:15; 15:5); he does not yet dwell among men. The point of the present passage is a symbolic representation of the opening up of the presence of God in the eschatological consummation. God's temple in heaven was opened that men may henceforth enter into unmediated fellowship with him. This is a symbolic way of proclaiming what is fulfilled in Rev. 21:3: "Behold, the dwelling of God is with men."

That this is a proleptic vision is seen from the fact that the temple is conceived as continuing to be in heaven (14:15, 17; 15:5; 16:17). The opening of the temple is a proleptic, symbolic act of the consummation which does not itself occur until chapters 21-22. In the consummation, God himself dwells among his people and there will be no need of a temple.

The ark of the covenant was seen within his temple. This is a reminder that God is the God of the covenant promises (Eph. 2:12); and in the eschatological consummation, all that he has promised, from the covenant with Abraham to the new covenant in Christ, will be fulfilled. In the Old Testament, the ark of the covenant stood within the Holy of Holies, to which none but the priests had access. It was symbolic of the very presence of God. What happened to the actual ark of the covenant we do not know. If it was not taken away by Shishak, king of Egypt, when he "took away the treasures of the house of the Lord" (I Kings 14:25), it must have been destroyed along with the temple when it was captured by the Babylonians in 586 B.C. (Jer. 3:16). A later Jewish legend said that Jeremiah had rescued the ark and hidden it in a cave on Mt. Sinai where it would be preserved until the final restoration of Israel (*II Macc.* 2:4-8). Jewish tradition, in any event, held that in the messianic age, the ark of the covenant would be restored. Here is a symbolic picture that the covenant is now confirmed because the Kingdom of God has come.

The **flashes of lightning, loud noises, peals of thunder, earthquake,** and **heavy hail** are conventional ways of expressing majesty and power attending the manifestation of the divine presence.

CHAPTER TWELVE

THE DRAGON, THE WOMAN, AND HER SEED

One of the central themes in the Revelation is the struggle between the Kingdom of God and the kingdom of Satan. The New Testament frequently recognizes that it is to be the normal experience of the church on earth to suffer tribulation and persecution. "In the world you have tribulation" (John 16:33). "Through many tribulations we must enter the kingdom of God" (Acts 14:22). At the end of the age, the church is destined to undergo the most intense persecution of her history — "great tribulation, such as has not been from the beginning of the world until now, no, and never will be" (Matt. 24:21). This persecution will be waged by a satanically inspired ruler, called the beast (11:7), better known as the Antichrist, who will try to frustrate the rule of God on earth by gaining universal power, demanding the worship of men, and inflicting martyrdom on all who remain loyal to Christ.

During this time of tribulation, God will assert his sovereignty and give forebodings of his final victory in judgment by pouring out judgments of his wrath upon those who worship the beast. The first of these judgments has been pictured in the series of seven trumpets (8:2 — 9:21) with their accompanying plagues. The sounding of the seventh trumpet (11:15-19) brought an announcement of the end, the establishment of the Kingdom of God, and the destruction of "the destroyers of the earth" (11:18).

Before the end actually comes, John must describe in greater detail the appearance of the Antichrist and his efforts to destroy the church (chap. 13). Before he enters upon this description of the time of the great tribulation, he parts the curtain that separates earth from heaven to depict a great warfare in the spiritual world. The experience of the church in suffering tribulation on earth is the manifestation in history of a spiritual battle. Behind the beast is the dragon — the devil, Satan — whose aim it is to frustrate the rule of God through his Messiah and destroy God's people. Chapter 12 describes in mythological terms this heavenly warfare. It explains to God's people on earth why they must face such satanic evil and persecution; but it assures them that in reality Satan has already been conquered and they are therefore able to conquer him by the blood of the Lamb (12:11).

(4) Interlude (12:1 — 14:20).

a. The Dragon, the Woman, and Her Seed (12:1-17).

The first vision of the interlude is pictured in mythological colors as a war in heaven between a great red dragon and a heavenly woman. The dragon represents Satan; the woman represents the ideal people of God — the church. The vision describes in mythological terms the effort of the dragon to destroy both the woman and the Messiah, the preservation of both from the wrath of the dragon, the overthrow of the dragon, and his effort to destroy the church on earth. This is not a vision of an event which is to take place at the end; it is a vision in highly imaginative terms of the heavenly warfare between God and Satan, which has its counterpart in history in the conflict between the church and demonic evil. As such, the vision completely transcends the usual categories of time and space. It is not meant to be a foretelling of history but a representation of the struggle in the spiritual world which lies behind history.

In the first few verses, John is represented as an observer of events which occur in heaven (vss. 1-12), but he suddenly and inexplicably finds himself on earth (vss. 13-17). The birth of Messiah is represented (vss. 2, 5), but there is no room in the story for his life and ministry; he is suddenly caught up in heaven (vs. 5); Satan is cast down, and in his wrath turns upon the church on earth. This is the background for the final eschatological persecution of the church by the Antichrist, which is elsewhere called the great tribulation (see on 7:14).

This chapter, in other words, embodies a surrealistic word-picture which describes the spiritual struggle standing behind historical events.

Verse 1. **And a great portent appeared in heaven, a woman clothed with the sun, with the moon under her feet, and on her head a crown of twelve stars.** The central feature of this heavenly woman is that she is the mother of the Messiah (vs. 2). Some commentators think she represents Mary, the mother of the Lord; others Israel, the people who gave birth to Messiah. It is true that Isaiah 66:7 pictures Zion as being in travail to give birth to the new redeemed Israel (see Isa. 26:17; Mic. 4:10); but this heavenly woman is mother both of Messiah and of the actual church on earth (her "offspring," vs. 17). Therefore, it is easier to understand the woman in a somewhat broader sense as the *ideal* Zion, the heavenly representative of the people of God (Isa. 54:1; 66:7-9).

Paul gives us the clue to the meaning of the heavenly woman when he speaks of the Jerusalem which is above, who is the mother of the people of God on earth (Gal. 4:26). She was the mother of the true Israel in the Old Testament, and of the people of the Messiah in the New Testament. The woman is the ideal church in heaven; her children are the actual historical people of God on earth.

We have to carry the symbolism further and apply it to what is pictured about Messiah. It is not at all clear that the birth of the Messiah (vs. 2) is meant to represent the birth of the historical Jesus, or that his catching up to heaven is his ascension. The picture seems to be altogether symbolic of a great struggle in heaven which in turn has consequences for the earthly experience of the church.

In this vision John seems still to be on earth. In chapter ten he saw an angel coming down from heaven to earth; in chapter eleven he was a participant in the drama of measuring the temple. In chapter thirteen he sees a beast rising out of the sea. In this vision he is apparently standing on earth and beholds the struggle in heaven against the backdrop of the sky.

The word translated "portent" is the usual word for a sign; it can also designate a striking phenomenon or a prodigy. He saw it in heaven; a better rendition would be "in the sky," for in vs. 4, the dragon swept down a third of the stars of heaven and cast them to earth.

167

It is difficult to envisage a heavenly figure "clothed with the sun." Are we to think of her as standing in the midst of the sun with its brilliance completely enveloping her? Obviously, this is a trait designed to describe the glory and majesty of her appearance. The description "with the moon under her feet" again is designed to represent no particular feature other than that of enhancing the heavenly glory of the woman. "On her head a crown of twelve stars" again may simply be a detail adding to the majesty of the woman's appearance. That it is highly symbolic is obvious from the fact that stars are invisible to the human eye in the presence of brilliant sunlight. It is possible that the twelve stars are symbolic of the twelve patriarchs and of the twelve tribes of Israel (Gen. 37:9).

Verse 2. **She was with child and she cried out in her pangs of birth in anguish for delivery.** The metaphor of Israel as a woman in travail is found several times in the Old Testament (Isa. 26:17; 66:7-8; Mic. 4:10; 5:3). However, it is doubtful if the verse intends to allude to the actual historical birth of Jesus. There is certainly no reference to the virgin birth of Christ.

Verse 3. **Another portent appeared in heaven; behold a great red dragon.** In vs. 9, this dragon is further identified as "that ancient serpent, who is called the Devil and Satan." This is obviously a mythological picture which represents a spiritual being as though he were a fierce sea monster. The idea of a dragon as the mythological embodiment of evil is found in the Old Testament references to Leviathan, Rahab, Behemoth (Pss. 74:14; 89:10; Isa. 27:1; 51:9; Job 40:15) and to a fearful sea monster (Job 7:12; Ezek. 32:2). He is also called the serpent (Amos 9:3; Isa. 27:1). There seems to be no particular significance in the fact that the dragon is red in color.

The dragon is further described as having **seven heads and ten horns, and seven diadems upon his heads.** A diadem was a kind of crown; the conquering Christ will be crowned with many diadems (Rev. 19:12). The number seven is the number of fullness (see the seven spirits in 1:4); the seven heads crowned with seven diadems suggest the great degree of power the dragon was allowed to exercise. The ten horns go back to Dan. 7:7, 24, and are symbolic of Satan's great might.

The symbolism is interesting. How are we to conceive of a dragon with seven heads and ten horns? Does one of the heads have four horns? Or do four of the seven heads have two horns each? Such questions refute themselves; all this is a symbolic portrayal of Satan's great power as the "god of this age" (II Cor. 4:4). This picture also provides background for the beast of chapter thirteen who has seven heads and ten horns (13:1; 17:3).

Verse 4. **His tail swept down a third of the stars of heaven, and cast them to the earth.** There is no need to see in these words anything more than the fearful appearance of this monster. There is no hint in this symbolism of a primeval war in heaven in which Satan was cast out of heaven down to the earth. Dan. 8:10 has a similar vision in which the "little horn" reached to heaven and cast some of the stars to the earth, but there they are called the "hosts of heaven." The dragon is such a colossal creature that with one sweep of his tail he can brush a third of the stars out of their natural position.

The dragon stood before the woman who was about to bear a child, that he might devour her child when she brought it forth. If the dragon is in the form of a giant serpent, standing would be a strange posture; but such details offer no problem in apocalyptic visions. The scene is still heaven. One might raise the question why the dragon did not devour the woman herself instead of her child, but such questions are irrelevant. John is describing spiritual realities in vivid mythological terms. Here is the ultimate purpose of Satan: to frustrate the work of Christ.

Verse 5. **She brought forth a male child, one who is to rule all the nations with a rod of iron.** These words clearly identify the child; he is God's anointed who is destined to reign in God's Kingdom over all the earth (Ps. 2:9; Rev. 2:27; 19:15). We are not to seek some specific event in the birth of the child. It does not refer to the birth of Jesus to Mary in Bethlehem; it has nothing to teach us about the pre-existent state of the Son; all is symbolism portraying the hostility of Satan to God's anointed one. Many commentators see here an allusion to Herod's effort to destroy the infant Jesus (Matt. 2:16). If this vision was intended to represent actual history, it ought to portray the crucifixion of Jesus, for the death of Jesus for a moment seemed to be the triumph of the powers of darkness (Luke 22:53).

But her child was caught up to God and to his throne. The scene is still heaven; there is no indication that the woman has descended to earth to give birth to her child. This can hardly be an allusion to the ascension of Christ, for his rapture did not have the purpose of escaping Satan's hostility. On the contrary, as the crucified and resurrected Christ he had already won his triumph over satanic power (Heb. 2:14; Col. 2:15). This is John's vivid way of asserting the victory of God's anointed over every satanic effort to destroy him.

Verse 6. **And the woman fled into the wilderness, where she has a place prepared by God.** The scene is still heaven, the earth does not come into the vision until vs. 9 when Satan is thrown down from heaven to earth. Commentators often allude to the flight of the Christian Jews from Jerusalem to Pella at the time of the Jewish war, when they escaped the fearful destruction which befell their countrymen; but no such historical events are intended. We must assume that the dragon, frustrated in his efforts to destroy the Messiah, turned on his mother — the heavenly woman. But his efforts again were in vain. God protected and preserved the woman even as he had saved his anointed one.

In the wilderness, the woman had a place **to be nourished for one thousand two hundred and sixty days.** Here again we meet the symbolic number of three and a half years which represents the period of evil during which Satan tries to frustrate the purposes of God, but particularly the last days of this period (see on 11:3). This verse asserts that even in the time of most severe trouble, God will preserve the heavenly woman; and this in turn includes the idea that he will preserve his church on earth.

Verses 7-8. **Now war arose in heaven, Michael and his angels fighting against the dragon; and the dragon and his angels fought, but they were defeated and there was no longer any place for them in heaven.** Here again, John employs apocalyptic mythological language to describe a spiritual fact. We misunderstand the character of John's thought if we try to place this heavenly battle somewhere in the stream of time. Some interpreters understand it to refer to a primordial battle describing "the fall of Satan"; others see in it an eschatological conflict which explains why such fierce persecution must befall God's people. Theologically, the clue to this battle is given in vs. 11: "And they have conquered him by the blood of the

Lamb." In redemptive history the victory over Satan was won by Christ through the shedding of his blood on the cross. John, however, is not here concerned with the way the victory is won but merely with the fact that Satan is defeated. We have no other scriptural support for the idea that the achievement of redemption, which includes the overthrow and the final defeat of evil, is the work of angels; it is altogether the work of Christ.

Michael appears a few times in Scripture. He is the guardian angel of Israel (Dan. 10:13, 21; 12:1) and fights on their behalf with the guardian angels of the gentile nations (Dan. 10-12). In the intertestamental literature, he is regarded as the patron of and intercessor for Israel (*Enoch* 20:5). In Jude 9, he is said to have contended with the devil for the body of Moses. In the present passage, he is represented as the defender of God's people as a whole against the evil power of Satan. The single intent of the passage is to assure those who meet satanic evil on earth that it is really a defeated power, however contrary it might seem to human experience.

Verse 9. **And the great dragon was thrown down, that ancient serpent, who is called the Devil and Satan.** The serpent appears to be an obvious allusion to Gen. 3:1-5. "Satan" is the transliteration of a Hebrew word which means "adversary," and is a term used of human adversaries (see I Kings 11:14, 23; I Sam. 29:4). When an angel stood in Balaam's way, he is called his adversary (Num. 22:22). The word came to be applied in particular to that enemy of mankind who accused men to God, as he accused Job (Job 1:6) and the high priest Joshua (Zech. 3:1). In Job, he appears before God as one of the "sons of God," yet he plays the role of adversary, for he accuses Job of insincerity in serving God.

"Devil" is another translation in the Greek Bible for Satan, carrying the sense of "accuser" or "adversary" (Job 2:1; Zech. 3:1-2; I Chr. 21:1 LXX). Properly, *diabolos* means "slanderer," but the word as applied to Satan does not carry this meaning. When Peter speaks of "your adversary the devil" (I Pet. 5:8), he succinctly expresses the meaning of the term. He is also called **the deceiver of the whole world** (see II Cor. 11:3).

He was thrown down to the earth, and his angels were thrown down with him. Satan's realm is often pictured as being the atmosphere above the earth. He is called "the prince of the power of the air" (Eph. 2:2); his angels are "spiritual

171

hosts of wickedness in heavenly places" (Eph. 6:12). However, in Job, he is pictured as having access to the very presence of God. The present passage describes a victory over Satan by virtue of which his accusations against God's people lose their force (vs. 10). We are not to think of any actual change of domicile. A parallel saying is found on the lips of our Lord: "I saw Satan fall like lightning from heaven" (Luke 10:18). Commentators have often tried to decide when in Jesus' thought this fall occurred. In the gospel context, the fall of Satan is associated with the mighty mission of his disciples. They were able to cast out demons because Jesus himself in his own mission had effected the fall of Satan. This again is obviously symbolic language, asserting that the presence of the power of the Kingdom of God on earth in the persons of Jesus and his disciples meant the toppling of Satan from his place of power. This also is John's meaning even though he expresses himself in mythological terms of a heavenly battle.

Verse 10. **And I heard a loud voice in heaven.** The voice is not identified, but it represents God's people, for it speaks of **our brethren.** The voice may be that of one of the martyrs of 6:9-11. The voice announces the triumph of God's Kingdom, that is, the establishment of his rule over every hostile demonic power. No distinction is to be made between the **power and the kingdom of God** and **the authority of his Christ;** the former is exercised and effectuated through the latter.

This announcement, like that in 11:15, is proleptic and looks forward to the consummation which has not yet occurred; but it has occurred in principle, for Satan is already a defeated foe. Even though John has described the heavenly warfare and the downfall of Satan in mythological terms, this defeat leads to the establishment of *the authority* of the Messiah in the world. The result is that Satan's accusations against God's people are frustrated.

Verse 11. **And they have conquered him by the blood of the Lamb.** This shows clearly that the victory over Satan which John has described in mythological terms actually was accomplished in history at the cross. The shed blood of Christ is the real means of victory over Satan. The secondary means of victory is the **word of their testimony;** i.e., their witness to the saving power of the blood of Christ. The background of martyrdom stands behind these words. They loved their Lord more than life itself and willingly suffered death rather than deny Christ. Jesus had said, "He who endures to the end [i.e., to the point of death] will be saved" (Matt. 24:13). Victory over Satan is not physical victory to be found in the preservation of life or escape from the persecution he wages against the saints. They stood fast in their testimony to Christ and **loved not their lives even unto death.** Their very martyrdom was their victory over Satan; it proved that his accusations against the brethren were empty. It is clear that victory over Satan is a spiritual victory which is often won even in the terrible experience of martyrdom.

Verse 12. **Rejoice then, O heaven, and you that dwell therein! But woe to you, O earth and sea, for the devil has come down to you in great wrath, because he knows that his time is short.** The defeat of Satan has a twofold result. It means rejoicing for the angelic hosts of heaven who surround God's throne; but it means woe to men who inhabit the earth and sail on the sea. While Satan has been overthrown, he has not yet been destroyed. He knows that his final doom is sealed, but he is still allowed to exercise great power. He is indeed powerless to make the martyrs deny their faith; his power as the accuser of the brethren is completely broken. No one, not even Satan himself, can lay any charge against God's elect (Rom. 8:33). The martyrs are safe and secure, having won their victory through the blood of the Lamb. But they are still martyrs. Satan is still able to attack the saints on earth and bring them to martyrdom, hoping that by doing so he may conquer them and compel them to deny their faith. This is the background for the last convulsive effort of Satan to crush the church and destroy the saints. Even though he knows his power is broken and his doom sure and soon, he attacks the church with great wrath.

Verse 13. **And when the dragon saw that he had been thrown to the earth, he pursued the woman who had borne the male child.** John now resumes the story of Satan's effort to destroy the heavenly woman — the ideal people of God. In vs. 6, the woman has fled from the dragon into the wilderness where she was preserved for three and a half years. Now, Satan pursues her into the wilderness and renews his efforts to destroy her.

Verse 14. **But the woman was given the two wings of the**

great eagle that she might fly from the serpent into the wilderness, to the place where she is to be nourished. No historical
equivalent is to be sought for the rescue of the woman. This
is John's way of assuring the church of their ultimate safety,
even in the face of martyrdom. The time, and times, and half
a time is taken from Dan. 7:25, and is the same as forty-two
months, three years and a half, or one thousand two hundred
and sixty days (see note on 11:2), the last terrible time of
unparalleled persecution and martyrdom. Even in death,
God will preserve his people; every effort of Satan to destroy
them will be in vain.

Verses 15-16. The serpent poured water like a river out of
his mouth after the woman, to sweep her away with the flood.
But the earth came to the help of the woman, and the earth
opened its mouth and swallowed the river which the dragon
had poured from his mouth. This continues the imaginative
picture of Satan's effort to destroy God's people. We have no
known parallels in ancient literature upon which John could
have drawn his vivid pictures. Nor are we to seek historical
counterparts. The message conveyed is simple and clear: Satan
will do everything in his power to destroy God's people, but
in vain.

Verse 17. Then the dragon was angry with the woman. This
is obviously picturesque language. The dragon has been
angry with the woman throughout the entire vision and has
been venting his rage upon her, utilizing every stratagem to
destroy her. Still, John can speak of the wrath of the dragon
against the woman as though it was a new turn in the narrative.

The key to this verse is the phrase the rest of her offspring.
The woman has already given birth to Messiah whom Satan
was unable to destroy. On the contrary, the Lamb by his
death (vs. 11) has provided the means for men to conquer
the dragon, and has guaranteed the eventual establishment
of Messiah's reign on the earth (vs. 10). The woman has other
children against whom Satan now directs his wrath. These
are actual Christians who constitute the empirical church on
earth. John turns from the ideal to the actual — from the
vision of the overthrow of Satan in heaven to the reality of
his persecution of the saints on earth. The spiritual conflict
is the backdrop for the actual struggle on earth between the
church and Antichrist. In the face of the time of great tribu-

lation, John has assured the church that Satan has already
been defeated and cannot win the victory over the church.
Nevertheless, he can inflict fearful persecution; and this final
persecution is reflected in the war on the rest of her offspring.

The translation of RSV, **Those who . . . bear testimony to
Jesus,** probably should be rendered, "hold the testimony of
Jesus."[1] The construction is a genitive case which can be either
subjective — the testimony which Jesus bore (see 1:2, 9; 6:9) to
which they held fast — or objective — the testimony which they
bore to Jesus (see 19:10; 20:4). The basic meaning is the same
in either case.

And he stood on the sand of the sea. The verse division is
different in AV and RSV, and the difference rests in turn upon
a difference in the text. The AV is based upon a later text,
and places John on the seashore where he beholds the beast
rising from its waters. Therefore, the words are included in
the first verse of chapter thirteen. However, the better text
reads, "and he stood on the sand of the sea," and refers to the
dragon. Having been frustrated in his efforts to destroy the
heavenly woman and the Messiah, the dragon now directs his
wrath against the church on earth; and to fulfill his purpose,
he takes his stand by the seashore that he may call forth from
the deep the beast who will be his primary instrument in the
last persecution.

[1]See G. B. Caird, *The Revelation of St. John the Divine* (New York:
Harper and Row, 1966), p. 158.

CHAPTER THIRTEEN

THE TWO BEASTS

Chapter thirteen continues the interlude between the sounding of the seven trumpets and the outpouring of the seven bowls. The seventh trumpet brought us to the last days of the age, when the mystery of God, both in salvation and judgment, would be fulfilled (10:7). Now we are in the time of the end, which is characterized by two outstanding features: the outpouring of divine judgments (the seven bowls) and the judgment of a rebellious civilization (Babylon), and the final persecution of the church. The time of the end is, in other words, the last climactic struggle between God and Satan. The present chapter describes the appearance of the Antichrist and his persecution of the church. The chapters which succeed will relate the outpouring of divine judgments.

John's readers have already been prepared for this time of persecution. The twelfth chapter has assured them that this time of martyrdom will be no new thing but only the final expression in history of a spiritual struggle which has been waged in heaven between Satan (the dragon) and the angels of God. Although martyrdom is impending, the final triumph of the saints is assured, because Satan is already a defeated foe. Defeated though he is, he will be allowed at the end time to wage one final convulsive warfare against the saints through the agency of the beast. For a brief history of the Antichrist concept, see the note at 11:7.

b. The Two Beasts (13:1-18).

176

Verse 1. **And I saw a beast rising out of the sea, with ten horns and seven heads, with ten diadems upon its horns.** The beast has appeared already in 11:7 as one who ascends from the bottomless pit to make war upon the two witnesses. This vision is directly dependent upon the vision recorded in Daniel 7, in which he saw four beasts coming up out of the sea, representing a succession of four worldly empires. Some commentators see in the sea a symbol of the agitated surface of unregenerate humanity (Isa. 57:20), which is likened to a seething cauldron of confused national and social life out of which great historical movements arise. Perhaps a clue is found in 17:15: "The waters that you saw . . . are peoples and multitudes and nations and tongues." The kinship between the beast and the dragon (Satan) is seen in the fact that both have ten horns and seven heads (cf. 12:3). The fourth beast of Daniel had ten horns. However, the dragon had seven diadems or crowns on its heads (12:3), while the beast has ten diadems upon its horns. The seven crowns of the dragon represent the fullness of his power. The ten crowned horns of the beast represent ten kings (17:12); they do not, however, play a significant role in the vision of the beast.

The crucial exegetical question is what the seven heads are intended to represent. At first sight the easiest solution is that the beast represents the historical Roman Empire of the first century, and the seven heads represent seven successive emperors. There are, however, exegetical difficulties in identifying the seven heads with any seven emperors. The beast may well be represented in the Roman Empire, but we have already noted that early Christian eschatology expected the appearance of Antichrist at the end of the age, and there are features about this beast and his colleague — the second beast — which were in no way consonant with Rome's rule. The beast then is the eschatological Antichrist who was foreshadowed in certain aspects of Rome, and in other totalitarian states as well.

There was **a blasphemous name upon its heads.** The beast is to claim divine prerogatives. The little horn of Dan. 7:25 "shall speak words against the Most High"; the desolating sacrilege in the Olivet Discourse (Matt. 24:15) will take his stand in the holy place; the man of lawlessness (II Thess. 2:4) "opposes and exalts himself against every so-called god

or object of worship, so that he takes his seat in the temple
of God, proclaiming himself to be God." Here, the beast wears
the name of deity upon his heads, demanding the worship of
men (vs. 4). This self-deification of Antichrist has had its
precursors in history. Deification of the emperor was prominent in the Roman Empire. Julius Caesar, Augustus, Claudius,
Vespasian, and Titus had been pronounced divine by the
Roman Senate after their death. Several emperors had used
the term *DIVUS* on coins when they were still alive. In the
East, coins often bore the Greek term *theos*. As we have seen in
the letters to the seven churches, the cities of Asia vied with
each other for the honor of having a temple dedicated to Rome
and the emperor to promote the imperial cult. The most
explicit claim to deity was made by Domitian (A.D. 81-96) who
demanded that he be addressed by the title, *Dominus et Deus*
— Lord and God. The deification of the state and its ruler is
not a phenomenon limited to the last days and the Antichrist;
we have witnessed manifestations essentially of the same
phenomenon in modern totalitarian states.

Verse 2. The beast that John saw was **like a leopard, its
feet were like a bear's, and its mouth was like a lion's mouth.**
The beast combined attributes of the first three beasts in
Daniel 7; the fourth beast is represented by ten horns. In the
beast, we find concentrated all the characteristics which have
been manifested in successive world empires.

**And to it the dragon gave his power and his throne and
great authority.** The beast, like Paul's man of lawlessness
(II Thess. 2:9), is not merely the concentration of political
and military power; it is the embodiment of satanic evil, draw-
ing its power and authority from the dragon.

Verse 3. **One of its heads seemed to have a mortal wound,
but its mortal wound was healed, and the whole earth followed the beast with wonder.** The wording of the English
may be a bit misleading; it does not mean to say that one of
the heads looked as though it was mortally wounded but really
was not. The words are the same as those used of the Lamb
in 5:6 who actually had been slain. Here, one of the heads is
wounded to death, but the death wound is healed.

Many interpreters understand John to mean that one of
the Roman emperors was killed and later brought back from
the dead as the embodiment of satanic evil. Support for this

view has been sought in the so-called myth of *Nero redivivus*. The Emperor Nero came to death by his own hand in A.D. 68, but the story arose that he was not really dead but had escaped to the East and would return in triumph. In the year 69, a pseudo-Nero appeared in Asia but came to naught; and in 88, another pretender appeared in Asia declaring that he was Nero and had been in hiding.

This myth was indeed used in certain circles of Christian apocalyptic where the return of a triumphant Nero is pictured, sometimes as the Antichrist (*Ascension of Isaiah* 4:1-14; *Sibylline Oracles* 4:119; 5:363; 8:70). The fatal objection to this view is that it is not only one of the heads of the beast which is slain, but the beast himself which received the mortal wound (13:12, 14). Later, it is spoken of as "the beast that . . . was, and is not, and is to ascend from the bottomless pit" (17:8). The murder or suicide of a Roman emperor might lead to a period of chaotic unrest, but it in no way interrupted the continuity of the empire itself. The fact that both one of the heads and the beast himself received the mortal wound suggests that the beast is in some way to be identified with his ten heads. The beast is the embodiment of all that was expressed in the four beasts of Daniel 7, and the seven heads are concrete embodiments of this imperial power. (See further notes on 17:8-12.) The beast himself, in the person of one of its heads, was slain but later revived. In this vision, John radically reworks the materials in Daniel 7.

Verse 4. **Men worshiped the dragon, for he had given his authority to the beast, and they worshiped the beast, saying, "Who is like the beast, and who can fight against it?"** Here is the key to the character and purpose of the beast; it is not merely the exercise of political power — it has the objective of capturing the loyalties of men and diverting them from the worship of God. To turn from God and submit to the beast is in reality to worship Satan. The time of the Antichrist is a struggle for the souls of men. The beast will manifest such mighty power that he will convince the world of the futility of resisting him (cf. II Thess. 2:9-10).

Verse 5. **And the beast was given a mouth uttering haughty and blasphemous words.** This is based directly on Dan. 7:8, 20, 25. The little horn had a mouth "speaking great things" and spoke "words against the Most High." The fact that he was given a mouth to utter these blasphemous words suggests that his power was not his own, but was granted to him by a higher authority. He received his power from the dragon. "Blasphemous words" are not words of derogation of God but of self-deification.

And it was allowed to exercise authority for forty-two months. See the note on 11:2. The forty-two months is a symbolic number for the entire period of persecution of the church, but particularly the end of this period — the time of the great tribulation.

Verse 6. **It opened its mouth to utter blasphemies against God.** This verse expands and particularizes what has been said in vs. 5. To blaspheme does not mean to curse, as in English, but in connection with God to do or say anything that desecrates the divine name or violates his glory and deity. Jesus was accused of blasphemy by the high priest (Matt. 26:65) because he claimed a place at the right hand of God. Blasphemy here is the exaltation of a human claim over the claim of God upon man's loyalty and worship. The blasphemy of God's **dwelling, that is, those who dwell in heaven** reflects Dan. 8:10, where the little horn grew great, "even to the host of heaven; and some of the host of the stars it cast down to the ground, and trampled upon them." The stars here appear to represent the saints[1] who are defamed and downtrodden by Antichrist. Those who dwell in heaven are those whose citizenship is in heaven (Phil. 3:20).

Verse 7. **Also it was allowed to make war on the saints and to conquer them.** This does not indicate any sort of military maneuver but hostility and complete mastery by whatever means (see 2:16; 13:4; 19:11). The chief objects of the beast's wrath are the saints — i.e., "those who keep the commandments of God and bear testimony to Jesus" (12:17). The primary purpose of the beast is to turn men away from Christ, which he attempts by fierce persecution. That he conquers them does not mean in this context that he succeeds in perverting their loyalty from Christ to the beast — i.e., in apostatizing them, but he does succeed in waging terrible persecution. "This horn made war with the saints and prevailed over them" (Dan. 7:21). However, those whom the beast had

[1]See E. J. Young, *The Prophecy of Daniel* (Grand Rapids: Eerdmans, 1949), p. 171.

seemed to conquer by their martyrdom had in reality won a victory. Later, John saw before the throne of God "those who had conquered the beast and its image" (15:2). "They have conquered him by the blood of the Lamb and by the word of their testimony, for they loved not their lives even unto death" (12:11). Their very martyrdom was their victory; they stood steadfast in their loyalty to Christ and refused to worship the beast or the dragon.

And authority was given it over every tribe and people and tongue and nation. The beast *was allowed* in the sovereignty of the divine purpose to exercise a worldwide authority. It is impossible to find a fulfillment in these words in any historical situation in the Roman Empire of the first century. The persecution under Nero (A.D. 54-68) was limited to Rome and involved only a relatively few martyrs; the persecution under Domitian (A.D. 81-96) was of very limited scope. While occasional persecution of Christians occurred in Asia, there was nothing like a general persecution. John looks far beyond his own horizon to a time when an anti-Christian ruler will be allowed to exercise a worldwide sovereignty.

Verse 8. **And all who dwell on earth will worship it.** John again foresees a situation in the future under Antichrist which transcends the worship of the Roman emperor. In the Roman Empire, Jews were exempt from the demand of the formality of emperor worship. In this last day no one will be exempt except Christians, who will pay for their loyalty to Christ with their lives. For the **book of life,** see 3:5. Here and in 21:27, it is called the Lamb's book of life. It is the register of those who have been saved by faith in the crucified Lamb of God. That their names were **written before the foundation of the world** carries the assurance that even though they seem to be powerless before the attacks of the beast, they are really in the keeping providence of God and have been since the foundation of the world. "Before the foundation of the world" grammatically can modify either "written" (as in RSV) or "slain" (as in AV), but the parallel thought in 17:8 decides in favor of the former construction. That the Lamb **was slain** refers both to the fact that he has wrought salvation for those who follow him, and that in his death he has led the way for those who would follow him. Jesus himself insisted that every

181

disciple must be willing to take up his cross (Mark 8:34), i.e., follow Jesus to death.

Verse 9. John concludes his portrayal of Antichrist with the serious admonition, which concludes each of the letters to the seven churches, **if anyone has an ear let him hear.**

Verse 10. This is followed by a sober affirmation which is, however, capable of different renderings. AV takes both parts of the verse to refer to persecutors who shall finally suffer the fate they inflict on others: "He that leadeth into captivity shall go into captivity: he that killeth with the sword must be killed with the sword." On the other hand, both couplets may refer to the persecuted: resistance to either captivity or the sword will be futile. The RSV takes the first half to refer to the persecuted and the second half to the persecutor: **If anyone is to be taken captive, to captivity he goes; if anyone slays with the sword, with the sword must he be slain.** The first couplet informs Christians that the persecution waged by the beast will be carried out within the providence of God and therefore violent resistance is out of place. If one is destined for captivity, he must be willing to go meekly as a Christian. However, persecution is not the last word; there is divine retribution, and the final punishment of those who kill with the sword will fit the crime. The last word is not with the persecutor.

Here is a call for the endurance and faith of the saints. Final judgment is in the hand of God and will surely come. Those who take up the sword against the people of God will meet their just retribution, but endurance is required in awaiting that day. Meanwhile, the beast will seem to have unlimited power to bring the saints to death. This will require of them unswerving faith that God is still God and is still ruling, and that his Kingdom is over all.

Chapter 13 tells of two beasts — one rising out of the sea and the second rising out of the earth. The second beast is the servant of the first. He has the sole objective of compelling men to worship the first beast. The details of his description make it clear that he represents organized religion, which in the Roman Empire was embodied in the imperial priesthood, particularly in Asia, whose purpose it was to promote worship of the city of Rome and its emperor. The Asiarchs of Acts 19:31 were probably local priests who promoted the worship of the emperor. In its eschatological form, the second beast suggests the capture of organized religion to help promote the aims of the first beast.

Verse 11. **Then I saw another beast.** Preterist interpreters admit that it is impossible to find any ancient historical figure who is the counterpart of the second beast. They almost unanimously see in him the priestly structure which supported emperor worship. But, as Hanns Lilje points out, the picture is largely prophetic.[2] The symbolism of emperor worship in Asia Minor forms only the background for the vision of the second beast, whose power and influence will go far beyond anything known in the ancient world. The experience of emperor worship provided only echoes of the terrible reality which will be fulfilled in the last days. No particular significance is to be seen in the fact that the second beast rises **out of the earth.** In Dan. 7:3, the four beasts rise out of the sea; in 7:17 they rise out of the earth.

This beast **had two horns like a lamb and it spoke like a dragon.** He is a parody of Christ — religion prostituted for evil ends. The second beast had the appearance of a lamb, but his voice belied his appearance: he spoke like a dragon. That the second beast represents religion employed in support of the worship of the beast is seen from the fact that hereafter he is called the false prophet (16:13; 19:20; 20:10). The first beast represents civil power, satanically inspired; the second beast represents religious power employed to support civil power.

Verse 12. **It exercises all the authority of the first beast in its presence, and makes the earth and the inhabitants worship the first beast, whose mortal wound was healed.** The second beast is no competitor of the first but his henchman. He has no power of his own but derives his power from his association with the beast. His single objective is to capture the religious loyalties of men for the first beast.

It is significant that in the language of this verse, as pointed out above (13:2), the beast is identified with its heads. It was not merely one of his heads which was wounded and then healed; the beast himself received a mortal wound and was then restored to life.

[2]Hanns Lilje, *The Last Book of the Bible* (Philadelphia: Muhlenberg Press, 1955), p. 195.

Verses 13:13-14a. **It works great signs, even making fire come down from heaven to earth in the sight of men; and by the signs which it is allowed to work in the presence of the beast, it deceives those who dwell on earth.** Paul had said that "the coming of the lawless one by the activity of Satan will be with all power and with pretended signs and wonders, and with all wicked deception for those who are to perish" (II Thess. 2:9-10). The main point is that the false prophet, like the beast, does not represent merely formal religion but actual satanic power. Magic played an important role in early pagan religion and was often used to deceive the gullible (Acts 13:6ff.; 16:16; 19:13ff.). The false prophet will not only engage in pseudomiracles; he will have power to make fire come down from heaven to earth. This is apparently not destructive fire but only a sign to deceive men with pretended divine powers, making them think it is in reality the power of Satan. "Those who dwell on earth" is a frequent idiom in the Revelation for unregenerate men; the false prophet will not deceive the saints (Mark 13:22).

Verses 14b-15. **Bidding them make an image for the beast which was wounded by the sword and yet lived; and it was allowed to give breath to the image of the beast so that the image of the beast should even speak.** The power to make statues speak was well known in the ancient world. There grew up a cycle of legend around the person of Simon Magus (Acts 8:9ff.), and early Christian literature relates stories of how he brought statues to life. Emphasis is placed again upon the fact that this power did not reside in the false prophet himself. *It was allowed* (literally, "it was given to him") to do this. The apparent quickening of the image of the beast is the supreme claim to divine power: the claim to be able to create life as God himself does.

Furthermore, it was allowed **to cause those who do not worship the image of the beast to be slain.** The language of the passage states that it was the speaking image of the beast who commanded the death of those who did not worship the beast. Here again the crucial issue is made clear. The conflict is not between religion and no religion, nor between one religion and another, but between Christ and Antichrist — between God and Satan.

In vs. 8, all whose names were not written in the Lamb's

book of life worship the beast; here all who do not worship the beast are put to death.

Verse 16. **Also it causes all, both small and great, both rich and poor, both free and slave, to be marked on the right hand or on the forehead.** In 7:3, the people of God, standing on the threshold of the great tribulation, are sealed on their foreheads, setting them apart as God's people, protecting them from the outpourings of divine wrath (9:4), and, we may suppose, confirming them in their witness and loyalty to Christ. The beast has a countermark which is branded on the hand or forehead of all those who worship him. Thus we have two bands of people — those sealed for God and those marked for the beast. The mark consisted of the name of the beast (vs. 17). It is not at all clear that John is thinking of a literal brand visible on the person of the worshipers of the beast. The seal of God placed on the forehead of the 144,000 (7:3) is surely not meant to be a visible mark; it is a symbolic way of expressing the divine protection (see Isa. 44:5). The mark of the beast may be intended to be a parody on the mark of God.

We know of no ancient practice which provides adequate background to explain the mark of the beast in historical terms. The word for "mark" was used for brands on animals. It was also a technical term for the imperial stamp on commercial documents and for the royal impression on Roman coins. Slaves were branded on their forehead, but this was a sign of servitude, not of loyalty. A few instances of branding captives have been known in Graeco-Roman history, and Ptolemy Philopator compelled certain Alexandrian Jews to be branded with the mark of Dionysus, which was the symbol of an ivy leaf (*III Macc.* 2:29). However, the practice of branding was not a common one and is not known in connection with emperor worship. The mark of the beast is a mark of fealty on the part of those who receive it and designates them as worshipers of the beast.

Verse 17. **No one can buy or sell unless he has the mark, that is, the name of the beast or the number of its name.** The mark of the beast served both a religious and an economic purpose. Again we have no historical situation associated with emperor worship which illustrates this prophecy. John expects the beast, aided by the false prophet, to achieve a totalitarian rule in which he has complete control over politics, religion, and economics with the purpose of compelling the worship of all men.

Verse 18. **This calls for wisdom: let him who has understanding reckon the number of the beast, for it is a human number, its number is six hundred and sixty-six.** John now gives the name of the beast in symbolic form, using a device known in the ancient world as gematria. Neither the Greek nor Hebrew tongues used a system of numbers. Instead of numbers, the letters of the alphabet stood for numbers; e.g., A-1, B-2, C-3, etc.[3] Thus a name could be converted into its corresponding letter. Deissmann records a wall-scribbling from Pompeii which reads, "I love her whose number is 545"[4] (ΦΜΕ).

In the *Sibylline Oracles,* we find a relevant illustration of gematria. Swete alludes to a passage where the numerical value of the name Jesus is given as 888 (I=10, H=8, Σ=200, O=70, Υ=400, Σ=200).[5] John calls for wisdom in calculating the name of the beast from its number and adds that it is a human number, whose equivalent is 666.

The prevailing interpretation by preterist scholars is that the number refers to the Emperor Nero *(Neron Kaisar).* However, the numerical total of *Neron Kaisar* in Greek is not 666, but 1005. The problem is solved by transplanting *Neron Kaisar* into Hebrew, which does indeed total 666. This is achieved, however, by a slight variation in the spelling of the Hebrew word for Caesar. Furthermore, no one has explained why John, writing to a Greek-reading public, would have used the elaborate symbolism of gematria with a Hebrew instead of a Greek form of the name. It is also significant that none of the ancient interpreters of Revelation recognized this solution. Our earliest interpreter, Irenaeus, suggested that 666 might represent either *euanthas, teitan* (Titus?), or *lateinos*

[3]For Greek numerology, see W. W. Goodwin and C. D. Gulick, *A Greek Grammar* (Boston: Ginn & Co., 1930), p. 93; for Hebrew see Gesenius' *Hebrew Grammar,* ed. by E. Kautzsch and A. E. Cowley (Oxford: University Press, 1946), p. 30.

[4]Adolf Deissmann, *Light from the Ancient East* (New York: Hodder and Stoughton, 1910), p. 276.

[5]H. B. Swete, *The Apocalypse of St. John* (London: Macmillan, 1917), p. 176. English text in Edgar Hennecke, *New Testament Apocrypha* (ed. by W. Schneemelcher; Philadelphia: Westminster, 1964), II, 710.

(the Latin Empire).[6] Many interpreters have felt that this last solution of Irenaeus was the best one.

Almost anything can be done with these numbers by clever manipulation. If A=100, B=101, C=102, etc., the name Hitler totals 666.

It is possible that the number was intended to be altogether symbolic. If the name of the Messiah IHΣΟΥΣ equals 888, and 7 is considered the perfect number, it is possible that 666 is intended to be a symbolic number for the best that man can do, which falls short of adequacy. This could be the meaning of the phrase "it is a human number." The most we can say is that if the number of the beast is a prophecy of a future situation, no one yet has solved the meaning of the number, but its meaning will be plain when the time comes.

[6]Irenaeus, *Against Heresies* V. 30.

CHAPTER FOURTEEN

VISIONS OF ASSURANCE

Chapter fourteen continues the interlude between the seven trumpets and the seven bowls. We must be reminded again that the seventh trumpet brought us to the very time of the end (10:7), but before the actual coming of the end John was given visions which represent to him that the end time will be the final manifestation of the age-long struggle between the Kingdom of God and the power of Satan. This is a struggle which has been waged in the spiritual realm unseen by men (chap. 12), but it will emerge in historical form in the person of Antichrist who will try by every possible stratagem to pervert the loyalty of the saints. Now, just before the outpouring of the bowls of God's wrath and the coming of the end, John is again assured that the consummation is in God's hands; that the wicked, godless civilization of the beast will fall under divine judgment, and that the saints will be brought into their eternal salvation. The chapter really consists of a series of disconnected short visions, of which the Lamb on Mt. Zion is only the first.

c. Visions of Assurance (14:1-20).

(i) The Lamb on Mount Zion (14:1-5).

The first vision is again proleptic (see 10:7; 11:15) and pictures the destiny of the people of God who have been preserved through the great tribulation but who have fallen prey to the wrath of the beast. They are seen in the messianic Kingdom.

188

This vision is not actually realized until chapters 20-22, but as he often does, John gives his readers anticipatory visions of what is yet to be to steady them for the hard experiences that lie immediately ahead.

Verse 1. **Then I looked, and lo, on Mount Zion stood the Lamb, and with him a hundred and forty-four thousand who had his name and his Father's name written on their foreheads.** John moves from the prophecy of the beast and those who bear his mark upon their hands and foreheads to the redeemed who bear the mark of God. Though they have fallen victims to the beast because they have refused to worship him, their salvation is assured. This is in a sense a repetition of the vision of the great multitude in 7:9-17, who have come through great tribulation and who are seen standing before the throne and before the Lamb. The present vision is a reassurance of their final victory in the face of martyrdom at the hands of the beast.

The last time we saw the Lamb, he was standing before the throne in heaven (7:9); here he is standing in the holy city, Zion or Jerusalem. It is possible that Mount Zion is to be understood symbolically as the place of deliverance and victory. The second Psalm promises the establishment of God's anointed upon "Zion, my holy hill" (Ps. 2:6), and continues the promise of victory with the words, "I will tell of the decree of the Lord: He said to me, 'You are my son, today I have begotten you'" (Ps. 2:7). In the New Testament, this promise is seen as fulfilled in the resurrection of Messiah from the dead (Acts 13:33; Heb. 1:5; 5:5). It is possible, therefore, that Mount Zion is intended to be understood spiritually of the victory of the saints.

However, it is more likely that Mount Zion stands for the eschatological victory which, according to the Revelation, is in the new Jerusalem which comes down from heaven from God (21:2). The earthly Zion or Jerusalem is constantly pictured in the Old Testament as the seat of God's rule on earth and the center of his final victory. "And it shall come to pass that all who call upon the name of the Lord shall be delivered; for in Mount Zion and in Jerusalem there shall be those who escape" (Joel 2:32). However, in the New Testament, Zion has become "the city of the living God, the heavenly Jerusalem" (Heb. 12:22), no longer an earthly city but a city above

(Gal. 4:26). Jerusalem-Zion is the heavenly dwelling place of God himself; it is no longer an earthly city where he is thought to dwell. On earth, he dwells in the living temples of the hearts of his people (Eph. 2:21-22). However, in the eschatological consummation, men will not leave the earth and take flight to the heavenly Jerusalem; rather, the heavenly Jerusalem will descend to earth and God will dwell among men.

The hundred and forty-four thousand is the same company which was sealed in 7:9-17; and here, as there, they represent the total body of the redeemed. Many interpreters insist that two of their characteristics — chastity and first fruits (vs. 4) — make them out as a special body of believers, either martyrs or celibates. But these words demand no such interpretation; the saints who were suffering martyrdom in the last chapter are now seen in their final salvation in the new Jerusalem.

Verse 2. John **heard a voice from heaven** whose source is not indicated. Apparently it comes from the presence of God. The voice of the glorified Christ was "like the sound of many waters" (1:15), and the four living creatures spoke with a voice of thunder (6:1). The musicians are distinguished from the four living creatures and the elders in vs. 3; apparently they are the angelic hosts of singers. Their voices rise in a mighty crescendo of sound.

Verse 3. **They sing a new song before the throne and before the four living creatures and before the elders. No one could learn that song except the hundred and forty-four thousand who had been redeemed from the earth.** In 5:9, the twenty-four elders sang a new song magnifying the Lamb who had ransomed men by his blood to reign in his Kingdom. The present song is also about redemption, because it can be learned only by those who had been redeemed from the earth. As the new song in 5:9 is sung by the elders even though it is a song of redemption, so this new song is sung by the angels but is designed primarily for redeemed men.

Verse 4. **It is these who have not defiled themselves with women, for they are chaste.** The Greek word translated "chaste" is the same word meaning virgins *(parthenoi).* Many interpreters understand these words to describe the hundred and forty-four thousand as a special class of Christians who had practiced a life of special self-denial and purity by abstain-

ing from marriage and becoming celibates. The basic meaning of *parthenoi* would seem to support this view. However,
this would be a violation of the whole biblical theology. Scripture nowhere looks upon sexual relations as such as being
sinful or involving defilement. Sexual relations are without
exception viewed as an important element in human relation-
ships; in fact, they are a gift of God. Chastity or the avoidance
of sexual defilement always stands in contrast to illicit sexual
relations. In the New Testament, marriage is a state to be
commended, and sex relations are an essential part of marriage
(I Cor. 7:4ff.). Paul does indeed assert that Christian ministers can often carry out their responsibilities more effectively
in the unmarried state (I Cor. 7:32-34), but this is not because
sex is viewed as something defiling but only because the
family relationship can be burdensome.

The word "chaste" (or "virgins") can refer to the spiritual
condition, not only to physical relations. Ignatius salutes his
brethren "with their wives and children, and the maidens
(parthenoi) who are called widows" *(Ignatius to the Smyrneans,*
13:1). Socially, these women had been married and were now
widows; but spiritually they were virgins. Paul uses the word
of the married state: "I betrothed you to Christ to present
you as a pure bride *(parthenon)* to her one husband" (II Cor.
11:2). This interpretation is supported by the fact that John
on several occasions speaks of the idolatrous worship of the
beast as *porneia* — fornication (14:8; 17:2, 4; 18:3, 9; 19:2).
This idea has an extensive background in the Old Testament
where apostasy from Israel's God to worship the gods of the
Canaanites is constantly described as adultery. We conclude,
therefore, that the one hundred and forty-four thousand are
virgins and undefiled in the sense that they have refused to
defile themselves by participating in the fornication of worshiping the beast but have kept themselves pure unto God.

**It is these who follow the Lamb wherever he goes; these
have been redeemed from mankind as first fruits for God and
the Lamb.** That this company is chaste and undefiled is the
negative aspect of their character; the positive side is stated
in the fact of their loyalty to the Lamb; they follow him even
unto death. Theirs is a perfect, uncomplaining discipleship.
As the path of perfect devotion to the will of the Father led
the Lamb to his sacrificial death on the cross, so discipleship

to him may well lead to sharing in his cross (Matt. 10:38; Mark 8:34). They follow the Lamb because they are not their own but have been redeemed — purchased for God at the cost of the blood of the Lamb (5:9).

As the redeemed, they constitute a "first fruits for God." This word is not altogether free from difficulty, for it usually designates part of the whole. The first fruits was the beginning of the harvest, a partial gathering with more to follow. The Greek word is used in this way of the resurrection of Christ from the dead; he is the first fruits of the resurrection of all the saints; he is the initial stage of which the saints constitute the whole (I Cor. 15:20, 23). This meaning would support the view that the hundred and forty-four thousand are a select class of Christians who stand over against believers as a whole. However, this meaning is by no means necessary. "First fruits" can be used of a total group with a view to their total consecration to God. In this sense, all Christians are viewed as "a kind of first fruits of his creatures" (Jas. 1:18). In the same way, Jeremiah says, "Israel was holy to the Lord, the first fruits of his harvest" (Jer. 2:3). There is no thought in the present passage that the redeemed are a first installment of men with the salvation of all to follow. To be sure, God lays a claim upon all mankind, but it is only the redeemed who are actually devoted to him; the emphasis of the term is upon the devotion and consecration of the redeemed.

Verse 5. **And in their mouth no lie was found, for they are spotless.** The word "spotless" is used in the Old Testament of unblemished sacrifices which were fit to be offered to God. Here, the redeemed belong to God with a faultless dedication. The particular nature of their flawless dedication is their complete truthfulness: "in their mouth no lie was found." The redeemed in Israel were those who "utter no lies nor shall there be found in their mouth a deceitful tongue" (Zeph. 3:13). Perfect honesty of speech was one of the characteristics of the servant of the Lord (Isa. 53:9). The redeemed, like their Lord, are utterly sincere and guileless (I Pet. 2:22).

(ii) A Call to Repentance (14:6-7).

Verse 6. **Then I saw another angel flying in midheaven.** As we have indicated, the fourteenth chapter consists of a series of loosely connected visions associated with the end. After a vision of the final salvation of the redeemed, John hears an angel summoning all men to repentance while there is yet time, before the last judgments fall and it will be too late. Why the angel is called "another" is not clear, unless we are to understand that the new song in heaven (vs. 2-3) was sung by angelic hosts. He flew in the midheaven, at the zenith where all could see him (see 8:13). The message of the angel was addressed **to those who dwell on earth** — John's usual idiom for unregenerate humans (see 3:10; 6:10; 8:13, etc.). This angel addressed himself not to the saints but to unbelievers. His message is an **eternal gospel.** The fact that the definite article is omitted presents a difficulty. It has led many commentators to see a special message to be proclaimed in connection with the coming of the end. One contemporary scholar thinks this refers to a special angelic ministry at the end which will issue in a great movement of salvation among the gentiles.[1] However, it is possible to understand the announcement of the end itself as a piece of good news. In 10:7, the fulfillment of the mystery of God is a piece of good news — a gospel announced to the prophets. To the worshipers of the beast and the unrepentant, the announcement of the end is not gospel; it is a word of doom and of judgment. Yet the announcement of the end is good news, for it will see the consummation of God's redemptive purpose. Perhaps too much ought not to be made of the omission of the definite article. Paul speaks of God's gospel (Rom. 1:1) without the definite article.

Verse 7. **And he said with a loud voice, "Fear God and give him glory, for the hour of his judgment has come; and worship him who made heaven and earth, the sea and the fountains of waters."** In light of the angel's proclamation that the end is about to take place and judgment is about to fall, men of all nations are summoned to repent. It is not yet too late; final judgment has not yet fallen; there is still time to turn in repentance and find the mercy of God. For the phrase, "give him glory," see notes on 11:13; it clearly implies repentance.

[1] Joachim Jeremias, *Jesus' Promise to the Nations* (London: SCM, 1958), p. 22.

God is here described primarily in terms of the judge and the creator. The inhabitants of the earth have been amazed by the powers displayed by the beast and his false prophet (13:12-14); they are now reminded that they have to do with one who is mightier than the beast — with him who is the source of all things in heaven and on earth.

(iii) The Fall of Babylon (14:8).

Verse 8. **Another angel, a second, followed.** The summons to repentance in view of the impending judgment is followed by a proleptic angelic announcement that Babylon has already fallen. This is analogous to the proleptic announcements of the coming of the Kingdom of God (11:15; 12:10). **Babylon** was the great enemy of Israel in Old Testament times (Isa. 21:9; Jer. 50:2; 51:8) and here stands for the capital city of the final apostate civilization, the symbol of human society organized politically, economically, and religiously in opposition to and defiance of God. Babylon had an embodiment in first-century Rome (I Pet. 5:13); and in Jewish-Christian apocalyptic, Babylon became a symbolic name for Rome *(Sibylline Oracles* V.143, 159, 434; *Apocalypse of Baruch* 11:1; 67:7). **The wine of her impure passion** is literally "the wine of the wrath of her fornication" (18:3). This combines two ideas: the wine used to intoxicate and to seduce to fornication; and "the wine of God's wrath" (vs. 10). Babylon has deceived and seduced **all the nations** by the enticements and allurements of her wealth and luxuries; but this cup of sensual delight will turn out to be the cup of God's wrath. The actual fall of Babylon which is here announced is described in 17:1 — 18:24.

(iv) The Doom of the Worshipers of the Beast (14:9-12).

The universal call to repentance is followed by a statement of the doom of those who refuse to repent. What will be the fate of those who persist in the worship of the beast? What will be the ultimate destiny of men who are unmoved by the loyalty of the martyrs who seal their faithful witness to Jesus with their blood? The present vision answers these questions.

Verses 9-10. **And another angel, a third, followed, saying with a loud voice, "If anyone worships the beast and its** image, and receives a mark on his forehead or on his hand, he also shall drink the wine of God's wrath, poured unmixed into the cup of his anger." We must be reminded again that behind the outpourings of God's wrath upon a rebellious civilization in the seven trumpet plagues — and in the immediate future of the seven bowl plagues — was a merciful purpose: to turn men to repentance while there was yet time (see notes on 9:20; 16:8). Those who have set themselves in irreversible hostility to God must become the objects of divine wrath before God's Kingdom is established. It is inconceivable that men who hate God's Messiah and join in the persecution of God's people should enter the Kingdom of God. The perfect reign of God and the establishment of his rule in the world includes of necessity the judgment of those who refuse to embrace his rule.

Two words are used to describe God's judgment: wrath *(thumos)* and anger *(orge)*. No sharp distinction can be drawn between the two words, but *orge* represents the kind of anger that rises out of a settled disposition, while *thumos* represents anger of a more passionate kind. In most of the New Testament, *orge* is the usual word to designate the divine wrath; outside of Revelation, *thumos* is used only once (Rom. 2:8). However, both words are frequently used together in the Greek Bible, and they are used here together to intensify the reality of God's wrath.

In any case, God's wrath is not a human emotion; it is the settled reaction of his holiness to man's sinfulness and rebellion. Unless God in his wrath finally purges the world of all evil and rebellion, his Kingdom cannot come. Therefore, in the largest sense of God's redemptive purpose for men, his wrath is a necessary correlative to his love and mercy. Two of the main themes of the Revelation are the recalcitrance of men against God's salvation, manifested in their subservience to the beast; and the judgment of God which must fall upon them. In Revelation John emphasizes God's wrath as does no other book in the New Testament (12:12; 14:8, 10, 19; 15:1, 7; 16:1, 19; 18:3; 19:15). Yet it is no inconsequential matter that his Gospel, which more than any other expresses the love of God, also insists, "He who does not obey the Son shall not see life, but the wrath of God rests upon him" (John 3:36). Paul introduces his most reasoned statement of the gospel of grace with the words, "The wrath of God is revealed from heaven against all ungodliness and wickedness of men" (Rom. 1:18; see Rom. 3:5; 12:19; Col. 3:6). Any interpretation of the New Testament gospel which does not include the wrath of God is an attenuated and apocopated message.

The wine of God's wrath is "poured unmixed into the cup of his anger." Literally translated, the words read "mixed unmixed." It was the ancient custom to mix wine with spices and herbs to render it more tasteful, so that the idiom "to mix wine" became the idiom "to pour wine" (Ps. 75:8). However, the wine of God's wrath is also unmixed, i.e., undiluted; it will be drunk full strength. The two words are used in a similar way in *Psalms of Solomon* where God *"mingled* for them a spirit of wandering; and gave them to drink a cup of *undiluted* wine" (8:15).

And he shall be tormented with fire and brimstone in the presence of the holy angels and in the presence of the Lamb. Here is the ultimate meaning of the cup of God's wrath. The lake of fire and brimstone is pictured as the final place of punishment of the beast and the false prophet, as well as all whose names are not found written in the Lamb's book of life (Rev. 20:10, 15). Such language, like John's description of the heavenly city, must be taken as symbolical of a fearful and final reality which no man can describe. The usual word describing the fate of the lost in the New Testament is *geenna* or Gehenna, while the intermediate state is referred to by the word *hades* (Old Testament *sheol*). *Geenna* does not appear in the Revelation; *hades* occurs four times where it is practically synonymous with the grave (1:18; 6:8; 20:13, 14). The AV badly confuses the situation by translating *hades* in these four passages by the word "hell." In fact, the AV usually translates both *geenna* and *hades* by the word "hell," whereas they have very different meanings.

Geenna comes from the Hebrew *ge-hinnom* which means "the Valley of Hinnom" and refers to a ravine south of the city of Jerusalem where in the days of the monarchy apostatizing Jews adopted the cultic practices of Palestine and cremated children in honor of Baal and Molech (II Kings 23:10; II Chr. 28:3; 33:6; Jer. 32:35). Thus the Valley of Hinnom became in Jewish tradition a place of destruction by fire.

196

Jeremiah sees the valley transformed into a valley of slaughter (Jer. 7:31-32; 19:5-6) in the day of vengeance. Our Lord himself made use of this metaphor to describe the fate of the wicked. He warned his hearers to employ any measures necessary to remove obstacles to avoid this fate: "it is better for you to enter life maimed than with two hands to go to hell (*geenna*), to the unquenchable fire" (Mark 9:43). Elsewhere, Jesus described the fate of the lost as final separation from God and from his Christ (Matt. 7:23; 25:12).

We cannot understand all that is meant in the statement that the wicked will be punished "in the presence of the holy angels and in the presence of the Lamb." Jesus himself had said that those who deny him would be denied before the presence of God and the angels (Mark 8:38; Luke 12:9). Jewish apocalyptic contains a note which is lacking in the Revelation, that the wicked will be punished in the presence of the saints (*Enoch* 48:9). The central point here seems to be, as Beckwith has suggested, that the sight of the Lamb, now triumphant and victorious, would be the most poignant factor in the pain of the wicked because, as worshipers of the beast, they had joined him in warfare against the Lamb.[2]

Verse 11. **And the smoke of their torment goes up for ever and ever; and they have no rest, day or night, these worshipers of the beast and its image, and whoever receives the mark of its name.** The language of this verse reminds us of another company, the twenty-four elders who "day and night . . . never cease to sing" praises and adoration unto God (4:8). The eternal duration of the punishment of the wicked is no new note in the New Testament. Jesus had spoken of the eternal punishment of the wicked (Matt. 25:46) and warned of the hell of fire where "their worm does not die, and the fire is not quenched" (Mark 9:48).

Verse 12. **Here is a call for the endurance of the saints, those who keep the commandments of God and the faith of Jesus.** In view of the certain doom of the beast and those who worship him, John inserts a call to patient endurance on the part of those who are about to suffer at the hands of the beast. The "faith of Jesus" is not the faith he gives but an objective genitive: *faith in Jesus.*

[2]I. T. Beckwith, *The Apocalypse of John* (Grand Rapids: Baker Book House, reprinted 1967), p. 659.

(v)   A Beatitude on the Martyrs (14:13).

Verse 13. And I heard a voice from heaven saying, "Write this: Blessed are the dead who die in the Lord henceforth." "Blessed indeed," says the Spirit, "that they may rest from their labors, for their deeds follow them." The saints who remain faithful to Jesus are not only summoned to endurance; they are assured of blessedness upon their death. This beatitude — a favorite among Christians in time of death — is pronounced primarily upon those who are about to suffer martyrdom, not upon the saints in general. However, we need not understand that this promises a blessing not to be enjoyed by all Christians. This is the same rest promised the martyrs in 6:11. The word "henceforth" does not mean that other saints are not blessed, but that those who shortly will fall before the beast are, contrary to all outward appearances, the blessed of God. To die *in the Lord* is the state of all believers, who both die and live in Christ (I Cor. 15:18; I Thess. 4:16). It does not designate a special group of Christians. The beatitude is confirmed and explained by the Holy Spirit; the blessed enter into rest. The Greek word translated "labors" means labor to the point of weariness. Their afflictions by the beast have worn the saints down to the point of exhaustion. Nevertheless, they have died *in the Lord* and their deeds (lit. works) follow them beyond the grave. Deeds here include their *endurance, obedience* to the commandments of God, and *faith* in Jesus mentioned in the preceding beatitude.

(vi)   The Harvest of the Grain (14:14-16).

John concludes this interlude with two visions: one of the harvest of grain and the second of the vintage of God's wrath. The first pictures the eschatological judgment with special reference to the gathering of the righteous into salvation; the second pictures the judgment of the wicked into condemnation. The presupposition of these two visions is that the final spiritual struggle has occurred between Christ and Antichrist and men have made their decision: loyalty to Christ even unto martyrdom, or worship of the beast. These two visions portray proleptically and dramatically the fate of these two companies. The actual fulfillment of these visions does not occur until chapters 19-20.

Verse 14. The natural way to understand the **one like a son of man** whom John sees is that he is the returning Messiah, Christ himself; and it is difficult to avoid this conclusion. The idea of "one like a son of man" goes back to the vision of the coming of the Kingdom of God in Dan. 7:13 where one like a son of man was presented to the Ancient of Days and received an everlasting kingdom that all peoples and nations should serve him. Jesus himself spoke of the role of the Son of man in the eschatological judgment, which he likened to a harvest (Matt. 13:37ff.); and again, he portrayed the eschatological mission of the Son of man in the separation of the righteous from the wicked (Matt. 25:31ff.). John has earlier likened the exalted Jesus to one like a son of man (1:13). In view of the fact that Son of man is a frequent term to designate the eschatological role of Christ, and the further fact that Son of man in the New Testament is never applied to angels, we must conclude that this is a vision of the returning Christ.

The objection to this is that this heavenly figure initiates the harvest at the command of "another angel" (vs. 15); and it is held to be incongruous that the Christ would undertake the eschatological harvest only at the command of an angel. This is not, however, a fatal objection, for in apocalyptic thought angels often play a role which we might attribute to the Messiah. In the parable of the wheat and the weeds, the Son of man sows the good seed, but the angels are the reapers at the harvest (Matt. 13:37, 41); yet the angels are the agents of the Son of man. In the parable of the net, the angels are the fishermen who separate the evil from the righteous (Matt. 13:49). In what may well be the key chapter in the book of Revelation which depicts the spiritual struggle going on behind the stage of history, it is Michael and his angels who win the victory over the dragon (12:7ff.), although in the rest of the New Testament, the victory is won by Christ. The relationship between Christ and his angels is a mystery we cannot solve, but it is clear that the relationship is a close one. So there can be no ultimate objection that an angel is the agent in calling for the hour of harvest.

The Son of man is seen **seated on a white cloud.** In the Revelation, white has a symbolic significance and is always associated with the things of God (see note on 6:2). The white cloud is reminiscent of the bright cloud seen on the Mount of

199

Transfiguration (Matt. 17:5). The return of Christ is often pictured as attended with clouds (Matt. 24:30; Rev. 1:7). The **golden crown** is symbolic of triumph, and the **sharp sickle** is the instrument of harvesting the grain.

Verse 15. **Another angel came out of the temple.** The fact that the angel comes out of the temple indicates that he comes from the presence of God and bears a message from God himself. The angel is only the emissary. The idiom "another angel" is a common one in the Revelation and cannot always be distinctly defined (see 7:2; 8:3; 14:6). The **harvest of the earth** is a frequent biblical symbol for the final judgment of men (Jer. 51:33; Hos. 6:11; Mark 4:29; Matt. 13:39). Usually the idea of harvesting includes both the righteous and the wicked. In the present context, since the following vision is concerned with the harvest (vintage) of the wicked, it is difficult to avoid the conclusion that the harvest of the grain has special reference to the righteous, even though this fact is not stressed. This is reinforced by the fact that the metaphor of harvesting is used of the ingathering of men into the Kingdom of God (Matt. 9:37f.; Luke 10:2; John 4:35-38).

The harvest of the earth is **fully ripe.** These words convey the idea that, contrary to human appearances, history is moving under the sovereignty of God. History and human affairs are not ruled by a blind meaningless fate which goes nowhere. God is watching over history, and the hour will come in his divine wisdom when mankind is ripe for judgment. History will not get out of control; in God's hour, the issues will be settled.

The Greek word for "fully ripe" is translated by some (RV, NEB) "over-ripe," but this is quite unnecessary. The idea is simply that the time of harvest has come and cannot be delayed.

Verse 16. **So he who sat upon the cloud swung his sickle on the earth, and the earth was reaped.** Christ may use the instrumentality of angels (see above), but he is himself the reaper. The actual reaping is described later in chapters 19-20.

(vii) The Vintage of God's Wrath (14:17-20).

The meaning of the second vision of the consummation is not in doubt; it clearly and vividly pictures the judgment of the wicked in terms of a harvest of grapes.

Verse 17. **And another angel came out of the temple in**

heaven, and he too had a sharp sickle. The harvest of the
vine is carried out by an angel, but he comes *out of the temple,*
i.e., from the very presence of God and serves as an angel of
God. In Matt. 25:41, it is the Son of man, accompanied by
angels, who sends the wicked to their doom; and in the Revelation, the eschatological judgment is an expression of the
wrath of the Lamb (6:16), even though it is more often described in terms of the wrath of God (14:10; 16:19; 19:15).

Verse 18. **Then another angel came out from the altar,**
probably the altar of incense, which has previously been mentioned in connection with the prayers of the saints (8:3f.).
We are reminded again of the efficacy of the prayers of God's
people on earth, persecuted though they be, in bringing about
the end. The prayers of the saints are now about to be answered. If, however, the altar is the altar of burnt offering,
the allusion is to the cry of the souls under the altar who pray
for vindication (6:9ff.) — a prayer which is about to be answered. In either case, the basic thought is the same. No explanation is given of the fact that this angel has **power over
fire:** possibly because of the fire on the altar, possibly because
fire is often associated with judgment.

The idea of a harvest of **grapes** occurs elsewhere in Scripture as a symbol of judgment. "I have trodden the wine press
alone. . . . I trod them in my anger and trampled them in my
wrath; their lifeblood is sprinkled upon my garments, and I
have stained all my raiment" (Isa. 63:2-3). "Put in the sickle,
for the harvest is ripe. Go in, tread, for the wine press is full.
The vats overflow, for their wickedness is great" (Joel 3:13).

Verse 19. **So the angel swung his sickle on the earth and
gathered the vintage of the earth, and threw it into the great
wine press of the wrath of God.** This verse makes it clear that
the harvest of grapes represents judgment, not salvation. The
same harvest is pictured in 19:15 as the mission of the conquering Messiah who "will tread the wine press of the fury of the
wrath of God the Almighty." There is no problem in the fact
that the judicial work of Messiah is here pictured as the work
of an angel.

Verse 20. **The wine press was trodden outside the city,** which
is not identified and probably is not meant to be identified
specifically. The city is here the symbol of God's dwelling in
the midst of his people — possibly the new Jerusalem — and the

thought is that judgment will fall upon the wicked as they are shut out from the presence of God. Possibly there is a vague allusion to the eschatological battle of Joel 3:2, 12. The metaphor suddenly changes from the treading of grapes to a military slaughter. The flow of **blood** is incredible, literally conceived; **one thousand six hundred stadia** is a distance of about a hundred and eighty-four miles — the entire length of Palestine. The entire land is pictured as being inundated in blood to a depth of about four feet. The thought is clear: a radical judgment that crushes every vestige of evil and hostility to the reign of God.

CHAPTER FIFTEEN

PREPARATION FOR THE BOWLS

The preceding three chapters have constituted an interlude between the sounding of the seven trumpets and the outpouring of the seven bowls. The time of the sounding of the seventh trumpet announced the period of the end (10:7); but when the trumpet was sounded, which was to be the third woe (11:14), no woe or plague occurred; instead we have a proleptic announcement of the coming of God's Kingdom. Since the seventh trumpet has no plague of its own, even though it is the third woe, we must conclude that the seven bowls constitute the third woe, with which "the wrath of God is ended" (15:1). These plagues are poured out only on those "who bore the mark of the beast and worshiped its image" (16:2), and, like the seven trumpets (9:20), have the oblique purpose of bringing men to their knees before God in the last opportunity for repentance (16:8).

4. THE SEVEN BOWLS (15:1 — 16:21).

(1) The Preparation (15:1-8).

Verse 1. **Then I saw another portent in heaven, great and wonderful, seven angels with seven plagues, which are the last, for with them the wrath of God is ended.** The word translated "portent" means marvel or wonderful appearance as in 12:1, 3. Through the symbolism of the sounding of seven trumpets, John has portrayed a series of divine visitations in the form of plagues and afflictions to awaken men to the ultimate reality of God. Now this series comes to its climax; with the visitation of the bowl plagues, God will have fully poured out his wrath in the particular context of the plagues which anticipate the final judgment. These words cannot be interpreted to mean that these plagues exhaust the totality of God's wrath. The beast, the false prophet, and all who persist in wickedness are yet to be cast into the lake of fire in the final manifestation of God's wrath against sin. These words must be taken in their particular eschatological context: the outpouring of God's wrath in the time of the great tribulation is the attempt to make the worshipers of the beast bow before the sovereignty of God.

Verse 2. **And I saw what appeared to be a sea of glass mingled with fire, and those who had conquered the beast and its image and the number of its name.** On the threshold of the last plagues, John has a proleptic vision of the conquerors of the beast. They are in fact the martyr-saints slain by the beast because of their endurance in the face of persecution, their steadfast obedience to the commandments of God and their faith in Jesus (14:12). They have conquered the beast by their martyrdom, for in death they have not denied the name of Jesus. They have refused to worship the beast, to bow before its image (13:15), and to receive the number of its name. Although the beast had power to slay them, in reality they have conquered him by remaining true to Jesus; his real purpose was frustrated. We must assume that the persecution waged against the saints by the beast continues throughout the period of the seven bowl plagues.

There is no compelling reason to interpret the sea of glass as other than that which stood before the throne of God (4:6). The central thought in the symbolism is that these conquerors of the beast are standing before the throne of God, in his very presence. The beast had supposed that in slaying them he had conquered them; but their death meant only that they moved from earth into the presence of God. Theirs was the final victory. That the sea of glass was mingled with fire is probably a symbolic allusion to the fact that this is a time of judgment for those who dwell on the earth; or it may refer to the bloody persecution through which the victors had passed. The **harps of God** which they hold **in their hands** form a further symbol of their victory. Harps are expressions of praise and worship to God (5:8; 14:2); the victors express their joy over their victory by songs of praise.

Verse 3. **And they sing the song of Moses, the servant of God, and the song of the Lamb.** Exegetes debate whether this means that the victors sing one song or two. Grammatically the language might seem to suggest two songs: one of Moses, and one of the Lamb. Contextually the idea is that the victors sing a song of triumph which both the saints of the Old Testament and the New Testament knew how to sing, because both sang of the deliverances of the one God. The song of Moses is perhaps the song of deliverance in Exodus when the Israelites praised God for their deliverance from Egypt. The song of the Lamb in the present context is not a song of personal salvation; it is a song of deliverance from the hatred and hostility of the beast. As God delivered Israel from Egypt, even while pouring out plagues on the Egyptians, so he has delivered the saints from worshiping the beast, while pouring out his judgments on the worshipers of the beast.

The song is not one of spiritual redemption but a song of acclamation to the mighty works of God. This must include the works of judgment by which God expresses his wrath against those who have persecuted the saints. The song is couched almost altogether in Old Testament language, because God is the God who delivers his people. His works of judgment are **great and wonderful** (see Pss. 92:5; 111:2; 139:14). He is the **Lord God the Almighty,** in whose light the powers of the beast are limited. His ways, even in allowing the saints to suffer, are **just and true.** He is in fact the **King of the ages.** The reading reflected in the AV, "King of saints," is a late reading in the Greek text with no substantial support. In this time of great tribulation when the beast seemed to have unlimited power to enforce his demonic purpose upon men and persecute the saints — in the darkest hour of human history when it truly seemed that Satan was the god of this age (II Cor. 4:4), the martyrs sing a hymn of praise to God, recognizing that he is the true and living God. They exalt the name of God because, contrary to outward appearances, he is indeed the King of all the ages, including the time of martyrdom. This song is one of the most moving expressions of faith in the entire biblical literature.

Verse 4. **Who shall not fear and glorify thy name, O Lord?**

For thou alone art holy. All nations shall come and worship thee, for thy judgments have been revealed. Taken out of context these words could be interpreted to mean a universal salvation of all nations. There are also statements in Paul's correspondence which, taken out of context, sound like universal salvation. It is God's purpose "to unite all things in him" (Eph. 1:10). "Every knee should bow, in heaven and on earth and under the earth, and every tongue confess that Jesus Christ is Lord, to the glory of God the Father" (Phil. 2:11). "And through him to reconcile to himself all things, whether on earth or in heaven" (Col. 1:20). However, such statements must be understood in their total biblical intent. The Bible constantly looks forward to a day when God will reign on the earth, surrounded only by those who find their joy in worshiping him. "All the nations thou hast made shall come and bow down before thee, O Lord, and shall glorify thy name" (Ps. 86:9). "And many people shall say, 'Come, let us go up to the mountain of the Lord, to the house of the God of Jacob.' ... He shall judge between the nations" (Isa. 2:4; cf. 66:23). "For from the rising of the sun to its setting thy name is great among the nations" (Mal. 1:11). This is the goal of the book of Revelation: the establishment of a city where all the nations shall find healing (Rev. 22:2). This does not mean universal salvation; it does mean that the Kingdom of God will witness a fellowship of people drawn from all the nations who gladly give themselves in worship and devotion to God.

It is worthy of note that even though the song is sung by the martyrs, they do not sing of themselves or the way in which they have overcome the beast; they are entirely occupied with the sovereignty, justice and glory of God. Furthermore, there is no trace of personal vengeance over their enemies upon whom the judgments of God have fallen.

The judgments of God which have been revealed are the judicial sentences of God in relation to the nations, either in the way of mercy or condemnation. On Babylon and its citizens who worshiped the beast, God has revealed his judgments in wrath; but men will recognize that "true and just are thy judgments" (16:7).

Verse 5. After this I looked, and the temple of the tent of witness in heaven was opened. The final seven plagues are about to begin and are pictured as occurring as the result of

the emptying of seven bowls carried by angels who come from
the very presence of God. The temple of God has already appeared in the Revelation. In a proleptic vision, the temple of
God in heaven was opened and the ark of his covenant was
seen (11:19). This was a reminder of God's faithfulness to his
covenant promises. Here, the faithfulness of God also demands
the judgment of evil.

This verse blends two historical references: the tent of witness in the wilderness, and the temple which was later constructed in Jerusalem. The tabernacle in the wilderness was
called "the tabernacle of the testimony" (Exod. 38:21; Num.
10:11; 17:7; Acts 7:44). This became the pattern for the temple
when it was constructed in Jerusalem, and this temple in turn
was used as the pattern for the dwelling of God in heaven.

Verse 6. **And out of the temple came the seven angels with
the seven plagues, robed in pure bright linen, and their breasts
girded with golden girdles.** Ordinarily John does not describe
the appearance of the many angels who play a role in his eschatological drama. The clothing of these angels is designed to
enhance the splendor of these celestial beings. There is no
reason to think that the golden girdles suggest priestly
functions.

Verse 7. **One of the four living creatures gave the seven
angels seven golden bowls full of the wrath of God.** The four
living creatures stood close to the throne of God (4:6); this is
a symbolic way of saying that the bowls have full divine sanc-
tion. A bowl was a shallow vessel used for drinking and for
libations. The same word was used of the golden bowls full
of incense, which are the prayers of the saints, in the hands
of the twenty-four elders (5:8). There may be a deliberate
allusion to the bowls containing the incense of prayer. The
prayers of the saints have their role in bringing upon the
world the final expression of God's justice and wrath. The emphasis upon the eternity of God — the one **who lives for ever
and ever** — is a reminder that, although evil may seem to dom-
inate affairs in human history, God is the eternal one whose
purposes cannot be frustrated, even by satanic and demonic
evil.

Verse 8. **And the temple was filled with smoke from the
glory of God and from his power, and no one could enter the
temple until the seven plagues of the seven angels were ended.**

In the Old Testament, when God manifested himself to men, he often appeared in such glory that men could not stand before it. "Moses was not able to enter the tent of meeting, because the cloud abode upon it, and the glory of the Lord filled the tabernacle" (Exod. 40:36). The priests were unable to enter Solomon's temple at its dedication because the glory of the divine presence filled the house (I Kings 8:10). When Isaiah was granted a vision of God sitting in his temple surrounded by the seraphim, the foundations of the thresholds shook at the divine voice and the house was filled with smoke (Isa. 6:4). Ezekiel fell on his face before his vision of the temple filled with the glory of the Lord (Ezek. 44:4). The emphasis is not so much the unapproachableness of God as his majesty and glory in comparison to all that is human and mundane.

CHAPTER SIXTEEN

THE SEVEN BOWLS

There are certain similarities between the seven bowl plagues and the seven trumpet plagues, and both series contain certain similarities to the plagues of Egypt. But the seven bowl plagues are much more severe and intense. While the first four trumpet plagues fall upon man's environment rather than upon man himself, the first bowl plague falls directly upon man. These plagues must be seen in the context of the titanic struggle between the Kingdom of God and the kingdom of Satan pictured so vividly in chapter twelve. These plagues are not the expression of God's wrath against sin in general, nor are they punishments for individual wrongdoing. They are the outpouring of his wrath upon him who would frustrate the divine purpose in the world — the beast — and upon those who have given their loyalty to him.

There was an interlude between the first six seals and the seventh, and between the first six trumpets and the seventh. But there is no interlude here; the seventh bowl plague is the overthrow of Babylon herself — the capital of the beast's empire. What is announced in the seventh bowl plague is described in detail in the two following chapters. These plagues are God's answer to Satan's last and greatest effort to frustrate the divine rule.

(2) The First Bowl (16:1-2).

Verse 1. **Then I heard a loud voice from the temple telling**

the seven angels, "Go and pour out on the earth the seven
bowls of the wrath of God." The loud voice must be that of
God himself, for all others had been excluded from the temple
until the seven plagues were ended. On the wrath of God,
see note on 14:10.

Verse 2. **So the first angel went and poured his bowl upon
the earth, and foul and evil sores came upon the men who
bore the mark of the beast and worshiped its image.** The first
plague falls directly upon men and is like the plague of boils in
Egypt (Exod. 9:10-11). These plagues are not inflicted upon
men in general but upon those who have surrendered to the
enticements of the beast. However, John views his empire as
worldwide in its scope; only those who are loyal to the Lamb
resist his satanic claims (13:7-8). In the end-time, religion will
be no longer a merely nominal thing; all men will have to
declare their loyalty for Christ or for Antichrist.

(3) The Second Bowl (16:3).

Verse 3. **The second angel poured his bowl into the sea, and
it became like the blood of a dead man, and every living thing
died that was in the sea.** In the first plague in Egypt, the waters
of the Nile were smitten and became blood (Exod. 7:17-21).
At the sounding of the second trumpet, something like a
mountain was cast into the sea and a third of its waters became
blood and a third of the creatures in the sea died (8:8-10). No
such limitation is placed upon this plague; all creatures in the
sea died.

(4) The Third Bowl (16:4-7).

Verse 4. **The third angel poured his bowl into the rivers
and the fountains of water, and they became blood.** The third
trumpet plague affected the rivers and the fountains of water
so that a third of them was turned poisonously bitter. Here,
there is no such limitation. The trumpet plague brought death
to many from the bitter water; and while the effect of this bowl
plague is not stated, we may assume that it brought great suffering and death.

Verses 5-6. **And I heard the angel of water say, "Just art
thou in these thy judgments, thou who art and wast, O Holy
One. For men have shed the blood of saints and prophets, and**

thou hast given them blood to drink. It is their due!" The angel of water is an expression which is found nowhere else. In 7:1, we have four angels who control the four winds, and in 14:18, the angel who has power over fire. In *Enoch* 66:2, we read of angels who were over the powers of the waters and who had the power to hold back the waters. The voice of this angel proclaims the justice of God's judgments upon those who have shed the blood of those who were loyal to God. The judgment of those who have martyred the saints is suited to the evil they have done. This is only what men deserve.

Verse 7. **And I heard the altar cry, "Yea, Lord God the Almighty, true and just are thy judgments!"** This is the only place in the Revelation where the altar is said to speak. Earlier, a voice came from the horns of the altar of incense (9:13), and voices had been heard from under the altar of burnt offerings (6:9). The context does not determine whether the altar is that of incense or of burnt offering; but in either case, the meaning is the same. The judgments of God have fallen upon a rebellious world as a vindication to those who have been martyred (6:9) in answer to the prayers of the persecuted saints (9:13). Furthermore, the angel who had commanded that the vineyard of the earth be reaped came from the altar (14:18). The altar affirms that God's judgments are not arbitrary and capricious but are true and just. In the end, God's acts of judgment will be completely vindicated.

(5) The Fourth Bowl (16:8-9).

Verses 8-9. **The fourth angel poured his bowl on the sun, and it was allowed to scorch men with fire; men were scorched by the fierce heat.** This bowl caused a plague of excessive heat which afflicted men with a fierce sunstroke. The phrase "it was allowed to scorch men with fire" indicates that this plague is due to nothing inherent in the sun's heat, but is due to the sovereign judgments of God overruling the processes of nature. It is important to note that the text states that the afflicted men recognized that this was a work of God; but so hard and recalcitrant are their hearts because of the choice they have made to follow the beast that, instead of being brought to their knees in humble confession of their dependence on God, they

211

curse his **name** and stubbornly refuse to **repent and give him glory.**

(6) The Fifth Bowl (16:10-11).

Verses 10-11. **The fifth angel poured his bowl on the throne of the beast, and its kingdom was in darkness.** This plague is poured out directly upon the center of the beast's power. This again makes it clear that these plagues embodying the wrath of God do not represent his wrath against the sins of men in a general sense, although this is a biblical theme (Rom. 1:18), but his wrath poured out upon the demonic civilization of the last time. The plague is one of supernatural darkness, similar to the plague of darkness in Egypt (Exod. 10:21-23). The darkness was accompanied by acute **anguish.** The text does not indicate the cause of the distress and pain that led men to **gnaw their tongues** in agony. We may suppose that the intense darkness served to magnify the pain inflicted by the preceding plague, which had brought upon them **pain and sores.** Again, men recognize the hand of God in judgment, but their hearts are adamant; they refuse to show any trace of repentance but instead **cursed the God of heaven.**

(7) The Sixth Bowl (16:12-16).

Verse 12. **The sixth angel poured his bowl on the great river Euphrates, and its water was dried up, to prepare the way for the kings from the east.** This bowl is different from the others in that it does not inflict a plague upon men but serves as a preparation for the final eschatological battle. This plague is similar to the sixth trumpet, when four angels were released from beyond the Euphrates to lead an invasion of practically innumerable hosts of demonic cavalry who killed a third of mankind (9:13-19). We have seen that the river Euphrates in the Old Testament is the boundary of the promised land, beyond which were hordes of heathen peoples waiting for the opportunity to invade the people of God (see note on 9:14). The prophets sometimes looked upon the drying up of the river Euphrates as the prelude to the gathering of God's dispersed people in their own land (Isa. 11:15-16; *IV Ezra* 13:47). In the present instance the drying of the river is represented symbolically as the removal of the barrier which holds back the pagan hordes.

"The kings from the east" are not further defined nor is their role described. Some commentators see a civil conflict between the kings of the east and the kings of the whole world (vs. 14), but nothing of the sort is hinted at in the text. The more natural assumption is that the kings of the east—the pagan hordes — join forces with the kings of the whole (civilized) world to do battle with Messiah, for it is clearly the eschatological "battle on the great day of God the Almighty" (vs. 14). Later, we read that the beast is supported by "ten kings who have not yet received royal power, but they are to receive authority as kings for one hour, together with the beast" (17:12). They join the beast in making war on the Lamb (17:14). These ten kings may be either the kings from the east, or else the kings of the whole world. In any case, John expects a confederation of two groups of kings in support of the beast to do battle with the Lamb.

Many commentators assert — as though it were a self-evident fact in the text — that the "kings from the east" represent the Parthians who now invade the civilized world under the leadership of *Nero redivivus*. This, however, is sheer speculation. The Nero myth expected him to attack and conquer Rome; in the present passage these kings ally themselves with the beast to oppose the Almighty. If this involved the *Nero redivivus* myth, the beast should be their leader coming from the east, whereas the beast already has his throne in Babylon and accepts the support of these foreign kings.

Verse 13. Now the "kings from the east" suddenly disappear from the narrative, and equally suddenly the **dragon** and the **beast** appear. For the first time, the term **the false prophet** occurs; he is the second beast who arose out of the land to support the first beast in his blasphemous claims. The **three foul spirits like frogs** issuing from their mouths is John's way of describing the demonic inspiration of the foes of God in the last great battle. In the sixth trumpet, a terrible demonic plague came from the east to afflict men, bringing death to a third of mankind. Here the motif is different; the evil spirits do not afflict men but inspire them to give their support to the dragon and the beast and the false prophet. John means to say that this is no mere military or political movement but the manifestation in eschatological history of the age-long struggle between God and Satan. The word translated "foul" is the word frequently used in the gospels which refers to demons as

unclean spirits (Mark 1:23; 3:11; 5:2). They are said to be
like frogs, probably to preserve the analogy to the plague of
frogs in Egypt (Exod. 8:6).

Verse 14. **For they are demonic spirits** is a much better translation than the AV: "for they are the spirits of devils" (literally, demons). Since demons are spiritual beings, we may not
think of demons having spirits; they *are* spirits. For **the kings
of the whole world,** see the discussion on vs. 12. John expects
a coalition of human rulers, demonically inspired, who will do
battle with Messiah.

The battle on the great day of God the Almighty is not a
common biblical phrase. The common idioms are the day of
the Lord (see I Thess. 5:2), the day of Christ (Phil. 1:10), or
the day of the Lord Jesus Christ (I Cor. 1:8). Some interpreters
try to find a difference in meaning between these terms, as
though they represented several distinct days, but this is impossible. In fact, so interchangeable are these idioms that the
word alone without further modifiers, "the day," or "that day,"
can be used to designate the last eschatological day (I Cor.
3:13; II Thess. 1:10). The Gospel of John often speaks of "the
last day" (John 6:39; 11:24; 12:48). Peter speaks of "the
day of God" (II Pet. 3:12). The day of the Lord is the time
when the total redemptive purpose of God will be consummated, both for salvation and judgment, both for individuals,
the church, and the whole creation. Here, John sees the hatred
that has expressed itself throughout the ages of human history
in terms of hostility and persecution of the people of God as
coming to a last grand finale when all the rulers of the earth
join hands in a final battle. Such a battle between God's people
and their pagan neighbors is frequently envisaged by the Old
Testament prophets (Ps. 2:2-3; Isa. 5:26-30; Jer. 6:1-5; Ezek.
38; Joel 3:9-15).

Verse 15. In view of the imminent crisis involved in the
battle between God and the forces of evil, Jesus himself inter-
jects a word to the church, both to warn his people and to assure them of the realities behind the immediate historical
events. The war of the united kings under the leadership of the
beast is not the ultimate reality; the ultimate reality is the
fact of the Lord's return. This is the event which is the focus of
the expectation of the saints. This verse is an interruption in

the context of the passage to give the church its proper perspective.

He will come **like a thief.** The coming of Christ is likened elsewhere to the coming of a thief (see notes on 3:3). There is no thought of the furtiveness, nor even of the suddenness of the Lord's return, but of its unexpectedness. Paul likens the coming of Christ to the coming of a thief (I Thess. 5:2), but this has reference only to those who are not prepared: "But you are not in darkness, brethren, for that day to surprise you like a thief" (I Thess. 5:4). For those who are awake to his coming, the return of the Lord will be no surprising, unexpected event but a glad deliverance from the tragic situation in the world in which they have found themselves. John assumes that such people will be **awake.** The translation of the AV, "Blessed is he that watcheth," somewhat obscures the meaning of the Greek. In English, to "watch" for something means to have the attention fixed on that object so that nothing distracts the watcher. This is perhaps the most logically effective argument for an "any-moment," i.e., pre-tribulation return of the Lord. It is impossible to "watch" for something unless that event is capable of occurring at any time, i.e., before the great tribulation. However, the Greek word means simply "to be awake." Jesus exhorts his disciples to be awake because they could not know the hour of his return (Matt. 24:42). He illustrated this by saying, "But know this, that if the householder had known in what part of the night the thief was coming, he would have watched [i.e., been awake] and would not have let his house be broken into. Therefore you also must be ready; for the Son of Man is coming at an hour you do not expect" (Matt. 24:43-44). The whole emphasis is upon the unexpectedness of the Lord's return, and in light of the uncertainty of the times, believers must never relax and sleep but must always be awake. To be asleep means to say, "There is peace and security" (I Thess. 5:3), i.e., to lose sight of the ultimate issues of life and to assume that security is to be found on the human level instead of in terms of one's relationship to Christ. For such, "sudden destruction will come upon them as travail comes upon a woman with child, and

215

there will be no escape" (I Thess. 5:3).[1] In the present context, John assumes that the church has not lost its perspective and has not lost sight of the ultimate spiritual values in spite of the triumphant rule of the beast among the nations.

The warning about **keeping his garments that he may not go naked and be seen exposed** is not common eschatological terminology, but the meaning is clear. The church in Laodicea had been warned against spiritual poverty and nakedness, and had been counseled to buy "white garments to clothe you and to keep the shame of your nakedness from being seen" (3:18). This is a summons to spiritual diligence.

Verse 16. **And they assembled them at the place which is called in Hebrew Armageddon.** After the exhortation to the church to watchfulness, John resumes the narrative of the three unclean spirits who gather the kings of the world to battle, adding that they bring them together in a place called Armageddon. This is preparatory for the actual battle which takes place in 19:11ff. when Christ comes as a victorious warrior to defeat his foes.

The word "Armageddon" is difficult; the Hebrew equivalent would be *har megiddon* — the mountain of Megiddo. The problem is that Megiddo is not a mountain, but a plain located between the Sea of Galilee and the Mediterranean, part of the valley of Jezreel (Esdraelon). It was a famous battleground in the history of Israel. At Megiddo, Barak and Deborah overthrew the Canaanite Jabin (Jud. 5:19); Ahaziah was slain by Jehu (II Kings 23:29; II Chr. 35:22). Why John calls it the mountain of Megiddo is not clear; R. H. Charles says that no convincing interpretation has yet been given of the phrase;[2] it is unknown in Hebrew literature. Charles suggests that the reference to the mountain as the final battlefield may be drawn from Ezek. 38:8, 21; 39:2, 4, 17, where an eschatological battle is seen on the mountains of Israel. Whatever the derivation of the name, it is clear that John means by Armageddon the place of the final struggle between the powers of evil and the Kingdom of God.

[1]For the entire subject, which has been vigorously debated in evangelical theology, see George E. Ladd, *The Blessed Hope* (Grand Rapids: Eerdmans, 1956), chap. 6, "Watch."

[2]R. H. Charles, *The Revelation of St. John* (New York: Scribners, 1920), II, 50.

216

(8) The Seventh Bowl (16:17-21).

The plague of the seventh bowl is a proleptic statement of the judgment of God upon Babylon, the seat of the beast's power. The detailed statement of the judgment and fall of Babylon follows in the next two chapters (17-18). Some commentators find here two different events: a preliminary overthrow of Rome which allows Antichrist to assume universal sway, followed by God's judgment of Rome.[3] However, John has frequently made proleptic statements of the coming of the end, both in terms of salvation and judgment, and then enlarged upon the events which will occur at the end (see notes on 6:12ff.; 11:15ff.; 14:8; 14:14ff.; 15:2ff.). In fact, John has already announced the fall of Babylon (14:8), and this is a declaration by way of anticipation. As the sixth seal brought us to the day of God's wrath (6:12-17), as the seventh trumpet brought a proclamation of the end (11:15ff.), so the seventh bowl brings the judgment of Babylon, with the actual detailing of this judgment yet to follow.

Verse 17. **The seventh angel poured his bowl into the air, and a great voice came out of the temple, from the throne, saying, "It is done!"** This is apparently the same voice as in vs. 1 — the voice of God — since it came from the temple and God's throne. The voice announced proleptically the consummation of God's judgment upon the beast's capital. The phrase, "It is done" represents a single Greek word indicating completed action. Here again, John employs the literary technique which we have frequently met of announcing a completed fact, and later expounding the content of that fact.

Verse 18. The pronouncement of the judgment of the beast's capital is followed by apocalyptic phenomena which are manifestations of the glory and power of God: **flashes of lightning, loud noises, peals of thunder, and a great earthquake such as had never been since men were on the earth.** Similar phenomena had followed the sounding of the seventh trumpet (11:19) and were associated with the vision of God in 4:5 and the preparation for the sounding of the seven trumpets (8:5). These phenomena are common manifestations of the divine power and glory.

[3] I. T. Beckwith, *The Apocalypse of John* (Grand Rapids: Baker, reprint 1967), pp. 408, 686.

Verse 19. The result of this theophany is the complete col-
lapse of the godless human civilization. **The great city,** Babylon, the capital of the beast, was **split into three parts;** that is,
it was brought to complete ruin. In 11:8, the same words, "the
great city," had been used to describe Jerusalem; but the context makes it quite clear that in the present passage, Babylon
is intended. Jerusalem has already been overthrown in a great
earthquake (11:13). While the present vision sees the utter ruin
of the city by an earthquake, all that this destruction means is
described in different terms in the two chapters that follow.

The cities of the nations fell. This again is a proleptic statement announcing the destruction of the nations which have
given their support to the beast. This detail is elaborated in
17:12-14 where we are told that the Lamb will make war
against ten kings who have supported the beast and will conquer them. See also 18:9 where the kings of the earth grieve
over the fall of the great city.

**God remembered great Babylon, to make her drain the cup
of the fury of his wrath.** Babylon has given to the nations of
the earth the "cup of the wine of her impure passion" and has
led "the kings of the earth to commit fornication with her" and
has enabled the merchants of the earth to "grow rich with the
wealth of her wantonness" (18:3). In return, God makes
Babylon, together with the nations who have followed her, to
drink another cup, the cup of his wrath. This theme has already been expounded in 14:8, 10.

"God remembered great Babylon." These are poignant
words. During the short period of the reign of Antichrist it
will seem as though God has forgotten his people. Evil will
seem to be the victor; no deliverance is in sight. But God does
not forget. God remembers, and he will remember to give the
mighty enemy of his people her just due.

Verse 20. Again John describes proleptically the consummation, which will involve a renovation of the entire created
order and the ushering in of new heavens and a new earth.
This event does not take place until after the return of Christ
(19:11ff.) and is described in terms of a completely transformed
order (21:1ff.). Yet John can signal the approach of this event
by apocalyptic language of the breakup of the old order: **and
every island fled away, and no mountains were to be found.**
John has already, early in his book, used similar language to

describe the coming of the end; the opening of the sixth seal witnessed the breakup of the present created order (6:12ff.).

Verse 21. **And great hailstones, heavy as a hundredweight, dropped on men from heaven, till men cursed God for the plague of the hail, so fearful was that plague.** We do not know with certainty the measure of weight indicated, but it seems to have been over a hundred pounds.

CHAPTER SEVENTEEN

THE MYSTERY OF BABYLON

John's apocalyptic narrative is now hastening to its end. He has carried us through the time of great tribulation with its terrible persecution of the saints by Antichrist, and he has shown us a rebellious, antichristian civilization unbowed and unrepentant under the outpourings of the wrath of God in the plagues of the seven trumpets and the seven bowls. The seventh bowl did not bring a plague upon mankind but announced the coming of the end, particularly in the overthrow of Babylon, an event which had already been announced (14:8). All that remains now is to tell of the coming of the end. John first gives the negative side of the divine victory, viz., the overthrow of the rebellious civilization announced in his seventh bowl (chapters 17-18), and then tells of the triumphant coming of Christ, his victorious reign, and finally the establishment of the new order in the new heavens and new earth (chapters 19-22).

IV. THE THIRD VISION (17:1 — 21:8).

From a literary point of view, as we have seen, the Revelation is structured in four visions. The first one contains the vision of Christ and his letters to the seven churches; the second contains the breaking of the seals of the scroll, the seven trumpets and the seven bowls. The third vision contains the revelation of the consummation of God's redemptive purpose.

1. THE MYSTERY OF BABYLON (17:1-18).

Twice before, John has suddenly and without explanation introduced Babylon into his prophecy (14:8; 16:19); now he picks up this motif to develop it at length as one of the most important facts in the coming of the end.

Verse 1. **Then one of the seven angels who had the seven bowls came and said to me, "Come, I will show you the judgment of the great harlot."** Why this particular mission was entrusted to one of the angels of the seven bowls is not explained. Another such angel fulfills a similar mission at the beginning of the final vision when John sees the new Jerusalem (21:9). It was an unidentified voice which had summoned John to behold his first vision (4:2; see 1:10); probably it too was an angelic summons. The call "Come," which had lifted John into an ecstatic trance (4:1f.; see also 21:9f.), signals a new revelation about to be given to him: the judgment of the great harlot.

In the Old Testament, the metaphor of adultery was frequently used of Israel as God's faithless wife who had proved unfaithful by turning to false gods. Foreign nations were never accused by the prophets of this form of sin. Sometimes Israel's sin was also described in terms of harlotry: "How the faithful city has become a harlot" (Isa. 1:21; see Jer. 2:20; 3:1; Ezek. 16:15; Hos. 2:5; 3:3; 4:15). She has not only been unfaithful to her God; she has sold herself wantonly to any who would ask. The metaphor of harlotry is also used by the prophets of heathen nations. Tyre is called a city who "will play the harlot with all the kingdoms of the world upon the face of the earth" (Isa. 23:17). The idea here is not one of spiritual faithlessness, but of the prostitution of everything to commercial gain. Nineveh is also described as a harlot (Nah. 3:4) because of the way she enticed weaker nations by her display of power and splendor only to scorn and enslave them. Here the harlot is Babylon, the symbol of human civilization with all its pomp and circumstance organized in opposition to God — "the city which has dominion over the kings of the earth" (vs. 18).

The great harlot is **seated upon many waters.** This is a very important statement and provides us with one of the clues in the identification of the harlot. This description does not fit historical Rome, for while the Tiber flows through the city,

Rome was not built upon many waters. The phrase does describe the historical Babylon, because the city was built on a network of canals. Jeremiah spoke of Babylon as the city which dwells by many waters (Jer. 51:13). John himself interprets the meaning of this phrase: "The waters that you saw, where the harlot is seated, are peoples and multitudes and nations and tongues" (vs. 15). Babylon became the personification of wickedness, and John has taken over the Old Testament symbolism and used Babylon to represent the final manifestation of the total history of godless nations. The city had a historical manifestation in first-century Rome, but the full significance of the wicked city is eschatological. Rome could be said to be seated on many waters in the sense that she drew her strength and sovereignty from her conquest of many nations; but it will be even more true of eschatological Babylon, who will seduce all the world to worship that which is not God.

Verse 2. **The kings of the earth have committed fornication** with the great harlot; that is, they have entered into intimate commerce with her to share her wealth and prosperity. In so doing they have also shared her vices and idolatries. Back of this is the symbolism of Jer. 51:7: "Babylon was a golden cup in the Lord's hand, making all the earth drunken; the nations drank of her wine, therefore the nations went mad." The particular form of fornication in the present instance is enticement of the peoples to worship the beast. **The wine of her fornication** is the means she uses as a form of seduction — the enticement by which she seduces the nations to share her ungodly character. They have joined in her sins against God. The seduction is an effective one; it affects first the rulers of the people and then in turn reaches to the **dwellers on earth.** This is a frequent Johannine idiom for ungodly men (3:10; 6:10; 8:13; 11:10; 13:8, 14).

Verse 3. **And he carried me away in the Spirit into a wilderness.** The active agent is the angel. These words indicate a new state of ecstasy in which John is given the vision of the great harlot. To be "in the Spirit" in the Revelation is to be in an ecstatic condition (1:10; 4:2). There seems to be no particular symbolic significance in the fact that John received the vision in the wilderness. The heavenly woman fled from the dragon into the wilderness (12:6, 14) that she might be protected by God from the wrath of the dragon. Here, the wilderness seems to be simply a solitary place where John could receive his vision. A wilderness in the biblical idiom was not necessarily a dry barren place; it could be simply an uncultivated region with sparse population.

John **saw a woman sitting on a scarlet beast,** obviously the same beast as 13:1 with its **seven heads and ten horns;** viz., the Antichrist. The color of the beast, not mentioned in chapter 13, is very similar to that of the dragon — Satan — in 12:3. The Greek words are different, but the basic color is the same. The beast is described as **scarlet** to indicate his intimate relationship to his ultimate master — Satan. For the meaning of the seven heads and ten horns, see note in 13:1.

There is no problem in the fact that in vs. 1 the woman was seated upon many waters while here she is seated upon the scarlet beast. The fluidity of apocalyptic language allows it to represent different facts by the use of concepts which may seem to be logically contradictory. That she was seated upon many waters reflects her relationship to the nations of earth; that she is seated upon the scarlet beast reflects her relationship to the Antichrist. As the seat of godless civilization, the great harlot has achieved her glory because she has been made great by the beast and is completely dependent upon it.

The beast was **full of blasphemous names.** One of the chief characteristics of the beast is his blasphemy. In 13:1, it had a blasphemous name upon its heads and it uttered blasphemies against God (13:5-6). The present verse is even more strongly expressed; the beast is full of blasphemous names. It is, of course, a reference to the self-deification of the Antichrist and his demand for the worship of his subjects. His blasphemies are not curses on the divine sovereignty uttered by men under the judgments of God (16:9); they consist of the derogation of deity by his own claim to self-deification.

Verse 4. The appearance of the great harlot is now described. She was **arrayed in purple and scarlet.** It is doubtful if any symbolic significance is intended by these colors; they merely reflect the splendor and luxury of her garb. Purple and scarlet clothing in the ancient world could be worn only by the wealthy because of the cost of obtaining these choice dyes. Interpreters of the historical school who understand the beast to represent the papacy (see chap. 1) have been fond of seeing in these colors the splendid robes of the bishops and cardinals of the church, but this can hardly have been John's intention. She was **bedecked with gold and jewels and pearls.** The word translated bedecked is literally "gilded." Her raiment was splendid and fabulously costly.

She held in her hand a **golden cup full of abominations and the impurities of her fornication.** This is a direct allusion to Jer. 51:7, quoted above. The golden cup was beautiful of appearance and promised the most delicious wine; but instead it was full of repulsive corruption. The word for abominations means anything foul and detestable; but in the Old Testament, it became particularly associated with idolatry. The phrase describing the Antichrist in our Lord's Olivet Discourse is, literally, the abomination of desolation (see AV), i.e., the abomination that brings desolation. The main thought is that with the promise of wealth and luxury, the woman entices men away from the worship of God.

Verse 5. **On her forehead was written a name of mystery: "Babylon the great, mother of harlots and of the earth's abominations."** This is not the first time that we have found names written on the forehead. The saints of God were sealed on their foreheads with the divine name (7:3; 9:4; 14:1). The followers of the beast also were sealed upon their foreheads and upon their hands with his name and the number of his name (13:17). In the new earth, the redeemed will have the name of God written on their foreheads (3:12; 22:4). This may also reflect the Roman custom for harlots to wear a headband bearing the name of the owner.

This name is a name of *mystery*. The structure of the passage allows the word "mystery" to be either a part of the title itself, or a part of the introductory words. Many scholars choose the former alternative (see AV), but it is easier to understand it as introducing the title and to mean that the title is not meant to be taken literally but has a hidden meaning, viz., the capital city of the Antichrist.

Babylon is the "mother of harlots." She was not satisfied herself alone to entice men away from God; she insisted that her daughters join her in her nefarious and blasphemous designs. Along with her blasphemous harlotry she gave birth to all sorts of abominations which fill the earth.

Verse 6. **And I saw the woman, drunk with the blood of the saints and the blood of the martyrs of Jesus.** The woman is a fit companion for the beast who made war on the saints and conquered them (13:7). As the capital of the beast, she will be the city most noted for the persecution and martyrdom of the saints. Nothing as far-reaching as this in scope had yet befallen the Christian church. A short persecution had been waged in the time of Nero which is described by Tacitus, the Roman historian, with the words: "A great crowd was convicted both of arson and of hatred for the human race. Not only were they put to death, but put to death with insult, in that they were either dressed in the skins of beasts to perish by worrying of dogs, or put on crosses or set on fire; and when daylight failed, they were burnt as lights for the night" (*Annals*, 15:44). But after this one outburst of hatred, Christians were comparatively untroubled in Rome. Furthermore, the brief persecution by Nero had nothing to do with the cult of the emperor. In contrast to this, the chief characteristic of the woman is her harlotry and her alliance with the beast. It was only under Domitian that we have evidence of the persecution of Christians on religious grounds. However, the persecution by Domitian was of a minor sort. John looks for a day when the chief city of the beast will be infamous for her persecution of the saints primarily on religious grounds; nothing in the first century provides an adequate counterpart to this. John is thinking of eschatological Babylon.

To be "drunk with blood" is a common ancient idiom (see Isa. 34:5, where the sword is pictured as being drunk with blood; see also Isa. 49:26).

No distinction can be made between the blood of the saints and the blood of the martyrs. They are saints because they belong to God; they are martyrs because they have shed their blood. Furthermore, they are martyrs *of Jesus;* they have been martyred because of their unswerving faith in him and their refusal to deny his name (12:17; 14:12; 19:10; 20:4).

When I saw her I marveled greatly. The AV reads, "with great admiration." This is an archaic use of the word and does not carry any sense of approval. The Greek would be literally translated, "I was amazed at her with great amazement." Possibly the cause of John's amazement was the fact that he had been told that he would see the judgment of the great harlot (vs. 1), but in the first part of his vision he saw a magnificently garbed woman attended with great splendor. His perplexity is easily understood.

Verse 7. In answer to his perplexity, the angel said, **"Why marvel? I will tell you the mystery of the woman, and of the beast with the seven heads and ten horns that carries her."** This is a rather perplexing answer. One would expect that the angel's explanation would deal largely with the mystery of the great harlot, but the angel says that he will explain also the mystery of the beast. This shows the inseparable relationship between the woman and the beast. The last center of civilization will derive its character altogether from the one fact that it is supported by the beast. There are not two mysteries; the one mystery includes both the beast and the harlot. John is promised not only the true meaning of the beast and the woman, but also the meaning of the seven heads and the ten horns of the beast.

Verse 8. **The beast that you saw was, and is not, and is to ascend from the bottomless pit and go to perdition.** This is another way of saying what John has already said about the beast. "One of its heads seemed to have a mortal wound, but the mortal wound was healed" (13:3). We have seen that this does not mean that one of the heads was wounded unto the point of death, but that it was actually slain. In the present passage, John makes it clear that the beast itself is to be identified with its heads. The slaying of one of the heads means the slaying of the beast. The beast is to pass through three stages: *it was*, i.e., it had an existence in the past; *it is not*, i.e., there will be a time when it does not exist; *it is to ascend from the bottomless pit,* i.e., it will have a future manifestation which will be the incarnation of satanic evil. The bottomless pit is the apocalyptic metaphor for the demonic, satanic realm of evil, and is pictured as the home of the beast before he appears on earth (11:7; see note in 12:1). The three stages of the existence of the beast are to be identified with the seven heads. He once existed in one or more of his heads; he ceased to exist when one of the heads received a mortal wound; but he will have a future existence when the head is healed. The healing of the head will involve a satanic embodiment that will exceed anything that has yet occurred. However, this final manifestation of the beast will be short-lived; it is destined to go to perdition. "Perdition" is a word occasionally used of the state

226

of final, eternal doom (Matt. 7:13; Phil. 1:28; 3:19; Heb. 10:39; II Pet. 3:7).

And the dwellers on earth whose names have not been written in the book of life from the foundation of the world, will marvel to behold the beast, because it was and is not and is to come. By a twofold designation, John identifies those who marvel at the beast. They are the worldlings (see note in vs. 2), and negatively, they are the unsaved. For the book of life, see note on 3:5. The cause of wonder will be the reappearance of the beast which disappears for a time and then returns to the scene of action.

Verse 9. **This calls for a mind with wisdom.** John is about to explain the mystery of the woman and the beast, but it is not a self-evident explanation; it is one that only those spiritually enlightened will understand.

The seven heads are seven hills on which the woman is seated. Most modern commentators see here a positive and inescapable identification of the great harlot with first-century Rome, because Rome was widely known as the city that was built on seven hills. As one writer says, "The local allusion is too plain to be doubted."[1] However, John immediately goes on to say in the next verse that "they are also seven kings." It is difficult to see any connection between the seven hills of Rome and seven of its emperors.

It is a biblical commonplace that a hill or mountain is a symbol of power or rule. In Dan. 2:35, the stone cut out without hands smites the nations of the world and in turn grows to become a great mountain. God said to Babylon, "Behold, I am against you, O destroying mountain . . . which destroys the whole earth" (Jer. 51:25). "In the latter days, the mountain of the house of the Lord shall be established as the highest of the mountains and shall be raised above the hills" (Isa. 2:2). God's servant "shall thresh the mountains and crush them, and . . . make the hills like chaff" (Isa. 41:15; see also Ps. 68:15-16; Hab. 3:6). It is easier, therefore, to understand the seven hills to stand for seven empires and the rulers who headed them.

It may be objected that John says the hills are also *seven kings,* not seven kingdoms; but this is biblical language. The four beasts of Dan. 7 were said to represent four kings (Dan.

[1]I. T. Beckwith, *The Apocalypse of John* (Grand Rapids: Baker, reprint 1967), p. 698.

7:17) when, more precisely, Daniel means the kingdoms over which they rule. The great harlot sits upon a succession of empires. She found her embodiment in historical Babylon, in the first century in historical Rome, and at the end of the age in eschatological Babylon. This may well be what John intended in speaking about the "mystery of the woman" (vs. 7). No simple identification with any single historical city is possible. The woman has formed an adulterous connection in every epoch of her history with the then existing world power.

Verse 10. **They are also seven kings, five of whom have fallen, one is, the other has not yet come, and when he comes he must remain only a little while.** This is one of the most debated verses in the book of Revelation. Preterist interpreters usually apply the verse to the succession of Roman emperors. Five emperors have reigned and passed from the scene; John is writing his Revelation during the rule of the sixth emperor. John expects this sixth ruler also to pass from the scene, to be followed by the seventh and last emperor, who will be the Antichrist in the person of *Nero redivivus*.

The problem with this apparently simple solution is that the dates simply do not work out. The Roman emperors were as follows:

Augustus	27 B.C.-A.D. 14
Tiberius	A.D. 14-37
Caligula	A.D. 37-41
Claudius	A.D. 41-54
Nero	A.D. 54-68
Galba	A.D. 68
Otho	A.D. 69
Vitellius	
Vespasian	A.D. 69-79
Titus	A.D. 79-81
Domitian	A.D. 81-96

Accordingly, the five kings who have fallen should be those from Augustus to Nero; Galba was the reigning emperor in the day when John wrote, and Otho was expected to be the last. This interpretation doesn't make sense, for Galba, Otho, and Vitellius all experienced very short reigns and were relatively unimportant in political and religious history. For this reason, many scholars suggest that they be left out of the reckoning, and Vespasian be seen as the sixth king, and Titus the seventh.

Such a procedure is arbitrary, for Galba, Otho and Vitellius, unimportant as they may have been, were bona fide emperors and were recognized as such by ancient historians.

However, this rather violent way of treating history does not really solve the problem, for nothing happened in the reign of Vespasian to disturb the Christian church and cause it to fear a time of fierce persecution, such as might give rise to the eschatological views of the Revelation and to the writing of the book. Furthermore, Vespasian did not promote the emperor cult.

All sorts of speculative solutions to the problem have been suggested. Some have suggested that this passage was an oracle written in the time of Vespasian which John incorporated into his book without modification; others that John deliberately projects himself back into the time of Vespasian; others that John began his reckoning with Caligula, as the first emperor who openly showed himself to be an enemy of God. No method of calculation satisfactorily leads to Domitian as the reigning emperor, and some scholars have given up any effort to relate the seven heads to specific kings but find in the number seven the ideal number that represents the completeness of imperial power.

This problem is altogether avoided if John does not mean to designate a succession of individual kings or emperors, but a succession of kingdoms. This finds some support in the statement, "five . . . have fallen." Several interpreters have pointed out that the word "fallen" is much better applied to the fall of a kingdom than to the death of an emperor (H. Alford, Th. Zahn). The great harlot who seduces the nations and persecutes the saints finds her support from the beast who appears in history in a succession of secular, godless kingdoms; five belong to past history; a sixth kingdom — Rome — ruled the world when John wrote. However, Rome is not Antichrist; a seventh kingdom is expected which will have only a short reign. This interpretation of the beast and its seven heads is supported by the verse that follows.

Verse 11. **As for the beast that was and is not, it is an eighth but it belongs to the seven, and it goes to perdition.** Three times in 17:8-11, John has said that the beast does not exist in the present, and twice that the beast will appear in the future. The beast has already once existed (he was); he does not now

229

exist (he is not), but he will come up again out of the abyss
(11:7; 17:8, 11). John has also said that the beast had seven
heads, one of which was wounded unto death and then healed
(13:3). He has also said that the beast itself received the mortal
wound but was healed (13:12, 14). Now he adds a new fact: the
beast is an eighth head, yet it belongs to the seven heads. The
symbolism is made difficult by the fact that the beast is sometimes identified with his heads, but is sometimes differentiated
from them. The solution to this involved symbolism lies in the
interpretation that the beast is the Antichrist, and yet he is not
the Antichrist; he is the Antichrist in two of his heads only.
As the Antichrist, he has already appeared in history (he was);
he does not exist in the present, but he is yet to arise in an
embodiment of satanic power. This is why John can say that
one of the heads was wounded to death, but the death wound
was healed; and also that the beast itself had received a death
stroke and had come to life again. In other words, the beast
is identified with two of its heads more closely than with the
other five. In one of the heads, the beast had himself appeared
in history; this head — and the beast himself — had been slain
(i.e., had disappeared from history) but is to be revived in a
final appearance, which will be a more complete manifestation
of the beast than the first (i.e., he shall ascend from the abyss).
Still, the other five heads are also heads of the beast, yet it is
not identified with them as with the two. The heads are successive manifestations of the worldly kingdoms at enmity with
God through all the changes of history.[2] The beast, then, has a
twofold meaning: broadly, it is the anti-God worldly power;
narrowly, it is one particular kingdom which has a twofold
manifestation. Five of the heads are manifestations of the
worldly kingdoms as such; two of the heads are specific embodiments of the beast himself. The clue to the understanding
of this is the prophecy of Daniel, on which John draws for his
symbolism of the beast (see notes on 13:2). In Daniel, the great
enemy of God's people is Antichrist, who has previously been
manifested in history in the person of Antiochus Epiphanes
(Dan. 8:9, 21). In typical prophetic manner, these two figures
are sometimes blended together so that they seem to be prac-

---

[2]See note on 11:15, where "the kingdom of the world" is viewed as a
single hostile sovereignty, however diversely it is manifested in actual historical forms and nations.

tically one (see p. 13). The beast that you saw was (vs. 8), i.e., it was embodied in Antiochus Epiphanes; it is not, i.e., it does not now exist in this same malevolent form; it is to ascend from the abyss (vs. 8) in the person of Antichrist.[3]

John adds a further specific detail about the last appearance of the beast — the Antichrist: "the beast ... is an eighth, but it belongs to the seven." This is difficult language. The second and final manifestation of the beast is in an eighth king; but it is not *the* eighth king for there are only seven; it is an eighth king which is one of the seven. This suggests that one of the seven is to experience two stages of his existence. This apparently is why John says that the seventh king "will remain only a little while" (vs. 10). He will be shortly followed by an eighth, who is the seventh in his full antichristian manifestation. John means to say that the eighth is like the seven, but yet is different from them. It belongs to the seven in that it succeeds them in world domination; but it stands apart in that it ascends from the abyss as the full satanic embodiment of the beast.

Verse 12. John now explains the ten horns. They are **ten kings** who **are to receive authority as kings** for a very short period of time — **for one hour** — and are to be the colleagues and supporters of the beast. Modern commentators who accept the *Nero redivivus* theory of the Antichrist usually understand these ten kings to be ten Persian satraps who will return in revived Nero's retinue to help him regain his empire. However, John expressly says that they **have not yet received royal power.** They are not yet kings; they will receive their power when the beast appears. This clearly casts John's thought into the future. It is idle to speculate as to the identity of these kings, or to understand them, as some do, as ten European kingdoms of a revived Roman empire. The idea of ten kings is based on Dan. 7:7, 24 where the fourth beast has ten horns who are ten kings, out from whom emerges a final king who fills the role of Antichrist. It is very possible that the number ten is meant to be symbolic designating the fullness of Antichrist's power and is not intended to be taken literally. The

[3]This interpretation of the beast is essentially that of Th. Zahn; see his *Introduction to the New Testament* (Edinburgh: T. & T. Clark, 1909), III, 436ff.; *Die Offenbarung des Johannes* (Leipzig: Deichert, 1926), II, 553ff.

ten kings are purely eschatological figures representing the
totality of the powers of all nations on the earth which are to
be made subservient to Antichrist.

Verse 13. **These are of one mind and give over their power
and authority to the beast.** These kings are not important in
and of themselves but only as allies of the beast. They do not
seek their own ends; they are complete in their devotion to
the beast.

Verse 14. **They will make war on the Lamb, and the Lamb
will conquer them.** This illustrates in particular their unan-
imous support of the beast; they join him in his hostility to the
Lamb, but in vain. This final conflict between the Antichrist
and Messiah does not occur at this point; it is pictured in 19:17-
21 at the return of Christ.

**For he is Lord of lords and King of kings, and those with
him are called and chosen and faithful.** The supreme lordship
of the Lamb assures his victory. This is the title inscribed upon
the robe and upon the thigh of the victorious Christ (19:16).
He does not conquer alone; in his retinue are those who have
been called and chosen by God and who have remained faithful to the Lamb in the face of the final persecution.

Verse 15. In the concluding verses of this chapter, John gives
us more specific information about the great harlot and then
tells of her destruction. This is a difficult passage, for it leaves
a number of important questions unanswered. At the beginning of the chapter, John had been summoned to witness "the
judgment of the great harlot" (vs. 1); but thus far, John has
learned more about the beast than about the woman. In this
concluding section, John turns his attention to the woman
and relates the means God uses to bring about her destruction. First, the angels explained to John the symbolism of
the **waters that you saw, where the harlot is seated.** These
waters represent many **peoples and multitudes and nations
and tongues,** which give their support to the woman. She is
the capital city of a complex civilization consisting of many
nations (see notes on vs. 1).

Verse 16. Now John states a fact which he does not explain
but which is the divinely decreed means to bring to pass the
judgment of the harlot. She has been the capital city of the
beast who has had the complete support of ten kings in his
hostility to the Lamb (vs. 13). At the beginning of the vision,

the woman was seen sitting on a scarlet beast (vs. 3), and as the city, Babylon, was the scene of the beast's persecution and martyrdom of the saints (vs. 6). Now, however, the picture changes, and for reasons which are not explained, a sort of civil war arises within the camp of the beast. The beast, followed by the ten kings, turns in hatred upon the harlot: **they will make her desolate and naked, and devour her flesh and burn her up with fire.** The prophets sometimes foresaw an eschatological state of chaos among the enemies of God when every man's sword will be against his brother (Ezek. 38:21; Hag. 2:22; Zech. 14:13). In Daniel's vision of the beast with ten horns, the little horn which boasted antichristlike pretensions attained to his place of power by destroying three of his colleagues (Dan. 7:24). John does not explain why the beast and the ten kings **will hate the harlot.** There is no question here of conquest; the city is already the capital of the beast.

John's language indicates the complete ruin and destruction of the erstwhile proud city. They will make her "desolate and naked"; i.e., they will strip her bare of all her beautiful adornments. They will "devour her flesh." This metaphor is taken from the fierceness of wild beasts and in the prophets denotes the utter destruction of men by their fellows (Ps. 27:2; Jer. 10:25; Mic. 3:3; Zeph. 3:3).

Many commentators see here a further allusion to the myth of *Nero redivivus,* according to which Nero was expected to return to Rome from the East, where he had been hiding among the Parthians, to wreak his vengeance upon his former capital. There is one possible relevant passage in the *Sibylline Oracles* where such an idea may be found: "There shall be at the last time, about the waning of the moon, a world-convulsing war deceitful in guilefulness. And there shall come from the ends of the earth a matricide (Nero) fleeing and devising sharp-edged plans in his mind. He shall ruin all the earth, and gain all power, and surpass all men in the cunning of his mind. That for which he perished he shall seize at once. And he shall destroy many men and great tyrants, and shall burn all men as none other ever did" (5:361-368). If this myth is in John's mind, it fails to explain the beast's hatred for the city and her complete destruction. In the myth, Nero recaptures Rome and assumedly makes her his capital again. Furthermore, the

Neronic myth as it is reflected in the *Sibylline Oracles* pictures the returning Nero as a military conqueror, not as the Antichrist. Nero did not promote the emperor cult, and his role in the *Sibylline Oracles* lost the religious note that is the most important characteristic of the beast in the Revelation.

Verse 17. John is himself conscious of the fact that the hatred of the beast for the woman is a surprising turn of events, and he adds a word of explanation: it is God's way of bringing judgment upon the woman. **God has put it into their hearts to carry out his purpose.** It is the divine sovereignty that has motivated the ten kings to a course of action which will fulfill the divine purpose. They are **of one mind** and they give over **their royal power to the beast, until the words of God shall be fulfilled.** When the beast turns in hatred upon the woman, the ten kings do not resist this surprising turn of events to defend the great city which has been the object of their admiration. They have complete unanimity in giving full support to the beast; but they do so because it is God's good purpose and his words must be fulfilled.

Verse 18. **And the woman that you saw is the great city which has dominion over the kings of the earth.** In the first century, this stood for Rome; but in the end time, it will stand for eschatological Babylon.

CHAPTER EIGHTEEN

THE JUDGMENT OF BABYLON

After foretelling the destruction of Babylon by the beast and his ten vassal kings in vivid but brief terms, John devotes a long section to the same theme, depicting in greater detail the desolation of the once proud and rich city. This chapter contains a series of announcements, dirges, and thanksgivings all dealing with the same theme: the judgment of the great city. Background for this section is found in the prophetic dirges over the fall of Tyre (Ezek. 26-28) and of Babylon (Isa. 13-14; 21; Jer. 50-51).

2. THE JUDGMENT OF BABYLON (18:1 — 19:5).

(1) Angelic Announcement of Babylon's Fall (18:1-3).

Verse 1. **After this I saw another angel coming down from heaven, having great authority; and the earth was made bright with his splendor.** The angel which had shown John the mystery of Babylon and had predicted the destruction of the city at the hands of the beast was one of the seven angels of the trumpet plagues; who this other angel is we are not told. John is now apparently on earth, for he sees the angel coming down from heaven; in chapters 15 and 16, he was in heaven. No explanation is given as to why this angel should have *great authority*. The word for "authority" is used in the Revelation synonymously with power (9:3, 10, 19). John saw an angel of great splendor whose radiance shone forth brilliantly (see Ezek. 43:2). Even though the message of the angel is one of doom for Babylon, the judgment of the wicked city means God's triumph.

Verse 2. **And he called out with a mighty voice, "Fallen, fallen, is Babylon the great!"** The fall of Babylon had already been announced by an angelic voice in precisely the same words (see 14:8). Both announcements proclaim the fall of the city as an accomplished event even though it actually lies in the future. As a matter of fact, the actual destruction of the city is nowhere described, apart from the brief prophecy of her destruction by the beast in 17:16. Both announcements reecho the words of Isa. 21:9. When this desolation has befallen the city, she will be no longer the mistress of civilization; no longer will she be inhabited by princes and merchants; she will be so desolated that no human being will set foot in her. She will become the **dwelling place of demons, a haunt of every foul spirit.** The devastation of Babylon echoes language from the prophecies of the ruin of Babylon, Edom, and Nineveh (Isa. 13:19-22; 34:11-15; Jer. 50:39; 51:37; Zeph. 2:15).

Verse 3. The cause of Babylon's judgment is that she has corrupted all the earth. **For all nations have drunk the wine of her impure passion.** This repeats the sin of Babylon mentioned in 14:8 (see notes). This language points not only to her luxury and immorality but to her seduction in enticing men to follow the beast. (See notes on the great harlot at 17:1-2.) This evil seduction has affected particularly the political and the economic leaders.

The kings of the earth have committed fornication with her, and the merchants of the earth have grown rich with the wealth of her wantonness. This tells us the means Babylon used to entice the world leaders to the worship of the beast. "Fornication" is a biblical word for idolatry. In the Revelation, it means the worship of the beast instead of worship of the Lamb. The great harlot has used promises of power and enticements of wealth and luxury as the attraction for following her lead. Power and wealth were employed in the name of demonic religion. The word translated delicacies (AV) really means "wantonness, luxury." The NEB translates this verse, "merchants the world over have grown rich on her bloated wealth." The word "wantonness" suggests self-indulgence and luxury accompanied by arrogance and wanton exercise of strength.

(2) Warning to God's People (18:4-5).

Verses 4-5. The sure fall of Babylon having been announced, John hears **another voice from heaven** calling upon the people of God to flee the city lest they share her sinfulness and her judgment. A similar summons was issued by the prophet Jeremiah to the Jews in Babylon (Jer. 51:6, 45). This suggests that the martyrdom of the church by the beast will not be complete. Jesus had described this period as the time of greatest tribulation that the world has ever seen (Matt. 24:21)—indeed, so severe that "if those days had not been shortened, no human being would be saved; but for the sake of the elect, those days will be shortened" (Matt. 24:22). John has indicated the beast's determination to destroy all who would not turn from their faith in Jesus to give their allegiance to him (13:7-8). While this will be a time of unprecedented martyrdom, this verse indicates that it will be far from total. God will have a people dwelling in the city who have been under constant danger of death because of their loyalty to Jesus. Now, as the Christian Jews fled Jerusalem to Pella just before the destruction of the city by the Roman armies, God's people are summoned to flee the city to avoid her doom. Under the unrelieved threat of martyrdom, there will be constant pressure that men will succumb and **take part in her sins,** and therefore **share in her plagues.** Babylon's doom is sure. Her sins are likened to a vast pile which reaches up to the very heaven (see Jer. 51:9); but God will remember **her iniquities.**

(3) Cry of Vengeance (18:6-8).

The theme of the heavenly voice changes. It has just summoned God's people to flee the doomed city; now it summons the angels of retribution to inflict a just vengeance upon the city. From the context, we would assume that the same voice is speaking, but since the theme changes so completely, this may be a different voice.

Verse 6. **Render to her as she herself has rendered, and repay her double for her deeds; mix a double draught for her in the cup she mixed.** This again sounds like language pleading for revenge (see notes on 6:10), but it echoes a theme which runs unbroken throughout the Bible. In their earthly experience, when followers of the Lamb witness to their faith in the crucified one and are persecuted because of their faith, their attitude toward their enemies is always to be one of forgiveness. A kindly spirit and love for one's enemies is one of the most characteristic marks of a disciple of Jesus (Matt. 5:43ff.). The Christian is to bless those who persecute him and never repay evil for evil (Rom. 12:14, 17).

However, this does not cancel out the final divine vindication. "Beloved, never avenge yourselves, but leave it to the wrath of God; for it is written, 'Vengeance is mine, I will repay, says the Lord'" (Rom. 12:19). God alone knows the motivations of the heart and can judge justly; but he remains the God of justice, and in the day of wrath, he will repay. The theme of divine vengeance and requital runs unbroken throughout the Bible (Deut. 32:35; Jer. 50:15, 29; 51:24, 26; Rom. 12:19; I Thess. 5:15; II Thess. 4:14; I Pet. 3:9). Since the great harlot has joined with the beast in trying to destroy the church, her just doom will be her own destruction.

The idea of rendering double for one's deeds is an Old Testament idiom indicating punishment in full measure (Jer. 16:18; 17:18).

Verses 7-8. The sin of Babylon is described as one of self-glorification and playing the wanton, i.e., of impious pride in exalting herself to the heavens. In her heart, she has said to herself, **A queen I sit, I am no widow, mourning I shall never see.** This echoes the vain self-exaltation of literal Babylon, which exalted herself above God, saying to herself, "I shall be mistress forever; . . . I am, and there is no one besides me; I shall not sit as a widow nor know the loss of children" (Isa. 47:7-9; see also Ezek. 28:2; Zeph. 2:15). Babylon has seduced the nations into thinking that they can dispense with God, that safety and security and prosperity will surely follow in the train of her luxury, self-indulgence, and wealth. However, this is self-deception. The final answer will be the decree of God, **for mighty is the Lord God who judges her.** He will requite her vanity and haughtiness with sudden destruction, which will befall her **in a single day;** she will suffer **plagues, pestilence and famine, and she shall be burned with fire.** The complete destruction of the city is sure.

(4) The Lament of the Kings and Merchants (18:9-19).

After proclaiming the divine retribution which will befall the great harlot, John voices the lament of political rulers (vs. 9) and economic leaders — "the merchants of the earth" (vs. 11) and the "seafarers" (vs. 17) — over the ruin of the great city. Their mourning does not reflect any sense of grief for the city herself but only for their personal loss because of the destruction of the city.

Verses 9-10. The **kings of the earth** are to be distinguished from the ten kings who joined with the beast to war against the Lamb (17:12-14). They were closely allied with the beast and willingly gave their royal power to support him in his demonic purposes (17:17). It is these ten vassal kings, together with the beast, whom God used to bring about the destruction of the great city (17:16). In addition to the ten who are actively aggressive in their support of the beast is a larger circle—the kings of the earth—whom the woman has enticed and **who have committed fornication and were wanton with her** (cf. 16:14; 17:2; 18:3). These have not been so openly devoted to the satanic purposes of the beast, but they have been enticed and deceived by the great harlot, by the glitter and glamour of her wealth and luxury, to share her fornication. Now they **weep and wail over her when they see the smoke of her burning** which has been inflicted on her by the beast and his ten vassal kings (17:16). They now realize how grossly they have been deceived by false promises of safety and security. **They will stand far off, in fear of** [sharing] **her torment, and say, "Alas! alas! thou great city, thou mighty city, Babylon! In one hour has thy judgment come."** Appearances were deceptive; Babylon had seemed to be a city both great and mighty, before whose power and might the strength of the church was as nothing. In her vanity, she seemed able to defy God and destroy his saints (17:6) with impunity. But God has the last word. In a single hour (see "in one day," vs. 8) divine judgment and destruction will befall her.

Verse 11. The lament of the kings of the earth is joined by **the merchants of the earth;** they **weep and mourn,** not as though they had lost a loved one, but because **no one buys their cargo any more.** Their grief is altogether selfish and mercenary; the destruction of the city means their economic ruin.

Verses 12-13. John gives a list of the merchandise for which there are no more buyers. Most of these items are found in the dirge over Tyre in Ezek. 27:5-24 (see also Ezek. 16:9-13). John's catalogue falls into several distinct groups: (1) precious stones: **gold, silver, jewels, and pearls;** (2) fine raiment, which was one of the distinctions of a rich man in the ancient world: **fine linen, purple, silk and scarlet;** (3) costly articles of decoration: **scented wood, ivory, costly wood, bronze, iron and marble;** (4) fragrances: **cinnamon, spice, incense, myrrh, frankincense;** (5) foods: **wine, oil, fine flour and wheat;** (6) beasts: **cattle, sheep, horses and chariots,** and (7) **slaves.** Purple and scarlet were two costly dyes highly prized by the wealthy. Silk was imported to Rome from China in great abundance. The word rendered "scented wood" was a hard dark wood used for costly furniture to make all sorts of luxurious articles. Bronze or brass and iron were used to make ornamental vessels. Spices and fragrances were imported to Rome from the East, and wheat was imported chiefly from Egypt.

The word translated "slaves" is literally "bodies" and reflects the low evaluation placed upon slaves by merchants in the ancient world. It is not clear why John adds to the trade in slaves the words, **that is, human souls.** In its Hebrew context, the word for soul, *nephesh,* does not designate a higher immortal element in man in contrast to his body, as *psyche* usually does in Greek thought, and as "soul" usually does in English. *Nephesh* simply designates human life or vitality (see Mark 10:45) and sometimes it is used of men as slaves (Ezek. 27:13; I Chr. 5:21). John probably used the word here to suggest that men, even though slaves, have a life which animals do not share. In any case, too much should not be read into the word.

In this catalogue of merchandise, John accurately reflects the luxury and opulence pursued by wealthy city dwellers in a city like Rome.

Verse 14. This verse continues the list of luxuries, but the literary form changes, and this verse is addressed to the city itself. The **fruit** in which she took delight is gone, and the dainty luxuries and slendors have disappeared forever.

Verse 15. These **merchants** who trafficked in this luxurious trade and became wealthy, like the kings of the earth (vs. 10),

will stand far off lest they too be caught up in the terrible
conflagration.

Verses 16-18. They will mourn for the great city which had
been so gorgeously arrayed in fine **linen, purple** and **scarlet,**
bejeweled with **gold,** with **jewels** and with **pearls.** Now, **in one
hour,** all the splendor and grandeur have perished.

The merchants of the earth are joined by **shipmasters and
seafaring men, sailors** and all those who had shared in the
wealth of the city by sea-traffic; they too stand far off when
they see the smoke of the burning city and lament her
destruction.

Verse 19. Their grief is pictured as being very intense.
They **threw dust on their heads** in a sign of grief (Ezek. 27:30)
as they mourned and cried and wailed. However, their grief
was a selfish one; they grieved not from a feeling of affection,
but because they had been among those who had ships at sea
and had grown **rich by her wealth. In one hour,** the city **has
been laid waste,** and along with the city, all their wealth has
perished.

(5) Outburst of Praise (18:20).

Verse 20. In contrast to the mournful lament of the kings
and merchants of earth, the judgment of the city is a cause
of rejoicing in heaven. These words are the words of the
prophet calling upon the people of God to rejoice in the
triumph of God's righteousness. First, heaven, i.e., the angels,
are summoned to rejoice, and the people of God on earth —
saints, apostles and **prophets** — are called to join with them.

The reason for rejoicing is that the destruction of Babylon
means that **God has given judgment for you against her.** This
is not a gleeful song of personal vengeance, but an announcement of the vindication of God's justice and righteousness. It
must always be kept in mind that background for such a song
of vindication is the question whether God's rule or Satan's
deceptive power is to triumph in human affairs. The time of
the great tribulation (7:15; Matt. 24:21) will be a period when
Satan will be allowed to do his worst. He will be incarnate in
the beast, who in turn will be allowed to exercise his will as
never before in human history, with the faithful followers of
Jesus the main objects of his venom. His capital city Babylon

will be drunk with the blood of the martyrs (17:6). As terrible
as this period is, it will be only temporary, and the destruction
of Babylon will mean that God, the eternal judge, has finally
given judgment for his people against Babylon. Such a judgment is necessary to vindicate God's righteousness, to extirpate
evil from the earth, and to save his people. Therefore, a song
of vindication of this sort, far from being one of personal
revenge, is a cry of rejoicing that God at the end will show
himself to be God in the face of all satanic foes.

(6) The Destruction of Babylon (18:21-24).

The fall of the city had already been announced at the
beginning of the chapter. Now the overthrow of Babylon is
again proclaimed by a symbolic act.

Verse 21. **Then a mighty angel took up a stone like a great
millstone and threw it into the sea, saying, "So shall Babylon
the great city be thrown down with violence, and shall be
found no more."** No problem exists in the fact that the fall of
Babylon has already twice been proclaimed as an accomplished
fact (14:8; 18:2), prophesied as an imminent event (17:16), and
is now once again announced. Apocalyptic language is not
prose but a series of pictures whose main concern is not chronology and sequence, but ultimate realities.

The casting of a great stone into the sea is a symbolic act
representing Babylon's overthrow. The prophets frequently
engaged in prophetic symbolic acts. Jeremiah wrote a book
describing the destruction of historical Babylon and then commanded that a stone be attached to it and it be thrown into
the Euphrates: "Thus shall Babylon sink, to rise no more,
because of the evil that I am bringing upon her" (Jer. 51:63).

Verses 22-23a. The completeness of Babylon's destruction
is vividly pictured in the cessation of the various activities
characteristic of the city. Babylon had been a patron of the
arts, but now all music will be stilled: **the sound of harpers
and minstrels, of flute players and trumpeters, shall be heard
in thee no more.** Business will die; no more craftsmen will be
found in the city. The pursuits of everyday daily life, such
as grinding flour for bread, will cease. The nights as well as
the days will be without life; no **light of a lamp shall shine in
thee** any more. Houses at night will be pitch black. The

usual human activities and festivities, such as weddings, will resound in the houses and streets no more. Babylon will become a dead city.

Verses 23b-24. The reason for Babylon's desolation is again stated. **For thy merchants were the great men of the earth.** The language used implies an attitude of arrogance on the part of Babylon's merchants. Her sin did not consist always in the fact of her wealth, but in the overweening pride and self-exaltation induced by her wealth. Furthermore, Babylon had deceived all nations by her **sorcery.** She was not satisfied to pursue her own course; she had insisted on enticing the nations of earth "with the wine of her impure passion" (18:3). She had seduced other nations to feel that ultimate security could be found in wealth and luxury. Finally, she had been an ally of the beast in shedding **the blood of prophets and saints** (cf. 17:6). Her sin was not alone wanton luxury, but a crass materialism which led her to exalt herself over God and persecute the people of God. Not only was Babylon the scene of martyrdom; she was the example for other cities, so that she could be said to be the scene of the martyrdom **of all who have been slain on earth.** It is obvious that John is not thinking of murder in general but is still concerned with the blood of saints and prophets. The influence of Babylon had extended throughout the world and inspired other cities to follow her example of persecuting the saints. No historical equivalent to this is known in the first century; John is thinking of eschatological Babylon.

CHAPTER NINETEEN

THE COMING OF CHRIST

(7) A Thanksgiving for the Judgment of Babylon (19:1-5).

The first paragraph of chapter nineteen continues the celebration of the fall of Babylon and consists of a song of thanksgiving in heaven that God has judged the great harlot. After this thanksgiving, John depicts the events of the consummation: the marriage of the Lamb, the coming of Christ, his messianic reign, the destruction of Satan and of death, and the coming of the new creation.

Verse 1. **After this I heard what seemed to be the mighty voice of a great multitude in heaven crying, "Hallelujah! Salvation and glory and power belong to our God."** The singers are not named, but they must be the hosts of angels who surround God's throne (cf. 5:11). "Hallelujah" is the word from Hebrew liturgy meaning "Praise ye Jahweh," and is found frequently in the Psalms (cf. Pss. 111:1; 112:1; 113:1; 146:1, etc.). The word occurs four times in this passage (vss. 1, 3, 4, 6) but nowhere else in the New Testament. The judgment of Babylon is one aspect of the divinely planned salvation. *Salvation* in this context means more than the deliverance of the saints from the hatred of the beast and Babylon; it is the safeguarding, the maintenance in triumph of the whole cause of God's Kingdom with its blessedness. But the triumph of God's Kingdom of necessity means the removal of all that stands in the way and attempts to frustrate the divine rule.

244

Verse 2. **For his judgments are true and just; he has judged the great harlot who corrupted the earth with her fornication, and he has avenged on her the blood of his servants.** So long as Babylon stands, the Kingdom of God cannot be established, for her corrupting influence affects the whole earth (14:8; 17:2; 18:3), but her removal makes way for the coming of God's Kingdom. Her fall also means the answer to the prayers of the martyrs who cry day and night to God that he avenge their blood (see 6:10).

Verse 3. **Once more they cried, "Hallelujah! The smoke from her goes up for ever and ever."** Babylon was destroyed by fire by the beast and the ten vassal kings (17:16; 18:8, 9, 18). This is a poetic metaphor drawn from the prophets (Isa. 34:10) to indicate the utter destruction of the city.

Verse 4. The hallelujah chorus of the angels is joined by the **twenty-four elders** (4:4) and the **four living creatures** (4:6 ff.) echoing the song, **"Amen. Hallelujah!"**

Verse 5. A voice **from the throne** could be the voice of God, but since the voice bids men to **praise our God,** it must be the voice of one of the four living creatures who stood closest to the throne. This voice calls on **all God's servants** on earth to join the chorus in heaven in praise to God. "Praise our God" is the equivalent of "Hallelujah!"

3. THE FINAL TRIUMPH AND CONSUMMATION (19:6 — 21:8).

(1) The Marriage of the Lamb (19:6-10).

Now that the judgment of Babylon has been celebrated, John moves on to proclaim the final triumph of the Kingdom of God and the consummation of God's redemptive purpose. This consummation has already been announced in 11:15 when the heavenly voices proclaimed, "The kingdom of the world has become the kingdom of our Lord and of his Christ." Actually this event does not occur until the return of Christ — an event portrayed in 19:11ff. In the same way, the event heralded in vss. 6-11 — the marriage of the Lamb — is a proleptic announcement of an event which actually takes place at the coming of Christ when he is united with his church on earth. It is John's custom to proclaim redemptive events

which he nowhere actually describes. This has been true of
the judgment of Babylon — a theme to which he has devoted
an entire chapter but which he nowhere describes, apart from
17:16. In the present pericope John heralds the marriage
supper of the Lamb, but he does not actually describe the
event; he merely announces it.

Verse 6. **Then I heard what seemed to be the voice of a
great multitude, like the sound of many waters and like the
sound of mighty thunderpeals.** This is the same voice which
John heard expressing thanksgiving for the judgment of
Babylon (19:1) — the voice of a host of angels. The voice of
the glorified Christ was like the sound of many waters (1:15);
the first summons John heard was like the voice of thunder
(6:2; see also 14:2).

The angelic host proclaimed that God has become King.
Both the AV and the RSV miss the idea, rendering the word
in the present tense: **the Almighty reigns.** The Greek verb is
a past tense and is what grammarians call an inceptive aorist,
emphasizing the initiation of an action. The NEB correctly
renders it: "The Lord our God . . . has entered on his reign!"
At this point in the Revelation, the reign of God has in fact
not yet been fully established; it awaits the return of Christ,
the chaining of Satan, and the inauguration of Christ's messianic reign — all events yet to be described. This is a proleptic
statement analogous to the announcements in 14:8 of the fall
of Babylon and 11:15ff. of the establishment of God's reign.
However, the judgment of Babylon has been announced as
the first great act in the establishment of God's Kingdom.
Human and demonic adversaries must be removed before
God's rule can prevail; their overthrow is the beginning of his
triumphant rule.

Verse 7. **"Let us rejoice and exult and give him the glory,
for the marriage of the Lamb has come, and his Bride has
made herself ready."** The voice announces the marriage of the
Lamb; it does not describe it. It proclaims that the marriage
of the Lamb is about to take place. The word rendered "bride"
is literally "wife" *(gune,* not *numphe)*. Some devout interpreters have tried to make a theological distinction between the
Lamb's wife and his bride. However, an engaged woman can
be called a wife in the sense that she is a betrothed wife, even
though the marriage has not yet taken place (see Gen. 29:21;

Deut. 22:24). Thus the angel told Joseph not to fear to take to himself Mary "his wife" (Matt. 1:20). The applicability of the metaphor of the wife to the church is seen in Eph. 5:25ff., 32, where Paul exhorts men to love their wives as Christ loved the church. Israel was often regarded as the wife of Jahweh or Jahweh as the husband of Israel (Isa. 54:5-6; 62:5; Jer. 31:32; Ezek. 16:8ff.) and the whole prophecy of Hosea is built around the theme of Israel as God's adulterous wife. However, the prophecy assures Israel of a new day when God promises, "I will betroth you to me forever; I will betroth you to me in righteousness and in justice, in steadfast love, and in mercy. I will betroth you to me in faithfulness; and you shall know the Lord" (Hos. 2:19f.).

Jesus used the wedding motif to represent his relationship to his disciples in both its present and future aspects. He asserted that he was the bridegroom come to his people. "Can the wedding guests fast while the bridegroom is with them?" (Mark 2:19). The fact that his disciples are here viewed as wedding guests rather than the bride is due to the flexible character of parabolic language. If this language is to be literally pressed, there is no bride — only the groom and the guests. John the Baptist also pointed to Jesus as the bridegroom, designating himself as only the friend of the the groom (John 3:29).

Jesus used the metaphor of a wedding feast to describe the eschatological coming of the Kingdom (Matt. 22:1-14). In this parable the bride plays no role whatsoever; attention is focused altogether upon the invited guests, some of whom accepted the invitation while others scorned it. Obviously, the responsive guests represent those who responded affirmatively to the invitation, while the unresponsive guests represent people like the scribes and Pharisees who rejected Jesus and his message. Again, Jesus likened the uncertain hour of the coming of the bridegroom to the unknown hour of the coming of the Kingdom of God (Matt. 25:1-13). In this parable, the bride is not identified; attention is altogether centered upon the ten maidens. The five wise maidens who found entrance into the wedding feast represent followers of Jesus who are ready and awake for his coming, while the five foolish ones represent those who claim admission but are unprepared. The bride plays no role whatsoever.

In Pauline thought the Old Testament idiom of Israel as Jahweh's wife is applied to the body of believers — the church. Before the coming of Christ, men had been bound to the law as a wife is bound to her husband; but in Christ, this bond to the law has been broken, and men are free to be joined to Christ as a wife is free to take a new husband (Rom. 7:1-4). Because believers are thus united to the Lord in the bonds of spiritual marriage, they are to abstain from all immorality (I Cor. 6:17). In these passages, the church is viewed as the actual wife who is bound by marriage to Christ. Nevertheless, Paul says that he has betrothed the Corinthians to Christ "as a pure bride [virgin] to her husband" (II Cor. 11:2). In this passage, the church is not yet the wife; the marriage is the eschatological union. This flexibility of meaning makes it clear that the entire idea of bride-wife is a metaphor which describes the relationship of the church to Christ in both its present and future aspects.

No real distinction can be made between Israel as the wife of Jahweh and the church as the bride of Christ; the church is also his wife. However, the consummation of this relationship is an eschatological event awaiting the return of Christ. Paul again likens the relationship of Christ to his church as that of a husband to his wife (Eph. 5:25ff.), but the actual wedding is viewed as future when the church is "presented before him in splendor, without spot or wrinkle or any such thing, that she might be holy and without blemish" (Eph. 5:27).

It is this eschatological event — the perfect union of Christ and his church — which John announced under the metaphor of the marriage of the Lamb. It must be again emphasized that John does not describe the marriage supper; he only proclaims that the time has come. The actual event is nowhere described; it is a metaphorical way of alluding to the final redemptive fact when "the dwelling of God is with men. He will dwell with them, and they shall be his people, and God himself will be with them" (Rev. 21:3). This is why John can apply the same metaphor of the bride prepared for her husband to the new Jerusalem which comes down from heaven to dwell among men (Rev. 21:2), and why the angel can refer to the new Jerusalem as "the bride, the wife of the Lamb" (Rev. 21:9). As Jerusalem is frequently used in Scripture to represent the people of God (Matt. 23:37), so in the vision of the new world, the people of God and their capital city — the church and the new Jerusalem — are so closely connected that the same figure — the bride — is used for both.

"His bride has made herself ready." In Eph. 5:25, the preparation of the bride for the marriage is represented as an act of Christ accomplished by the giving of his life; here preparation is demanded on the part of Christians. While redemption is altogether the work of God in Christ, there must be a human response. "When he appears, we shall be like him, for we shall see him as he is. And every one who thus hopes in him purifies himself as he is pure" (I John 3:2-3). "Since we have these promises, beloved, let us cleanse ourselves from every defilement of body and spirit, and make holiness perfect in the fear of God" (II Cor. 7:1).

Verse 8. While the bride must make herself ready for the marriage, her glorious raiment is not something she can acquire for herself; it must be **granted her,** i.e., given to her as a divine gift. The **fine linen, bright and pure,** stands in sharp contrast to the brilliant robes of the harlot. The wedding garment is a simple white garment which has been washed and "made . . . white in the blood of the Lamb" (Rev. 7:14).

It is not altogether certain that **righteous deeds** is the correct translation of *dikaiomata*. The basic meaning of the word is "statute" or "ordinance." It is used in 15:4 of the decrees of God in judgment and sentence of condemnation of the nations. Paul uses the word of God's decree in general (Rom. 1:32) and of his decree of justification in particular (Rom. 5:16), and it is possible that this is the meaning intended by John. The fine linen of the saints consists of the decree of justification of God for believers.[1] However, the plural is difficult to render in this way, and in Rom. 5:18 the word stands in contrast to *paraptoma* — an act of transgression — and refers to the act of righteousness accomplished by Christ in his death. Therefore, it seems easier to translate the word with the RSV: "righteous deeds." While the wedding garment is a divine gift, this is no arbitrary or formal matter but a dynamic one. The saints who are summoned to the Lamb's feast are those who have exercised steadfast endurance, who have kept the commandments of God, and have persevered in their faith in Jesus (Rev. 14:12).

[1]See Leon Morris, *The Revelation of St. John* (Grand Rapids: Eerdmans, 1970), *in loc.*

Verse 9. The **angel** speaking to John is not identified; possibly it is the angel of 17:1 who showed him the judgment of Babylon. The announcement of the marriage of the Lamb came from a great host of angels (19:6). Now, a single angel pronounces a beatitude upon those who will participate in the marriage feast.

Superficially, there appears to be confusion in the Seer's thought because his attention shifts from the bride to the wedding guests. Are these two different companies? A recent commentator sees here a distinction between the church (the bride) and the invited guests (the saints of the Old Testament and millennial periods).[2] This ignores the fluidity of metaphorical language; and the concept of the church as a bride and that of the eschatological consummation as a marriage are metaphors. Even as in our Lord's parables (see above), attention is sometimes focused on the guests while the bride is ignored altogether, so attention can shift from the bride to the guests without loss of meaning. Christ is both the Lamb and the shepherd of the sheep (Rev. 7:17) and a conquering warrior as well (Rev. 19:11ff.). So the church is both the bride and those invited.

The marriage supper. The messianic consummation is pictured not only as a marriage supper but as a joyous banquet. Jesus said that many would come from the east and west and sit at the table with the patriarchs in the Kingdom of Heaven (Matt. 8:11). He told his disciples at the last supper that he would not drink of the fruit of the vine until he should drink it with them in the Kingdom of God (Matt. 26:29).

Those who are invited *(hoi keklemenoi).* Men cannot find access to the marriage feast on their own merits; they must receive a divine invitation (see Matt. 22:3; Luke 14:17; Rev. 17:14). The initiative to salvation is always the call of God.

The angel says to John, **"These are true words of God."** In the face of all the evil that the church experiences on earth, the angel adds a solemn assurance that this promise of blessing in the messianic feast is the unfailing word of God.

Verse 10. John was overwhelmed with awe by what he had just heard and by the presence of the angel declaring that the words of beatitude upon those invited to the marriage supper

2John Walvoord, *The Revelation of Jesus Christ* (Chicago: Moody, 1966), p. 273.

were indeed the words of God. While there was a tendency
in the early church to worship angels (Col. 2:18), this tendency
fell under the criticism of the apostles, and it is possible that
John confused the voice of the angel with the voice of Christ.
The angel gently rebuked John, telling him that he was only
a fellow servant with John and with his **brethren who hold the
testimony of Jesus.**

The last phrase may be interpreted in two different ways.
The phrase first occurred in 1:2 where the angel "bore witness
to the word of God and to the testimony of Jesus Christ."
There it was a subjective genitive, indicating the testimony
which Jesus Christ bore to his churches. See also 1:9; 6:9;
12:17, where "the testimony which they held" designates the
witness Christ bore to his people, which they in turn accepted
and to which they bore witness. This is a very possible rendition of the present passage: the testimony to the truth and to
God's redemptive plan. The theme of the entire book of
Revelation is the final deliverance in the eschatological Kingdom of God of those who hold fast to the revelation Christ
has mediated to men. However, the phrase as it is repeated in
the next sentence may more easily be understood as an objective genitive: the witness borne by the church to Jesus. This is
probably the meaning of the same phrase in 20:4. See also
22:16.

Worship God, the angel tells John; God alone, and not the
angels, has an exclusive claim to human worship.

For the testimony of Jesus is the spirit of prophecy. This
may again be either a subjective or an objective genitive. It
may mean that the witness to God's redemptive purpose borne
to men by Jesus is accomplished only through the spirit of
prophecy. The letters to the seven churches are the voice of
the Holy Spirit (Rev. 2:7); this refrain is repeated at the end
of each of the letters. On the other hand, it may mean that any
true testimony to the person and redemptive work of Jesus
must have its source in the spirit of prophecy. In any case, both
ideas are true; in the present context, the objective genitive is
the easier resolution.

As punctuated in RSV, the last sentence is not a part of the
words of the angel to John but is John's explanation of the
angel's words, explaining why the angel is considered unworthy
of worship. The angel is not the object of the prophetic word;

on the contrary, the angels, together with John's brethren who
are inspired by the spirit of prophecy, bear witness to Jesus,
and in this regard, the angel is no more than a fellow servant
with the saints in their relationship to Christ.

(2) The Coming of Christ (19:11-16).

The preceding pericope has announced the imminent marriage of the Lamb which assumes the return of Christ when
the perfect union of Christ and his people will take place. This
union — the marriage and the marriage feast — is nowhere
described. John's new vision of the returning Christ emphasizes only one aspect of his coming: his victory over the powers
of evil. This is a motif often developed in the Old Testament
prophets; but in the prophets, it is usually Jahweh himself
who marches forth to a victorious warfare to establish his
reign over his enemies (Isa. 13:4; 31:4; Ezek. 38-39; Joel 3;
Zech. 14:3). The most vivid prophetic picture is that of an
unnamed conqueror who strides forth in crimsoned garments
for vindication, who had trodden the wine press of God's
wrath and stained his garments with his enemies' blood, who
trod the hostile peoples in his wrath and established the day
of vengeance (Isa. 63:1-6). John sees Christ coming as a conquering warrior in bloodstained garments, destroying all hostile and opposing powers with his mighty sword.

Some commentators hold that this portrayal of Christ contradicts the concept of the gracious and merciful Christ found
in the rest of the New Testament. This simply is not true;
everywhere in the New Testament the element of victory
through judgment is an inescapable aspect of Christ's total
work. (See Matt. 13:41-42; 25:41; Rom. 2:5; II Thess. 1:7; 2:8.)

While the Apocalypse employs symbolism to describe redemptive events and while this pericope is also filled with
symbolism, it would violate the nature of apocalyptic language
to spiritualize this passage to the point where it is taken to
designate God's judicial acts in ordinary historical events.
Apocalyptic symbolism in a passage like this, as in 6:12-17,
represents what the apocalyptist felt would be real objective
events in history — acts of God which transcend all ordinary
historical experience. The second coming of Christ is an absolutely essential theme in New Testament theology. In his cross

and resurrection, Christ won a great victory over the powers of evil; by his second coming, he will execute that victory. Apart from his return to purge his creation of evil, redemption remains forever incomplete. As Hanns Lilje has written, "Those who believe in the reality of the resurrection of Jesus Christ must also look for his return."[3]

Verse 11. **Then I saw heaven opened.** At the beginning of his prophecy John saw a door opened in heaven and was summoned into the heavenly realm to behold divine secrets. In the course of his visions, he saw the temple in heaven opened and the ark of the covenant disclosed to men (Rev. 11:19). What was suggested in these visions is now fulfilled as heaven is opened to make way for the triumphant coming of Messiah.

And behold, a white horse! The horse that rode forth when the first seal was broken (6:2) was white, and some interpreters identify the two. This, however, is highly unlikely. There can be no mistaking the identity of the rider of the present horse: he is "The Word of God" (vs. 13). White is a symbol of victory, and everywhere in the Revelation white is associated with the things of God and the divine victory. The white horse here represents Christ in his final victory over the evil powers which have oppressed the people of God throughout the course of the age.

He who sat upon it is called Faithful and True. These words were attributed to Christ in 3:14. The two words are practically synonymous in meaning, for the Hebrew idea of truth was not basically correspondence to reality as in Greek thought, but reliability. The "God of truth" (Jer. 10:10) is not the God who reveals eternal truth, but the God who can be trusted to keep his covenant. When John in his gospel wrote that "grace and truth came through Jesus Christ" (John 1:17), he meant that in the life, death, and resurrection of Christ, the faithfulness of God was revealed in fulfillment of his covenant. The return of Christ will be the reappearance of him who has already appeared among men to bring God's covenant promises to their final and full consummation.

In righteousness he judges and makes war. The present tense of the verbs indicates the permanent character of Messiah in all his acts. The great prophecy of the Davidic king de-

[3]Hanns Lilje, *The Last Book of the Bible* (Philadelphia: Muhlenberg Press, 1955), p. 244.

scribed him as one who judges the poor with righteousness and
decides with equity for the meek of the earth (Isa. 11:4). The
return of Christ in victory over his enemies will be no act of
personal vengefulness nor an arbitrary manifestation of divine
power; it will be an act of righteousness reflecting the faithfulness of God, for the extirpation of evil is the negative side
of the divine salvation.

Verse 12. **His eyes are like a flame of fire** (see 1:14). This
represents the all-searching gaze of Christ. Human experience
is full of mysteries and unresolved riddles; but the eyes of
Christ search all things; nothing is hidden from his gaze.

On his head are many diadems. He wears the crown of
royalty because he is the King of kings and Lord of lords
(17:14). The coming of Christ will mean the public manifestation and the universal enforcement of the sovereignty which is
already his by virtue of his death and resurrection. In his
resurrection and ascension, he began his reign as Davidic king
(Messiah) and Lord (Acts 2:36). He is even now the highly
exalted Lord (Phil. 2:9), and he must reign as king until he
has put all his enemies under his feet (I Cor. 15:25). His
messianic reign will be incomplete until he has destroyed
"every rule and every authority and power" (I Cor. 15:24).
While he is now reigning as Lord and King, great authority
and power remain in the hands of evil. The triumph of Christ
over all hostile powers is the meaning of his second coming
which has already been announced: "Hallelujah! for the Lord
our God the Almighty has begun his reign" (see note on 19:6).

He has a name inscribed which no one knows but himself.
Christ has already been named "Faithful and True" (vs. 11),
and again, "The Word of God" (vs. 13). That he also has a
secret name means that the human mind cannot grasp the
depth of his being.

Verse 13. The picture of the conquering Christ draws some
of its substance from the vision in Isa. 63 of the conqueror
who treads the wine press of God's wrath, whose garments are
splashed with the life-blood of his foes. We must agree with
the majority of modern commentators that the **robe dipped in
blood** refers to garments bloodied from conflict and battle,
not from Christ's own blood on the cross. The picture here is
of Christ the warrior and conqueror of evil, not of Christ the
redeemer. The objection is made that it cannot be the blood

of battle, for the battle has not yet been joined; Christ comes
to battle. This objection overlooks the fluidity and symbolic
nature of apocalyptic language. Christ can be pictured as the
warrior even before the battle is joined.

The designation of Christ as **The Word of God** is a distinctive fact which binds the Revelation to the other Johannine writings (John 1:1; I John 1:1). To modern Christians
"the Word of God" is primarily the Bible. In the New Testament, the Word of God is primarily the good news of the
gospel, whether proclaimed by Jesus (Luke 5:1; 8:11; 11:28) or
by the apostles (I Cor. 14:36; II Cor. 2:17; 4:2; I Thess. 2:13).
Christ in his own person is the Word of God *par excellence* —
the embodiment of God's total redemptive plan.

Verse 14. **The armies of heaven, arrayed in fine linen, white
and pure, followed him on white horses.** It is possible that
these hosts represent the saints, but it is more likely that they
are the heavenly hosts of angels. The presence of angels on
the apocalyptic day is a common feature in biblical thought.
"The Lord your God will come, and all the holy ones with
him" (Zech. 14:5). The Son of man at his coming will be
accompanied by angels (Mark 8:38; Luke 9:26; I Thess. 3:13;
II Thess. 1:7). The pure, white garb of the heavenly armies
indicates that they share in Messiah's victory. However, nothing is said about their engagement in the conflict; this belongs
to Messiah alone. They wear no armor and carry no weapons.
As the Lamb, Christ is followed by the saints (17:14); as the
heavenly Warrior, he is followed by the angels.

Verse 15. **From his mouth issues a sharp sword with which
to smite the nations, and he will rule them with a rod of iron.**
The only weapon involved in the warfare is the word of Christ.
This language looks back to Isa. 11:4: "And he shall smite the
earth with the rod of his mouth, and with the breath of his lips
he shall slay the wicked." Here is a symbolic representation of
victory by the power of a word which is impossible to be literally envisaged. The idea goes back to creation. God created the
worlds by his word. He spoke and it was done. This creation
was mediated through the living word, Christ (John 1:3; Heb.
1:2). The judgment on the old order will also be mediated
through the word of Christ. Just how John visualized this
victory is impossible to say. It is, however, certain that he expected actual objective events to occur which would transform

the structure of human society, purging out the evil. The
idea of a literal battle with military weapons is of course
impossible. The metaphor of a sword for the word of God is
not unknown (Heb. 4:12). The radical spiritualization of this
concept which sees a conflict of human ideologies in human
history and the triumph of Christianity does not accord with
the nature of apocalyptic thought.

**He will tread the wine press of the fury of the wrath of
God the Almighty.** This is a further allusion to Isa. 63:3,
which we have already met in the vision of the grape harvest
(14:19).

Verse 16. **On his robe and on his thigh he has a name
inscribed, King of kings and Lord of lords.** Here is a fourth
name given to the returning Christ. He is known to himself by
his hidden name; he is known to the churches as the Faithful
and True, the Word of God; he is known to the world as King
of kings and Lord of lords. It is possible that the first connective *and* is epexegetical, further defining the preceding phrase:
on his robe, that is, where it covers the thigh. No reason is
suggested as to why this name should actually be inscribed on
his thigh. The name designates the absolute sovereignty of
Christ. For the believer, this is already true (I Cor. 8:5-6); at
Christ's return, it will become a reality acknowledged by all.

(3)   The Battle of Christ and Antichrist   (19:17-21).

One of the major themes of the Revelation is the conflict
between God and Satan, which manifests itself in history in the
conflict between Christ and Antichrist. In the final sections
describing the triumph of Christ, John first sets forth the triumph of Christ over Antichrist and his supporters, which is
depicted in terms of a great battle, and then the triumph of
Christ over Satan himself, which takes place in two stages: his
binding in the abyss and his destruction in the lake of fire. The
battle itself with Antichrist is not described; it is only affirmed.
The victory over Antichrist necessarily includes a victory over
the kings and nations of the earth who have given their support
and allegiance to Antichrist. This is the battle of Armageddon,
which has already been proleptically announced at the sounding of the sixth trumpet (16:12-16), when demonic spirits
gathered the kings of the earth in allegiance to Antichrist "on

the great day of God the Almighty." The idiom with which John describes this great battle is drawn from Ezek. 39:17-20, where the final victory of God over the pagan nations, particularly against Gog, Meshech and Tubal, is described in terms of a sacrificial feast which God is preparing for the birds of the air and the beasts of the field when they shall eat flesh and drink blood, when "you shall be filled at my table with horses and riders, with mighty men and all kinds of warriors, says the Lord God" (Ezek. 39:20). Obviously this is a vivid, picturesque way of describing a great and decisive destruction of the enemies of God and cannot be taken literally.

Verse 17. John sees **an angel standing in the sun** where all the birds of the earth could see him. The angel cried out with a **loud voice,** summoning **all the birds that fly in midheaven** to gather together to partake of **the great supper of God.** This supper stands in contrast to the marriage supper of the Lamb to which the saints were invited. The supper is called the supper of God because, like the feast in Ezek. 39, it is given by God, provided by him.

Verse 18. The metaphor of a battle likened to a great feast is continued. As in Ezek. 39, the fare is **the flesh of kings, the flesh of captains, the flesh of mighty men, the flesh of horses and their riders, and the flesh of all men, both free and slave, both small and great.** It is obvious that in its context, "all men" designates those who have accepted the mark of the beast and have chosen allegiance to Antichrist rather than humble their hearts in response to the judgments of God which they have suffered and acknowledge the sovereignty of Christ. The details in the description are meant to designate the totality of the overthrow of evil and of evil men.

Verse 19. John now sees the forces of the enemy drawn up, apparently at Armageddon, **to make war against him who sits upon the horse and against his army.** At the head of these forces is the beast — Antichrist himself; and supporting him are **the kings of the earth** (16:14; 17:2, 18; 18:3).

Verse 20. One would expect some description of the battle with the kings of the earth, but instead, John turns at once to his main theme, the defeat of Antichrist. The defeat of the supporting kings is an altogether secondary feature. John merely states that **the beast was captured, and with it the false prophet,** and they **were thrown alive into the lake of fire that**

257

burns with brimstone. The lake of fire is Gehenna, although
the word itself is not used in the Revelation. In the New Testament, Hades and Gehenna are clearly distinguished from each
other, although the Authorized Version does not make this
distinction clear. Hades is the intermediate state between death
and the resurrection (Matt. 16:18; Luke 16:23; Acts 2:27) and
is sometimes used synonymously with the grave (Rev. 1:18;
6:8; 20:13). It is the equivalent of the Old Testament Sheol.
For the Old Testament background for the idea of Gehenna,
see the notes on 14:9-10. Because Ge Hinnom or the Valley of
Hinnom was a place of human sacrifices, it came to be the hell
of final punishment in apocalyptic literature (*Enoch* 27:1ff.;
54:1ff.; 56:3ff.; 90:26; *IV Ezra* 7:36; *Apoc.* of *Baruch* 59:10;
85:13). The fact that in the gospels hell is pictured not only as
a place of fire but also as a place of darkness (Matt. 8:12;
22:13; 25:30) suggests that both descriptions use metaphorical
language drawn from contemporary Judaism to describe final
and irremedial judgment. It is also significant that in Paul's
important passage about the man of lawlessness, he — the
Antichrist — is not to be cast into the lake of fire but is to be
slain by the breath of Messiah's mouth (II Thess. 2:8). Obviously this is metaphorical language describing complete destruction. The lake of fire appears again in 20:10, 14, 15; 21:8.

Verse 21.   John now speaks in very concise form of the
destruction of the armies of Antichrist, consisting of the kings
of the earth and those who had been seduced by the false
prophet to receive the mark of the beast and to worship its
image (vs. 20). All he says is that they were **slain by the sword
of him who sits upon his horse, the sword that issues from
his mouth.** Just how John conceived of this slaughter being
actually carried out, we cannot say. It is, however, certain that
he means to indicate the actual destruction of the hosts of
evil. He concludes by resuming the theme of the great supper:
all the birds were gorged with their flesh. Some scholars find
elements of universalism in the New Testament; this, however, can be done only when certain verses are taken out of
their biblical context. The New Testament expects masses
of men to remain unrepentant and obdurate in heart, who can
anticipate nothing but the judgment and wrath of the Lamb.

CHAPTER TWENTY

THE MESSIANIC TRIUMPH

Having related the destruction of Antichrist, John now relates the conquest and destruction of the beast's master — Satan himself. This takes place in two different stages. First, Satan is bound and shut up in the abyss; the first resurrection occurs and the resurrected saints join Christ in his messianic reign of a thousand years. At the end of this interim kingdom, Satan is loosed from his prison and finds the hearts of men over whom Christ has reigned to be still responsive to his entice-ments. He again deceives them and gathers them together for a second battle against Christ. After his defeat, Satan is cast into Gehenna where the beast and false prophet are; there follows (presumably) the second resurrection, for the dead stand before the throne of God in the final judgment. The wicked join Antichrist and Satan in Gehenna, and the righte-ous enter into the final state of blessedness in the new heaven and new earth.

The interpretation of this chapter has been a source of great debate and even conflict in the church. Systems of escha-tology have often been identified in terms of the way they treat the question of the millennium — the thousand-year reign of Christ. A postmillennial view was popular among interpreters of the historical school, who saw in the Revelation a prophecy of the course of history down to the end. *Postmillennialism* means that the return of Christ would not occur until the Kingdom of God had been established by the church in human history. In this view, chapter 19 does not describe the coming of Christ but is a very symbolic way of describing the triumph of Christian principles in human affairs and the triumph of Christ through his church. After this "golden age," Christ will return to raise the dead, judge the world, and inaugurate the new eternal order.

Amillennialism is the term used to describe the view of those who do not look for a millennial reign of Christ either before or after his second coming. This way of interpreting Rev. 20 involves the principle of recapitulation, viz., that the structure of Revelation does not relate consecutive events but frequently covers the same ground from different perspectives.

Interpreters of this viewpoint often identify the binding of Satan and his incarceration in the abyss with the victory over Satan accomplished by our Lord in his earthly ministry. It is clear that the gospels do represent Jesus as having bound Satan (Matt. 12:29) and toppled him from his place of power (Luke 10:18); and this victory over Satan is reflected in the Revelation (see note on 12:9); it is an open question as to whether the binding of Satan in Rev. 20 is the same as that in Matt. 12 or is an eschatological event.

Amillennialists usually understand the "first resurrection" in one of two different ways. Some see here the resurrection unto eternal life, which is an altogether spiritual reality that occurs for each believer when he becomes a Christian (John 5:25; Eph. 2:5-6). The reign of Christ with his saints is either the reign of Christ manifested in history through his church, or the spiritual reign of believers with Christ "in the heavenly places" (Eph. 2:6). The thousand-year period is no literal piece of history; it is a symbolic number coextensive with the history of the church on earth between the resurrection of Christ and his return.

A different amillennial interpretation understands the resurrection and reign of the saints with Christ to represent the destiny of the martyrs. Though they were slain, the martyrs did not really die. In fact, they lived and reigned with Christ in heaven. The "millennium" is the church age when martyred saints reign with Christ in heaven, awaiting the resurrection.

Premillennialism is the view that Rev. 20 is altogether eschatological. The coming of Christ will be followed by a binding of Satan and the resurrection of the saints who will join him in a temporal kingdom when he reigns over the earth.

This millennial kingdom will end with a final rebellion and the last judgment.

A variant form of premillennialism is Dispensationalism, which sees the millennial kingdom primarily in terms of God's theocratic promises to Israel. The entire book of Revelation is interpreted in terms of these dispensational presuppositions and is concerned with the fate of restored Israel in the last days and not with the church. In many circles the only form of pre-millennialism known is Dispensationalism. The form of pre-millennialism which sees the Revelation as a prophecy of the destiny of the church is not widely held today but it is the theology expounded in the present commentary.[1]

A key issue in our understanding of the millennium is whether chapter 20 involves recapitulation, looking back from the end to the whole history of the church. In chapter 12, it is unmistakably clear that the passage looks back to the birth of Messiah. However, in the present passage, no such indication is to be found. On the contrary, chapters 18-20 appear to present a connected series of visions. Chapter 18 tells of the destruction of Babylon; chapter 19 tells of the destruction of the beast and the false prophet; and chapter 20 moves on to tell of the destruction of Satan himself — a destruction accomplished in two stages. Antichrist, the false prophet, and Satan form an evil triumvirate, and are closely linked in chapter 13 (see also 16:13 where they are mentioned together in a single verse).

(4) The Binding of Satan, the Resurrection, and the Millennial Kingdom (20:1-6).

Verse 1. **Then I saw an angel coming down from heaven, holding in his hand the key of the bottomless pit and a great chain.** The bottomless pit is the abyss from which demonic locusts swarmed forth to torture men (9:1-6). In that vision an angel had the key to the abyss which he used to open the shaft releasing the demonic locusts. The abyss is also the home

[1]For a more detailed discussion of these issues, see G. E. Ladd, *Crucial Questions About the Kingdom of God* (Grand Rapids: Eerdmans, 1952), pp. 135-183; and for a more complete presentation of the different schools of eschatology, see John F. Walvoord, *The Revelation of Jesus Christ* (Chicago: Moody Press, 1966), pp. 282-290. Walvoord's commentary is of the dispensational type.

of the beast; he "ascends from the bottomless pit" (11:7; see our note on 9:1ff.). In the present instance, Satan is bound and incarcerated in the abyss. This is obviously symbolic language describing a radical curbing of Satan's power and activities.

Verse 2. **And he seized the dragon, that ancient serpent, who is the Devil and Satan.** Satan is here identified by the same complex of names as in 12:9, which depicts a prior overthrow of Satan. It is difficult to understand the **thousand years** for which he was bound with strict literalness in view of the obvious symbolic use of numbers in the Revelation. A thousand equals the third power of ten — an ideal time. While we need not take it literally, the thousand years does appear to represent a real period of time, however long or short it may be.

Verse 3. The meaning of this binding and incarceration is that **he should deceive the nations no more** during the millennial period. This idea of the deception of the nations reappears after Satan is loosed (20:8); he gathers the nations again in a further revolt against the Messiah, like the revolt which has already occurred under Antichrist (13:14; 16:14). This suggests that this binding is different from the binding of Satan accomplished by our Lord in his earthly ministry; the latter had special reference to demon exorcism by which individuals were delivered from satanic bondage (Matt. 12:28-29). We must remember that the very idea of binding Satan is a symbolic way of describing a curbing of his power and activity; it does not mean his complete immobility. His incarceration in the abyss does not mean that all of his activities and powers are nullified, only that he may no longer deceive the nations as he has done through human history and lead them into active aggression against the saints during the thousand years.

The mention of the nations raises a difficult question. One would suppose from the preceding chapters of the Revelation that the entirety of mankind had been involved in the struggle between Christ and the Antichrist. In the days of Antichrist, Satan the great deceiver (12:9) seduced the "kings of the earth" by the glamour and glitter of Babylon to give their allegiance to the devil's representative (16:12, 14; 17:2; 18:3, 9). One might suppose that this satanic deception embraced all the nations of the earth, including both their kings and their subjects. Now, however, it seems clear that the "kings of the earth" represent a select number who have supported Antichrist. There apparently remain nations outside the scope of this struggle who are now delivered from satanic deception.

The binding of Satan is not punitive but precautionary: **after that he must be loosed for a little while.** After the divine purpose in Christ's millennial reign is accomplished, Satan must be loosed and go about again to deceive the nations. These words are difficult to understand if they are applied to our Lord's binding of Satan in his earthly ministry. The victory he won over Satan was won once and for all. Satan will never be loosed from bondage to Christ won by his death and resurrection.

Verse 4. **Then I saw thrones, and seated on them were those to whom judgment was committed. Also I saw the souls of those who had been beheaded for their testimony to Jesus, and for the word of God, and who had not worshiped the beast or its image and had not received its mark on their foreheads or their hands.** This is a very difficult verse. The question is: How many groups does John see? Many interpreters recognize only one group and limit this "first resurrection" to the martyrs, maintaining that God has some special blessing for those who have died because of their faithful witness to Jesus. However, the RSV correctly reflects the Greek idiom, which could be literally translated: "And I saw thrones, and [people] sat upon them, and judgment was given to them; and [I saw] the souls of those who had been beheaded . . . ." The language suggests two different groups: one group to whom judgment was given, and a smaller group who are the martyrs of the great tribulation. In Greek, the language is quite ungrammatical, which leads Charles to treat the first phrase as a gloss.[2] However, it may well be that John actually envisaged two groups: a larger group of all the saints and then a smaller group — the martyrs — whom he singles out for special attention.

This would accord with the biblical theology as a whole, which gives to the saints a share in the eschatological rule of Christ. Christ himself had promised through John the prophet

[2]R. H. Charles, *The Revelation of St. John* (New York: Scribners, 1920), II, 182.

a share in his throne to all who overcame (3:21); and we found no reason to limit this promise to martyrs. It is a promise to all victorious believers. In 2:26 the promise was given, "He who conquers and who keeps my works until the end, I will give him power over the nations, and he shall rule them with a rod of iron, as when earthen pots are broken in pieces, even as I myself have received power from my Father." Here again is a clear promise that the saints will share Christ's authority and rule. The promise of reigning with Christ as king is repeated in 5:9-10, and it is addressed to all the saints: "Thou . . . didst ransom men for God from every tribe and tongue and people and nation, and hast made them a kingdom and priests to our God, and they shall reign on earth." The saints constitute a kingdom not because they are the people over whom Christ reigns, but because they share his reign. Daniel's vision of the Son of man sees not only the throne of God but a plurality of thrones (Dan. 7:9), and this is interpreted to mean that "the kingdom and the dominion . . . shall be given to the saints of the Most High; their kingdom shall be an everlasting kingdom, and all dominions shall serve and obey them" (Dan. 7:27). Jesus promised his disciples, "In the new world, when the Son of man shall sit on his glorious throne, you who have followed me will also sit on twelve thrones, judging the twelve tribes of Israel" (Matt. 19:28). Paul says, without explanation, "Do you not know that the saints will judge the world?" (I Cor. 6:2). The verb "to judge" (*krino*) can have the broader meaning of "to rule,"[3] and this is probably the meaning in I Cor. 6:2.[4] In the Revelation, the meaning of the judgment given to those seated upon thrones is further defined in the last sentence of vs. 4: "they came to life again, and reigned with Christ a thousand years."

Many commentators emphasize the statement "I saw the souls of those who had been beheaded," insisting that the passage has reference to the fate of the martyrs in the intermediate state rather than in the resurrection. The souls of the martyrs have already appeared in the Revelation. Upon the

---

[3]See F. Büchsel in Kittel's *Theological Dictionary of the New Testament* (Grand Rapids: Eerdmans, 1965), III, 923.

[4]See A. Robertson and H. Plummer, *First Epistle of Paul to the Corinthians* (New York: Scribners, 1911), p. 111. "It is in the Messianic Kingdom that the saints will share Christ's reign over the created universe."

opening of the fifth seal, John saw the souls of the martyrs under the altar (6:9ff.), asking the plaintive question, "How long before thou wilt judge and avenge our blood?" They were told to rest a little longer until the number of their fellow servants should be complete. Now, John again sees the souls of the martyrs; but he immediately adds, "they came to life again." This is the most important word in the entire passage. The exegete must decide whether or not it means resurrection; and upon this decision will be determined how he interprets the entire passage. The present commentator is convinced that it means resurrection (see note below), and for this reason, no weight can be placed on the statement that John saw the souls of the martyrs.

Some commentators see three groups in this passage: the saints in general (those who sat in the thrones), the martyrs (those beheaded), and the living saints (those who had not worshiped the beast nor received its mark). It is a fact that the language of the Greek text is irregular and could allow for such an interpretation. "Souls" is in the accusative case, and the following phrase — "who had not worshiped the beast" — is in the nominative. But it is John's grammatical style to be careless about his cases and to follow oblique cases by a nominative. Furthermore, the following statement — "they came to life again" — governs both groups and cannot be applied to living saints.

The phrase "their testimony to Jesus" (literally, "because of the testimony of Jesus") is difficult to interpret. See the note on 19:10 and references. Often this idiom in John is a subjective genitive and refers to the witness which Jesus bore to the salvation of God which his followers accepted (see 1:2, 9). In the present passage, as in 19:10, the objective genitive fits the context better. The faithful saints had been beheaded because of the testimony they had borne to Jesus Christ.

The phrase "they came to life again" is the translation of a single Greek word, *ezesan*. The crux of the entire exegetical problem is the meaning of this word. It is true that the word can mean entrance into spiritual life (John 5:25), but it is not used of any "spiritual resurrection" of the souls of the righteous at death. The word is, however, used of bodily resurrection in John 11:25; Rom. 14:9; Rev. 1:18; 2:8; 13:14; and most commentators admit that this is the meaning in vs. 5:

265

"The rest of the dead did not come to life again until the thousand years were ended." If *ezesan* in vs. 4 designates spiritual life at conversion, or life after death in the intermediate state, we are faced with the problem of the same word being used in the same context with two entirely different meanings, with no indication whatsoever as to the change of meaning.

No objection can be raised on the ground that it is not possible to speak of a spiritual and of a literal reality in the same context. Jesus does this very thing in speaking of the dead and of the resurrection (John 5:25-29). However, this passage does not provide a true analogy to the passage in the Apocalypse. There is this all-important difference. In the gospel, the context itself provides the clues for the spiritual interpretation in the one instance and the literal in the other. Concerning the first group who are to "live," the hour has already come. This makes it clear that the reference is to those who are spiritually dead and who enter into life upon hearing the voice of the Son of God. The second group, however, are "in the tombs," i.e., they are not the spiritually dead but the physically dead. Such dead are to be brought back to life again. Part of them will experience a "resurrection of life," i.e., a bodily resurrection which will lead them to the full experience of the spiritual life that is already theirs. The rest will be revived to a "resurrection of condemnation," i.e., to the execution of the decree of divine judgment which rests upon them already because they have rejected the Son of God and the life he came to bring (John 3:18, 36). The language of these words makes it indubitable that Jesus wishes his hearers to know that he is speaking of two experiences of "living": a present spiritual resurrection, and a future bodily resurrection.

In Rev. 20:4-6, there is no such contextual clue for a similar variation of interpretation. The language of the passage is quite clear and unambiguous. There is no necessity to interpret either word spiritually in order to introduce meaning to the passage. At the beginning of the millennial period, part of the dead come to life; at its conclusion, the rest of the dead come to life. There is no evident play upon words. The passage makes perfectly good sense when interpreted literally. Natural, inductive exegesis suggests that both uses of *ezesan* are to be taken in the same way, referring to a literal resurrection. We can do no better than to repeat the oft-quoted words of Henry Alford,

> If, in a passage where *two resurrections* are mentioned, where certain *psychai ezesan* at the first, and the rest of the *nekroi ezesan* only at the end of a specified period after that first, — if in such a passage the first resurrection may be understood to mean *spiritual* rising with Christ, while the second means *literal* rising from the grave; — then there is an end of all significance in language, and Scripture is wiped out as a definite testimony to anything.[5]

There is an obvious parallelism between this passage and Dan. 7.

Dan. 7	Rev. 20
9. As I looked, the thrones were placed	Then I saw thrones
10. The court sat in judgment	seated upon them were those to whom judgment was committed
22. Judgment was given to the saints of the Most High	
And the time came when the saints received the kingdom.	They came to life again and reigned with Christ a thousand years.[6]

They . . . reigned with Christ a thousand years. Our note on the earlier part of the verse proves that the idea of saints sharing Christ's messianic reign is a common one in the New Testament. However, this is the only passage in the entire Bible which teaches a temporal *millennial* kingdom, and there is only one other passage in the New Testament which may envisage a temporal reign of Christ between his parousia and the *telos*: I Cor. 15:23-24.[7]

Verse 5. **The rest of the dead did not come to life again (*ezesan*) until the thousand years were ended. This is the first resurrection.** The *first resurrection* refers back to vs. 4 to the

[5]Henry Alford, *The Greek Testament* (Boston: Lee and Shepard, 1872), IV, 732.

[6]See Hans Bietenhard, *Das tausendjährige Reich* (Zürich: Zwingli Verlag, 1955), pp. 21-2.

[7]For a discussion of this passage, see G. E. Ladd, *Crucial Questions About the Kingdom of God* (Grand Rapids: Eerdmans, 1952), pp. 177ff.; for chiliasm in Jewish apocalyptic, see *ibid.*, pp. 159ff.

souls of the saints and martyrs who came to life. Commentators usually recognize that the resurrection of "the rest of the dead" is the eschatological resurrection. Emphasis is often laid on the fact that John does not speak of a *second* resurrection; but it is implied in the statement, "the rest of the dead did not come to life again [as the participants in the first resurrection had done] until the thousand years were ended." As a matter of fact, if the first resurrection is different from the resurrection of vs. 5, "the rest of the dead" never do come to life as the others had done. Two resurrections are implied in the twofold use of *ezesan;* and a "second resurrection" is described if not labeled as such in vs. 12. The New Testament does not elsewhere clearly teach a twofold resurrection, although it is implied in such passages as John 5:29 and I Cor. 15:24-25. Paul nowhere in his epistles speaks of the resurrection of unbelievers; he is altogether concerned with the destiny of those who are in Christ. If the first resurrection includes all saints and martyrs, "the rest of the dead" includes all who have not known and believed in Christ. Their resurrection does not occur until after the millennium; it is described in vs. 12, when the rest of the dead are raised to stand before God's throne of judgment.

Verse 6. **Blessed and holy is he who shares in the first resurrection. Over such the second death has no power.** The "first death" is the death of the body which all men, except those living at the parousia, experience. The second death is eternal death in the lake of fire (vs. 14; see Matt. 10:28 where the death of the body and soul are contrasted). These blessed ones are called **priests of God and of Christ** because they have access into the immediate presence of God, and because they also share his reign in his messianic kingdom (1:6; 5:10). Just how we are to conceive of their participation in Christ's reign we cannot know. The saints will be in their resurrection bodies, while the people who make up "the nations" (vs. 8) are living out their natural existence. Many have taken offense at the thought of such mingling of the redeemed and unredeemed orders. We can only suggest that after the first Easter morning, Jesus in his resurrection body enjoyed forty days of intercourse with his disciples (Acts 1:3). God has yet many marvels in his redemptive purpose.

(5) The Final Destruction of Satan and Death (20:7-15).

Verses 7-8. **And when the thousand years are ended, Satan will be loosed from his prison and will come out to deceive the nations which are at the four corners of the earth.** This verse possibly suggests the reason for the temporal reign of Christ during the millennium. A burning theological question is the justice of God in judgment and condemnation. Paul is concerned "that every mouth may be stopped, and the whole world may be held accountable to God" (Rom. 3:19). While God does not need to vindicate his righteousness, Paul is concerned to make it crystal clear that God has so dealt with men that those who suppress the truth are without excuse (Rom. 1:20). In the present instance, even after Christ himself has reigned over men during the millennium, when the deceiver is set free from his prison, he finds the hearts of men still responsive to his seductions. This makes it plain that the ultimate root of sin is not poverty or inadequate social conditions or an unfortunate environment; it is the rebelliousness of the human heart. The millennium and the subsequent rebellion of men will prove that men cannot blame their sinfulness on their environment or unfortunate circumstances; in the final judgment, the decrees of God will be shown to be just and righteous.

Gog and Magog are biblical names for the nations who are rebellious against God and hostile to his people. In Ezek. 38:1, Gog is the prince of the land of Magog and comes from the north in the latter days to do battle with God's people. In Revelation, both words represent the hostile nations.

While the New Testament has little to say about a temporal messianic kingdom, Ezekiel's prophecy has the same basic structure as Rev. 20. Chapters 36-37 picture the salvation of Israel, restored to their land and blessed with the messianic salvation (see 36:24-29). The goal of the prophetic expectation, "you shall be my people, and I will be your God" (Ezek. 36:28) is now realized. David, God's servant, will rule over his people, and God will dwell in their midst (37:25, 28). However, the blessing of the messianic kingdom is not the end. The kingdom is disturbed by an eschatological war led by Gog from Magog (chapters 38-39); and only after the divine victory do we have a picture of the eternal new order, which in Ezekiel is described in terms of a rebuilt temple in the new Jerusalem (chapters 40-48).[8] This structure of a temporal messianic kingdom followed by the eternal kingdom in the new age is the same as that in Revelation.

Verse 9. The armies of evil march up against **the camp of the saints and the beloved city** as though to do battle with them, but no battle ensues. **Fire came down from heaven and consumed them.** The word for "camp" is properly a military installation; but here, it is used of the residence of the saints. Clearly, they are pictured as having their capital in the beloved city, Jerusalem. No actual battle occurs; God intervenes and destroys those who would destroy his people. It is impossible, in view of progressive revelation, to believe with the dispensationalists that the Jewish temple is to be restored and the literal bloody sacrificial system reinstituted. These belong to the old covenant which has passed away (Heb. 8:13). However, the saints in the millennium must have some center, and there is no difficulty in supposing that the millennial rule of Christ will have an earthly center in the holy city in the holy land.[9]

Verse 10. Again as in the battle of Armageddon, the emphasis in the divine victory is not on the defeat of the hosts of men who have fought against the Messiah and his people, but upon the destruction of the powers which have stood behind them. **The devil who had deceived them was thrown into the lake of fire and brimstone where the beast and the false prophet were.** Here is the final destruction of the ultimate root of evil. Jesus himself had spoken of "the eternal fire prepared for the devil and his angels" (Matt. 25:41). Hell was planned not for men but for the devil; but those who follow him must share his destiny.

They will be tormented day and night for ever and ever. It is impossible to visualize the actual terms of this verse. The devil and his angels are spirits, not physical beings; fire belongs to the material physical order. How a lake of literal fire can bring everlasting torture to nonphysical beings is impossible to imagine. It is obvious that this is picturesque language describing a real fact in the spiritual world: the final and ever-

[8]See G. Ernest Wright, "The Faith of Israel" in *The Interpreter's Bible*, I, 372.

[9]W. H. Simcox, *The Revelation of S. John the Divine* (Cambridge: University Press, 1893), p. 185.

lasting destruction of the forces of evil which have plagued men since the garden of Eden.

Verse 11. After the destruction of Satan, John witnesses the final judgment, the destruction of the old order, and the inauguration of the eternal state.

Then I saw a great white throne and him who sat upon it. This is the preparation for the final judgment. Some interpreters are greatly interested in the time and place of judgment and theorize that there are several different and distinct judgments taught in the New Testament: the judgment of the nations to decide which nations enter the millennial kingdom (Matt. 25:31-40); the judgment of believers before the judgment seat of Christ in heaven to receive their rewards for what they have done in the body (II Cor. 5:10); and the great white throne judgment of the present passage which is a judgment only of unbelievers. Such a scheme of eschatology cannot be proved but rests upon unsupported inferences. For instance, the final issue of the judgment of the nations is not the millennial kingdom but is either eternal life or eternal punishment (Matt. 25:46). This is clearly the final judgment which decides the eternal destiny of men. The judgment seat of Christ is also the judgment seat of God before which all believers must stand (Rom. 14:10). Scripture is not primarily interested in what concerns many students of the Bible, viz., in a scheme or chronology of prophetic events, and such efforts to differentiate between several different judgments do not have sound biblical support. However, the fact of judgment is solidly rooted in biblical thought. Paul affirms it unequivocally (Rom. 2:6-10).

The throne is *white* displaying the glory and majesty of God. John does not identify "him who sat upon it," but usually in the Revelation, it is God who sits on the throne (5:1, 7, 13).

From his presence earth and sky fled away, and no place was found for them. This statement undoubtedly involves poetic imagery; in the face of the glory and grandeur of the presence of God, the natural universe flees away. But it is more than poetry; it is the expression of an important theological truth. This statement takes us back to the first anticipation of the end at the opening of the sixth seal (6:12ff.). This describes a great cosmic convulsion when the sun became black, the moon became like blood, the stars fell, the sky vanished,

271

and the mountains were shaken (see our note *in loc.*). This announcement of the end is now fulfilled in the statement of our passage.

Behind such statements is a profound theology. Earth was created to be the dwelling place of man, and man as a creature of God stands in solidarity with the rest of creation. Therefore, the created world is pictured as sharing the results of man's sin, finding itself in bondage to decay, groaning and travailing until now (Rom. 8:19-22). The old order is a fallen order, laboring under the curse of man's rebellion. Therefore, before the new redeemed order can be inaugurated, God's judgment must fall upon the old order; but this judgment is not one of destruction but the prelude to re-creation. This motif of the judgment of nature and the new creation runs throughout the Old Testament prophets and is pictured with great variety of detail, but always with the same basic motif. Sometimes the picture is one of a simple regeneration of the old order as it stands with the curse lifted (Isa. 11:6-9); sometimes it is pictured in terms of a complete transformation in a new heaven and a new earth (Isa. 65:17).[10] In the prophetic hope, there is considerable variety of emphasis on the elements of continuity and discontinuity between the old and the new orders; in the New Testament, the element of discontinuity is more strongly emphasized than in the Old Testament, except in Isa. 65:6. Thus Peter anticipates a dissolution of the heavens and the melting of the elements with fire. However, the end of this judgment upon the old order is not its final destruction but the emergence of a new order. "We wait for new heavens and a new earth in which righteousness dwells" (II Pet. 3:13). The same is true of John's vision. The old order passes away to make room for the new.

Verse 12. John **saw the dead, great and small, standing before the throne.** This statement clearly implies, if it does not explicitly affirm, the resurrection of the "rest of the dead" (vs. 5) who did not experience the first resurrection.

Books were opened . . . and the dead were judged by what was written in the books, by what they had done. John does not further identify these books, but the last phrase suggests that they are the books in which have been recorded the deeds

[10]This theme is worked out in detail by the present author in his book, *Jesus and the Kingdom* (Waco: Word Books, 1964), chap. 2.

of men, both good and evil. Books of judgment are referred to in Dan. 7:10. The New Testament is insistent on the justice of God's final judgment in that it will not be arbitrary and capricious, but based squarely upon the deeds of men (Rom. 2:6ff.). Jewish apocalyptic picked up this idea and frequently mentions the books in which God has kept a record of men's deeds (*Enoch* 90:20; *IV Ezra* 6:20; *Apoc. Baruch* 24:1).

It is significant that the text does not intimate that anyone was saved on the basis of his good works. This is different from Jewish apocalyptic. In the *Testament of Abraham* (13) two angels record men's deeds; on the right good deeds, and on the left evil deeds. Another angel holds scales in which he weighs the deeds of men. Another angel tests men's deeds through fire; if their works are burned, they are carried off to a place of punishment; if their works are not burned, they are declared righteous.

Also another book was opened, which is the book of life. If no one is saved by his works, there is yet another possibility: the book of life. This includes the names of all who have believed in Christ. The idea of a book in which the names of the righteous are written goes back to the Old Testament (Exod. 32:32-33; Dan. 12:1), and appears several times in the New Testament (Luke 10:20; Phil. 4:3; Rev. 3:5; 13:8; 21:27).

Verse 13. **And the sea gave up the dead in it, Death and Hades gave up the dead in them, and all were judged by what they had done.** "Hades" (improperly translated "hell" in AV) is the abode of souls in the intermediate state and is here used synonymously with the grave (cf. 6:8). John does not mean to say that men who died on land and on the sea experienced a different fate after death; he merely means to affirm that *all* the dead, however they died, were included in this final judgment (see note on 19:20). When John says that the sea, Death and Hades *gave up the dead in them,* he obviously means resurrection, even though this is not explicitly affirmed. Certainly, we are not to think of the souls of those who had met death by drowning remaining in the sea until the time of judgment. John merely means that all who have drowned, all who have suffered death, are revived to stand before God in judgment.

Verse 14. **Then Death and Hades were thrown into the lake of fire.** This statement makes it clear that the very idea of a lake of fire is expressed symbolically. Death and Hades are personified and pictured as being cast into the lake of fire along with the beast, the false prophet, and Satan. Obviously, it is impossible to construe this literally. John means to affirm the final and complete destruction of death and the grave. It is true that Christ has "abolished," i.e., broken the power of death by his own death and resurrection (II Tim. 1:10); but the saints still die. All that eternal life means cannot be experienced until death itself is banished from the universe.

This is the second death, the lake of fire. This statement looks forward to the next verse. The idea of a second death for Death does not make much sense. John's mind moves from the destruction of Death to the judgment of the wicked.

Verse 15. **And if any one's name was not found written in the book of life, he was thrown into the lake of fire.** Apparently no one was saved by his works — i.e., on the basis of the good things which he had done which had been recorded in the books (vs. 12). Salvation is to be found alone through the Lamb of God. This accords with the teaching of Paul that "none is righteous, no, not one" (Rom. 3:10), and that justification can be found not by works of righteousness but only through faith in Christ.

CHAPTER TWENTY-ONE

THE CONSUMMATION

The chapter divisions in the Bible often do not coincide with the units of thought. The first unit in chapter 21 is directly continuous with chapter 20, giving a brief statement of the inauguration of the new age with its new Jerusalem (21:1-8). There follows another vision which describes in detail the new Jerusalem (21:9 — 22:5) whose descent has already been mentioned. After the final vision is appended an epilogue (22:6-21), which concludes the entire book.

(6) The New Creation (21:1-8).

Verse 1. **Then I saw a new heaven and a new earth; for the first heaven and the first earth had passed away.** This dissolution of the old order — the disappearance of the earth and sky — has already been announced (20:11). In its place John sees a new heaven and a new earth. Throughout the entire Bible, the ultimate destiny of God's people is an earthly destiny. In typical dualistic Greek thought, the universe was divided into two realms: the earthly or transitory, and the eternal spiritual world. Salvation consisted of the flight of the soul from the sphere of the transitory and ephemeral to the realm of eternal reality.[1] However, biblical thought always places man on a redeemed earth, not in a heavenly realm removed from earthly existence.

[1] For this view as found in Plato, Plutarch, and Philo, see G. E. Ladd, *The Pattern of New Testament Truth* (Grand Rapids: Eerdmans, 1968), pp. 13-31.

The statement that **the sea was no more** indicates the radical difference between the redeemed order and the old fallen order. This idea appears in Jewish apocalyptic (*Sibylline Oracles* 5:447; *Assumption of Moses* 10:6). Our modern scientific miracles have practically conquered the seas; but in the ancient world with its tiny ships, the sea represented the realm of the dark, the mysterious, and the treacherous. "But the wicked are like the tossing of the sea; for it cannot rest, and its waters toss up mire and dirt. There is no peace" (Isa. 57:20; see Ps. 107:25-28; Ezek. 28:8). The abolition of the sea suggests that there is practically no substantial continuity between the old fallen order and the new redeemed order, but that the old order is completely swept away and replaced by something altogether new and different. However, the statement in vs. 5, "Behold, I make all things new," suggests the renovation of what already exists. But it is improbable that the apocalyptist was much concerned about such details; his attention is fixed on the coming of the new order.

Verse 2. **And I saw the holy city, new Jerusalem, coming down out of heaven from God, prepared as a bride adorned for her husband.** In this verse, John merely mentions the descent of the holy city; in the final vision which begins at 21:9, he describes the city in considerable detail.

The New Testament conceives of a heavenly Jerusalem as the dwelling place of God, the true homeland of the saints, and the dwelling place of "the spirits of just men made perfect" (Heb. 12:22; see Gal. 4:26; Phil. 3:20). While this heavenly Jerusalem is represented as the dwelling place of the departed saints, heaven is not their ultimate destiny, but only the temporary abode of the saints between death and the resurrection (Rev. 6:9-11; II Cor. 5:8; Phil. 1:23). In the consummation after the resurrection (20:4), the heavenly Jerusalem will descend from heaven to take up its permanent location in the new earth.

The redeemed church has already been likened to a bride (19:7) who is joined with her Lord at the marriage supper of the Lamb. The heavenly Jerusalem, the seat of the abode of the redeemed in the new order, is also likened to a bride. One wonders if John means to identify the heavenly Jerusalem with God's redeemed people, even as the church is likened to the temple of God in the New Testament (I Cor. 3:16; Eph.

2:21). If so, the details of the description of the holy city are altogether symbolic terms in describing the redeemed church. In any case, it is at this point that the marriage supper of the Lamb takes place, as the next verse shows.

Verse 3. The meaning of the descent of the new Jerusalem is now stated: **the dwelling of God is with men. He will dwell with them, and they shall be his people, and God himself will be with them.** In the Old Testament times, God's dwelling place *(skene)* first was the tabernacle in the wilderness, and later the temple; and his presence was manifested by the shekinah glory. In the coming of Christ, God took up his dwelling temporarily among men (John 1:14 "The Word... *dwelt* among us." The same Greek root is used: *eskenosen*). During the church age, God indwells his church, which is his temple (Eph. 2:22); but this is a dwelling "in the Spirit," which can be apprehended only by faith, not by sight (II Cor. 5:17). In the consummation, all this is changed; faith will be changed to sight, and "they shall see his face" (22:4).

This is a reality which we cannot visualize; but direct, unmarred fellowship between God and his people is the goal of all redemption. This is further expressed by the phrase "they shall be his people." This is an echo of the Old Testament idiom, "I shall be their God and they shall be my people," which expresses the oft-repeated aim of the divine self-revelation and of all of God's dealings with his people.[2] All the promises of God's covenant with men, made first through Abraham, renewed through Moses, and embodied in Christ, are at last brought to full realization.

Verse 4. The essential blessing is direct, untroubled fellowship with God. However, other great blessings flow necessarily from this central reality. **He shall wipe away every tear from their eyes.** Tears here represent all human sorrow, tragedy, and evil. Accompanying the glorious vision of God will be a transformed mode of existence in which the sorrows and evils of existence in the old order are left far behind.

The most fearful cause of tears is the awful reality of dying; but in the presence of God, **death shall be no more.** The abolition of death has already been described when Death and

[2]See Gen. 17:7; Exod. 6:7; 29:45; Lev. 26:12; Num. 15:41; Deut. 29:13; II Sam. 7:24; Jer. 7:23; 11:4; 24:7; 30:22; Ezek. 11:20; 34:24; 36:28; 37:23, 27; Zech. 8:8.

Hades were thrown into the lake of fire (20:14). This triumph
over death is not, however, an end in itself; it is a blessing
which flows from fellowship with God. Not only is death
destroyed; there shall be neither **mourning** nor **crying** nor
pain any more, **for the former things have passed away.** In the
new order, all the evils that have burdened and cursed human
existence will flee from the presence of God.

Verse 5. **And he who sat upon the throne said, "Behold, I
make all things new."** This is the reason for the great transformation. Contrary to external appearances, existence is not
static. Back of creation is the Creator, the one who makes all
things new. This renovation has been already wrought in principle in Christ: "If anyone is in Christ, he is a new creation;
the old has passed away, behold the new has come" (II Cor.
5:17). However, it awaits the return of the Lord for its consummation. This process of renewal will finally include the
physical world itself. "Creation itself will be set free from its
bondage to decay and obtain the glorious liberty of the sons
of God" (Rom. 8:21). Salvation in the biblical sense is not
only the salvation of the souls of men; it includes the redemption of the body and even of their physical environment.

John is instructed to write down what he has heard, for the
words he has heard are **trustworthy and true;** they can be
relied upon to come to pass.

Verse 6. The voice John has heard has come from the
throne; i.e., it is the voice of God himself. Only a few times
in the Revelation is God said to speak (1:8; cf. 16:1, 17). Now
the voice assures John, **It is done.** The Greek verb is in the
plural: *"they* are done," i.e., the things spoken to John. Contrary to the confusing and chaotic picture presented to man
in his human experiences, the purposes of God in redemption
are as sure as though they have already taken place. The future
is not uncertain to those who trust God.

The future is secure because God is the eternal one. He
again affirms that he is **the Alpha and the Omega** (the first and
last letters of the Greek alphabet; see 1:8) who encompasses
all reality in himself. He is **the beginning and the end.** The
eternal one, who brought all things into existence, will make
all things new in the eternal order.

The renewal of all things includes the satisfaction of man's
deepest need; and therefore God summons men with the

invitation, **to the thirsty I will give water without price from the fountain of the water of life.** The figure of thirst represents the sense of spiritual need — of hunger and thirst after God. The final decree of salvation will not be arbitrary; the way is open to all who will sense their need and turn to God to be satisfied. Perhaps a contrast is intended with those who drink from the golden cup full of the wine of impure passion (17:4; 18:3) offered men by the great harlot.

Verse 7. The draught from the fountain of the water of life is not arbitrarily given to men but belongs to him **who conquers.** We are reminded of the promises made in the seven letters to those who conquer. The one prerequisite is abiding loyalty to Christ in the face of all evil and persecution. To such, God says, **I will be his God and he shall be my son.**

Verse 8. John now lists several kinds of people who will not have access to the water of life, whom God is unwilling to call his sons. The **cowardly** are those who have not had the courage to suffer hardship, including death, for the name of Christ (Matt. 13:21). Here again John emphasizes the enduring courage in the face of Antichrist which will characterize true disciples (1:9). The **faithless** may be either those who do not hold the faith in Jesus (14:12), unbelievers (AV), or it may mean those who cannot be trusted by God to bear the testimony of Jesus (1:2, 9; 12:17), the faithless (RSV). The **polluted** probably refers to those who have polluted themselves by worship of the beast (17:4), or it may have a broader meaning and designate all who are morally unclean (vs. 27). **Murderers, fornicators,** and **sorcerers** recall sins already referred to (9:21). The thought is not so much directed to these sins in general as to these sins as practiced by those who have been enticed by the great harlot. **Idolaters** designates not only those who worship false gods but particularly those who have worshiped the beast. **Liars:** falseness is frequently condemned in the Apocalypse (2:2; 3:9; 14:5; 21:27; 22:15). All such find **their lot in the lake that burns with fire and brimstone, which is the second death** (20:6, 14).

V. THE FOURTH VISION:
THE HEAVENLY JERUSALEM (21:9 — 22:5).

John has already mentioned briefly the descent of the heavenly city, the new Jerusalem, coming down out of heaven to take up its permanent location among men on earth. Now John retraces his steps and adds a detailed description of the holy city. The description presents some difficulties, in that it does not seem to represent a situation in which all things have been made new and God's new order purged of all evil. On the contrary, the earth is seen as being inhabited by nations who walk in the light of the city, who apparently are not residents of the city itself, and by kings who bring their glory into it (vs. 24). The leaves of the tree of life are for the healing of the nations (22:2) — a strange statement with reference to a redeemed, glorified humanity. Furthermore, a verse in the epilogue, looking back to the holy city, pictures dogs and sorcerers and fornicators as cowering outside the city walls, excluded from the city itself; in the new Jerusalem and the new earth, all evil will have been completely purged from the new creation. Such considerations have led some scholars to the conclusion that this is a description of the Jerusalem of the millennial kingdom with its mixed conditions in earthly affairs, not the eternal city.[3] This solution raises more difficulties than it solves. John nowhere else mentions a millennial Jerusalem, and there is no particular difficulty in concluding that John is using earthly language and idiom to describe the Jerusalem of the eternal order.

Verse 9. This section contains a new vision, and John is summoned by **one of the seven angels, who had the seven bowls,** as he had been summoned before (4:1; 17:1), to receive the further revelation. The content of this final vision is the **Bride, the wife of the Lamb.** In view of this identification, it is difficult to resist the conclusion that this Jerusalem is identical with the new Jerusalem of vs. 2 — the chief residence of the redeemed in the new redeemed earth. The language of John's summons is almost identical with the language of 17:1 where John was summoned to see the judgment of the great harlot — Babylon. This can hardly be accidental. John intends a deliberate contrast between the harlot city of the beast and the heavenly city of God's dwelling.

[3]Th. Zahn, *Die Offenbarung des Johannes* (Leipzig: Deichert, 1926), II, 608ff.; R. H. Charles, *The Revelation of St. John* (New York: Scribners, 1920), II, 177ff.; G. R. Beasley-Murray in *The New Bible Commentary* (F. Davidson, ed.; Grand Rapids: Eerdmans, 1953), p. 1197.

Verse 10. Again, John was **in the Spirit** (1:10; 4:1; 17:3), in a state of spiritual ecstasy. John was **carried . . . away to a great high mountain,** apparently to gain a good vantage point from which he could behold the new disclosures. There he saw what he had already mentioned (21:2): **the holy city Jerusalem coming down out of heaven from God.**

Verse 11. The most striking characteristic of the city was that it bore **the glory of God.** Glory or radiance is a common biblical term designating the presence of God. There are many parallels between John's description of the new Jerusalem and Ezekiel's vision of the temple. "Behold, the glory of the Lord filled the temple" (Ezek. 43:5). When John tried to describe the glory of the city, he could only do what he did when he attempted to describe the presence of God himself, viz., speak of it in terms of precious stones (4:3). The radiance of the new Jerusalem was **like a jasper, clear as crystal.** The word for "jasper" in antiquity was not limited to the type of stone we call jasper, but could designate any transparent precious stone. This jasper was possibly like a diamond.

Verse 12. The city **had a great, high wall, with twelve gates.** According to vs. 13, the gates were arranged with three on each side of the wall. This feature is taken directly from Ezek. 48:31ff.

And at the gates twelve angels, who stand guard on the gate towers as watchers. See Isa. 62:6, where watchmen are set in the walls to intercede for Israel and pray for the coming of the messianic kingdom. On the gates the names of the twelve tribes of the sons of Israel were inscribed (see Ezek. 48:31).

Verse 14. **The wall of the city had twelve foundations, and on them the twelve names of the twelve apostles of the Lamb.** This is an obvious allusion to the theology of the church, which is built upon the foundation of the apostles and prophets (Eph. 2:20). By this symbolism of the twelve gates bearing the names of the twelve tribes of Israel, and the twelve foundations bearing the names of the twelve apostles, John indicates that the city encompasses both dispensations, and that both the Israel of the Old Testament and of the church of the New Testament have their place in God's final establishment.

Verse 15. The angel who talked with John held in his hand **a measuring rod of gold to measure the city and its gates and**

walls. In 11:1, John was given a measuring rod to measure the inner temple, its courts, and its worshipers, setting them off from the outer courts and the city as a whole. The idea of measuring in the present passage does not have reference to preservation or judgment, as in chap. 11, but suggests the magnificence of the city and is patterned on Ezek. 40:3ff.

Verse 16. The measurements of the city resemble no earthly city; it is built in quadrangular form embodying perfect symmetry: **twelve thousand stadia,** or 1500 miles long on each of its four sides. According to ancient historians, Babylon was built in the form of a square; but the new Jerusalem is not only 1500 miles long on each of its four sides; it is built in the shape of a cube, **its length and breadth and height are equal.** Obviously, a city which is literally 1500 miles long, 1500 miles wide, and 1500 miles high beggars the imagination, especially when we recall that the distance from the Sea of Galilee to the Dead Sea was a scant sixty miles. Obviously, these measurements represent the ideal symmetry, perfection, vastness, and completeness of the new Jerusalem. Possibly the foursquare structure of the city, which has now become the dwelling place of God, is meant to recall the Holy of Holies (I Kings 6:20).

Verse 17. The dimensions of the walls of the city are now given: **a hundred and forty-four cubits,** or 216 feet. The text does not explain whether or not this is the height of the wall. For a city 1500 miles high, a wall only 216 feet high would be completely out of proportion. Possibly the measurement represents the thickness of the wall. When we reflect upon the structure of the new Jerusalem, we are bound to ask why it needed walls at all. Modern cities do not have walls, but ancient cities needed walls to protect them against the assaults of their enemies. But in the land of the new Jerusalem, there will be no enemies; only the people of God will inhabit it. It is obvious that John is trying to use human language to describe the indescribable and the unimaginable. Although an angel has measured the city and its walls, its size is given in the dimensions of **a man's measure,** i.e., ordinary human calculation, which in this instance is the same as **an angel's.**

Verse 18. The building materials of the city are like no human city. The **wall** of the city **was built of jasper,** a stone already mentioned to describe the transparent glory of the city as a whole (vs. 11; cf. Isa. 54:11ff.). The city itself was built of **pure gold, clear as glass.** This again indicates the transparent quality of the city. Gold has always been a precious metal, but transparent gold is not a human substance. The new city will reflect the glory of God, which human language cannot describe.

Verses 19-20. The twelve foundations supporting the wall of the city, on which were written the names of the twelve apostles, did not rest beneath the level of the ground as foundations usually do, but were visible to all. They were beautifully adorned with every sort of jewel. John names twelve precious ornaments in this foundation, not all of which are known to us. Each of the twelve foundations was adorned with its own particular jewel. It is doubtful if any symbolic significance is intended by this description of the foundations, beyond the beauty and majesty of the whole.

Verse 21. John adds another feature which again is inconceivable in terms of the cities of the present temporal order. The twelve gates were **twelve pearls,** each pearl constituting one of the twelve gates. Usually in ancient cities the gate was built into the wall as part of a tower; so each pearl was larger than the wall itself, constituting both the gate and its tower. Such pearls are beyond our imagination.

The street of the city was pure gold, transparent as glass. It is not clear whether the singular form of the noun — street — is meant collectively to include all the streets of the city, or whether the city, like many ancient cities, was conceived as having one broad main street running through its midst. In either case, transparent gold is no ordinary human building material.

Verse 22. **And I saw no temple in the city, for its temple is the Lord God the Almighty and the Lamb.** In the early days of Israel, God was conceived of as dwelling in the Holy of Holies in the tabernacle, and later, after Solomon's time, in the temple. The temple was the center of Jewish worship both in the time of the monarchy and the restoration. The sectarian group at Qumran in New Testament times rejected the established temple, even though it contained many priests in its fellowship, and developed the idea of the community as a new temple.[4]

[4]See Bertil Gärtner, *The Temple and the Community in Qumran and the New Testament* (Cambridge: University Press, 1965).

The early Christian church developed the theology of the church as the true temple of God (I Cor. 3:16; Eph. 2:21). In the age to come, there will be no need of a temple, for God himself will dwell among his people and direct unmediated communion.

Verse 23. **And the city has no need of sun or moon to shine upon it.** In reflecting upon the glories of the new Jerusalem, John was overwhelmed by the vision of the presence of God and recalled the prophecy of Isaiah, "The sun shall be no more your light by day, nor for brightness shall the moon give light to you by night, but the Lord shall be your everlasting light, and your God will be your glory" (Isa. 60:19). It is doubtful that John intended to give astronomical information about the new world; his purpose is to affirm the unsurpassed splendor which radiates from the presence of God and the Lamb. **The glory of God is its light, and its lamp is the Lamb.** This accords with the fact, found frequently in the New Testament, that God and Christ stand in the same relationship to men.

Verse 24. **By its light shall the nations walk; and the kings of the earth shall bring their glory into it.** Taken literally, this verse suggests that in the new earth there will be two companies of people: the redeemed who inhabit the new Jerusalem, and unregenerate nations of earth who live outside the city but who are influenced by its presence, walking in its light, and bringing their glory to the city. This fact has led many scholars to the conclusion that John is here describing the millennial Jerusalem, not the Jerusalem of the eternal order when all wicked men shall have been cast into the lake of fire. However, it is equally possible that John is using conventional human language to describe the universality of the knowledge of God in the eternal order. In the divine consummation, the redeemed will consist of peoples from every nation and tribe and people and tongue (7:9) who will not lose their national identity. John's language means no more than the statements of the prophets: "and many peoples shall come and say: 'Come, let us go up to the mountain of the Lord, to the house of the God of Jacob'" (Isa. 2:3); "and nations shall come to your light, and kings to the brightness of your rising" (Isa. 60:3). This is the affirmation of the universality of the knowledge of God.

Verse 25. When John says that **its gates shall never be shut** by day, he merely affirms the absolute safety and openness of the new Jerusalem. Isaiah had said, "Foreigners shall build up your walls, and kings shall minister to you; . . . your gates shall be open continually; day and night they shall not be shut; that men may bring to you the wealth of the nations" (Isa. 60:11). There will be no need to shut the gates in the face of enemies and hostile forces; the gates will stand open to allow all men immediate access to the presence of God.

And there shall be no night there. John has already asserted that there will be no need of the sun in the new city (vs. 23) because God will provide its light. So the presence of God will banish all darkness and night. In the Bible, darkness is a standard metaphor for existence apart from the presence of God (Matt. 6:23; 8:12; 22:13; 25:30); all darkness will be abolished in the presence of the radiance of God and the Lamb.

Verse 26. This verse repeats and reaffirms what was said in vs. 24.

Verse 27. If this verse is taken out of its context, it suggests that the **unclean** and those who practice **abomination or falsehood** are still in the earth, but though the gates are open day and night, they cannot enter the city. However, the flexibility of apocalyptic language allows John to use contemporary earthly idiom to describe future eschatological situations. Those who are now unclean and who practice abominations or falsehood will have no access into the heavenly city.

Only those who are written in the Lamb's book of life can enter the city. This fact has already been asserted. At the judgment of the great white throne, only those written in the Lamb's book of life received the divine vindication (20:15). In the former passage, John states it negatively; here he affirms it positively.

CHAPTER TWENTY-TWO

CONCLUSION

The chapter and verse divisions of the Bible are a relatively modern invention and do not always represent units of thought. In the present instance, the vision in the last chapter of the Revelation is directly continuous with what has preceded.

Verse 1. **Then he showed me the river of the water of life, bright as crystal, flowing from the throne of God and of the Lamb.** This is a symbolic way of describing the reign of eternal life in the age to come. The symbolism of a river of life is a common one in biblical thought. The Psalmist wrote of a "river whose streams make glad the city of God" (46:4). Jesus spoke of the living water (John 4:10, 14) which he offered men. Ezekiel's vision of the new Jerusalem pictured a river of water flowing from under the temple (which was not located in Jerusalem itself), which brought healing and life to the waters of the Dead Sea (Ezek. 47:1-12). Zechariah had a vision of the Kingdom of God in which rivers of water flowed from Jerusalem both eastward and westward (Zech. 14:8). The presence of the river of life in the new Jerusalem is a picturesque way of saying that death with all its baleful accompaniments has been abolished and life reigns supreme.

The fact that the river flows from the throne of God and of the Lamb means simply that God is the source of all life. Here, as in 3:21, there is only one throne on which are seated both the Father and the Son. This fact makes it difficult to distinguish between different thrones and different judgments, as some interpreters do. The judgment seat of Christ before which believers must appear (II Cor. 5:10) is also the judgment seat of God (Rom. 14:10).

Verse 2. The river flows **through the middle of the street of the city.** This is not to be taken in a literal sense to mean that down the center of Main Street in the new Jerusalem flows a river like the canals which flow down the center of the streets in Amsterdam. It merely expresses the centrality of eternal life in the new Jerusalem.

Verse 2b is a bit difficult to translate, but most commentators understand it to mean the same as the RSV translates it: **On either side of the river, the tree of life.** This is another traditional feature in Jewish apocalyptic going back to the Genesis narrative. God planted in Eden the tree of life (Gen. 2:9); but after man sinned, God excluded him from access to the tree of life lest in his sinful state he eat of this tree and live forever (Gen. 3:22). Jewish thought looked forward to access to the tree of life by whose fruit men would attain to eternal life (*Enoch* 25:2ff.; *IV Ezra* 7:53; 8:52; *II Enoch* 8:3). Jesus brought to men this eternal life in the midst of history through his incarnation, death and resurrection (John 3:36; 6:54; 20:31); and the present reference to the tree of life means the consummation of what Jesus accomplished in his earthly mission. It has particular reference to the eschatological hope; and in its eschatological aspect, it includes the complete transformation of that which is mortal into the likeness of the immortal (II Cor. 5:4). However, the condition of eternal life is relationship to God through Christ (John 17:3), and the eschatological transformation into immortality is a blessing resulting from direct, unmediated fellowship with God and with his Christ. "We shall be like him, for we shall see him as he is" (I John 3:2).

The tree bore **twelve kinds of fruit, yielding its fruit each month; and the leaves of the tree were for the healing of the nations.** The description of the tree of life follows very closely the language of Ezek. 47:12: "And on the banks, on both sides of the river, there will grow all kinds of trees for food. Their leaves will not wither nor their fruit fail, but they will bear fresh fruit every month, because the water for them flows from the sanctuary. Their fruits will be for food, and their leaves for healing."

The tree is pictured as bearing a different kind of fruit each month. This obviously has no parallel in the human experience of this age. The meaning is that the tree will not pass through the ordinary cycles of budding, blossoming, fruit-setting, and harvest, giving a crop once or twice a year, but will be loaded with fruit every month of the year. This expresses the absolute triumph of life over death.

In Ezekiel, the tree was primarily for fruit. John emphasizes the healing powers of the leaves of the tree. When he speaks of "the healing of the nations" by the leaves of the tree, we are not to think of nations of men living on the new earth in the age to come who will need healing from pain, sickness, and dying. The contrast is between this age, inhabited by suffering and dying peoples, and the age to come. All who have access to that age will partake of the tree of life and find perfect surcease from their afflictions.

Verse 3. John continues his contrast between life in this age and the age to come. This age is characterized by evil, sin, and many things which fall under the divine curse. Conditions in the new age will be completely transformed, and **there shall no more be anything accursed** (Zech. 14:11). The reason for this transformation is nothing less than the presence of God himself: **the throne of God and of the Lamb shall be in it, and his servants shall worship him.** This repeats the central motif of the new age (21:3). The chief joy of the redeemed — God's servants — will be the service of worship they render him.

Verse 4. **They shall see his face.** This is the hope and the goal of individual salvation throughout the Scriptures: the beatific vision of God. Throughout all redemptive history, God's presence was mediated to men in different ways. In the Old Testament it was mediated through the prophetic word, theophanies, dreams, angels and the cult. To come face to face with the living God meant death (Exod. 33:20). Jesus in his incarnation brought the presence of God to men in his own person (Matt. 1:23); to see and to know Christ was to see and know the Father (John 14:7, 9; 17:3). This vision of God was still a mediated vision, realized only in faith. In the age to come, faith will give way to sight (Ps. 17:15; Matt. 5:8; I John 3:2).

His name shall be on their foreheads. See note on 13:16; also 3:12; 14:1). The redeemed shall be perfectly possessed by God.

Verse 5. John repeats a promise already made that in the new age there shall be no night, for the presence of God will make unnecessary any other light and will abolish the darkness.

They shall reign for ever and ever. The text does not say whom they reign over, nor is it important. They shall share the royal office of Christ.

VI. EPILOGUE (22:6-21).

With the vision of the new Jerusalem, John's prophecy is complete. Now he appends an epilogue whose primary purpose is to affirm the authority of his book. The epilogue consists of a group of exhortations and affirmations loosely strung together which authenticate the prophecy, assert the certainty of the Lord's coming, and bid his readers to heed the words of his prophecy.

Verse 6. It is not clear who is speaking in this verse. Since no change of subject is indicated, we should conclude that the voice is that of the angel who has shown John the new Jerusalem (21:9, 15; 22:1). If so, then vs. 7 stands alone as an affirmation of Christ and not a part of the words of the angel. However, RSV punctuates vss. 6 and 7 together as the words of Christ.

And he said to me, "These words are trustworthy and true." The angel assures John that what he has seen and heard in the whole revelation of the future is true and reliable (cf. 3:14; 19:11).

"And the Lord, the God of the spirits of the prophets, has sent his angel to show his servants what must soon take place." Here, John claims again (cf. 1:3) that the book he has written is a prophecy. John has already said that "the testimony of Jesus is the spirit of prophecy" (19:10). This is the Holy Spirit who is sent by God into the world to inspire the prophets to proclaim divine truth. While the "spirits of prophets are subject to prophets" (I Cor. 14:32), their inspiration comes from God and enunciates divine truth. The purpose of this statement is to reaffirm the fact that John considers his book to be a genuine work of prophecy. The prophecy has been mediated through an angel (1:1); God who is the author of all prophetic utterance has spoken through his angel to convey to men *what*

289

must soon take place. The last phrase reiterates what John has already said in his introduction (1:1).

Verse 7. **"And behold, I am coming soon."** This must be taken either as a quotation by the angel of the words of the Lord, or as a new statement in which the Lord himself speaks. It reiterates what Christ said in the earlier part of the Revelation (2:16; 3:11). The word may mean "quickly" (AV) or "soon" (RSV). The Christian community should always live under the expectancy of the imminent coming of the Lord. No man knows the day nor hour (Matt. 24:36) and no one can set dates or calculate the time of his coming; but every generation must be awake as though the coming of Christ was at the threshold (Matt. 24:42-44). The biblical warnings involve a spiritual and moral tension of expectancy and perspective.

Blessed is he who keeps the words of the prophecy of this book. It is possible that this statement embodies the words of Christ himself who has just spoken; otherwise, they are a beatitude of the apocalyptist. In view of the beatitude in 1:3, the latter choice is the more probable. The prophecies of the Revelation were not written to satisfy intellectual curiosity about the future; they were written that the church might be able to live in the will of God by keeping the words of the prophecy. The church of the first century, the church of the last generation, as well as the church of every age finds herself caught up in the struggle between Christ and Antichrist. John wrote his prophecy not only to inform the church about the events of the consummation but to admonish her to steadfast and unswerving loyalty to Jesus Christ in the face of demonic pressures and persecution. He therefore pronounces a beatitude on those who heed and stand fast and who endure to the end.

Verse 8. John, in conclusion, identifies himself again: **I John am he who heard and saw these things.** Here again (see 1:1, 4) John identifies himself as one who is known by the churches in Asia, who needs no other identification than the simple name John.

The next sentence is a bit difficult to locate in the author's flow of thought. **And when I heard and saw them** [these things — the whole contents of the book] **I fell down to worship at the feet of the angel who showed them to me.** On a previous occasion John had fallen to his face to worship the interpreting angel (19:10). These words represent John's stance as the recipient of revelation. The understanding of the consummation of God's redemptive purpose was mediated to him by an angel, and he was so overcome by awe and wonder that his natural reaction was to fall down and worship the angel.

Verse 9. The angel reiterates what he had said on the previous occasion (19:10). John must not give worship to an angel, for an angel does not fill the role of deity but is only a mediator of the divine revelation and therefore a **fellow servant** with John and with his **brethren the prophets,** and also **with those who keep the words of this book,** i.e., with all the saints. God alone is the worthy object of worship.

Verse 10. **And he said to me, "Do not seal up the words of the prophecy of this book, for the time is near."** The speaker must still be the angel who spoke in 19:9; 21:9. In his first vision of the heavenly throne room, John saw a papyrus scroll sealed along the edge with seven seals, indicating that the contents of the book were not accessible to men. On occasions when prophets received revelations which did not concern their own immediate contemporaries but some future time, they were told to seal up the book of their prophecy (Isa. 8:16; Dan. 8:26; 12:4, 9). However, John's prophecy was not designed for some remote generation but for the entire Christian church, including John's own generation. Therefore he is not to seal his book (note that it is again called a prophecy) but is to leave it unsealed that all may read.

This commentary has taken the viewpoint that the contents of John's prophecy have primarily a twofold perspective. It is concerned with the struggle between Christ and Antichrist which will come to its terrible climax at the end of the age. However, this struggle also expressed itself in the relationship between the state and the church in the first century, particularly in the deification of the emperors and the growing demand of the state that its citizens recognize the emperor's deity by a formal act of- worship. We might add that this same demonic struggle is apparent wherever the state makes totalitarian demands. John's prophecy outlines the spiritual struggle between God and Satan (chap. 12) which expresses itself wherever the state exceeds its divinely ordained role as the supporter of law and order (Rom. 13:1-7). Therefore, while the book is primarily concerned with the climax of the struggle in the appearance of Antichrist, it is also relevant to Christian experience wherever and whenever the antichristian principle of totalitarianism manifests itself.

Without doubt the early church lived in expectancy of the imminent return of the Lord; but so should every generation of believers. The New Testament expresses a tension between imminence and perspective; the time is near, yet the end is delayed (Matt. 24:42-44; Luke 19:11ff.).

Verse 11. This sounds like a harsh verse which leaves no room for repentance. The evildoer is to continue in his evil and the filthy in his filthiness, while the righteous and the holy are set in the doing of good. However, as John approaches the conclusion of his book, he holds forth the invitation to repentance: "Let him who is thirsty come, let him who desires take the water of life without price" (vs. 17). Still, there will come a time when it will be too late for repentance. "It is not only true that the troubles of the last days will tend to fix the character of each individual according to the habits which he has already formed, but there will come a time when change will be impossible — when no further opportunity will be given for repentance on the one hand or for apostasy on the other."[1] In view of his sense of the imminence of the end, John in imagination transports himself to the end when repentance will indeed be impossible — when the stand one has taken for Christ or Antichrist will be finally and irrevocably determinative.

Verse 12. **"Behold, I am coming soon."** Without warning, John inserts words of Jesus as he has done in vs. 7. See note on that verse.

"Bringing my recompense, to repay every one for what he has done." The purpose of the coming of Christ, so far as men are concerned, is to fill the role of judge. The New Testament constantly emphasizes the fact of judgment on the basis of works (Rom. 2:26; Rev. 2:23). From the perspective of the Apocalypse, patience in tribulation, steadfastness under persecution, faithfulness to Christ constitute the good works of Christians (13:10; 14:12).

Verse 13. The ground of Christ's authority to be judge of

---

[1]H. B. Swete, *The Apocalypse of St. John* (London: Macmillan, 1917), p. 305.

men rests in the fact that he is **the Alpha and the Omega, the first and the last, the beginning and the end.** The attributes expressed in these words are attributed to God himself in 1:8 and 21:6. Christ can be the judge of men because he transcends all human experience, sharing the eternal nature of God himself.

Verse 14. Having said that Christ is coming as the judge of men, judging them according to their works, John now contrasts the destiny of the saints with the fate of the wicked. The saints are not those who have achieved a human righteousness of good works, but **those who wash their robes.** This idea has already appeared in the Revelation; the martyred but redeemed church is described as those who "have washed their robes and made them white in the blood of the Lamb" (7:14; see also 3:4). The tense of the verb "wash" is not an aorist denoting a single act in past time but a present indicating durative, continuing action. All cleansing from sin, whether the sin of unbelieving days or the sins committed by disciples of Christ (I John 1:8-9), is accomplished only by the blood of Christ. Such **have the right to the tree of life** and **enter the city by the gates.** John is affirming a basic principle; he has already concluded his prophecy and described the heavenly city's descent to earth with the tree of life growing within. Here, one would suppose that eating of the tree of life gives access to the city; but such logical sequences do not disturb the apocalyptic way of thinking. Only those washed in the blood of the Lamb have access either to the tree or to the city. This is simply John's vivid way of saying that eternal life and a blessed destiny are found only through the atoning work of Christ.

Verse 15. John now adds a statement which seems incongruous and out of place: **Outside** [i.e., of the city] **are the dogs and sorcerers and fornicators and murderers and idolaters, and every one who loves and practices falsehood.** Taken literally, this suggests that only the redeemed inhabit the holy city, while the wicked, like dogs cowering at the city gates, are excluded from the holy city and find their destiny somewhere in the final order outside. As a matter of fact, John has already asserted that their doom is not merely exclusion from the city but is the lake of fire (21:8). The present verse is John's picturesque way of contrasting the fate of the wicked with that of the righteous. The wicked are indeed excluded from the city. "Dogs" is a term sometimes used to describe wicked, malicious persons (Phil. 3:2; Ps. 22:16, 20).

Verse 16. John again inserts words of Jesus giving his attestation and authorization of the book. **I Jesus have sent my angel to you with this testimony for the churches.** This reaffirms the introduction of the book. God gave the revelation to Jesus Christ who in turn gave it to his angel to reveal to John (1:1). The clear statement that Jesus gave his testimony to the churches through the angel helps us to interpret the difficult phrase "the testimony of Jesus," which we have decided in most instances means the testimony given by Jesus and received and held by the churches (subjective genitive; see 1:2, 9; 6:9; 12:11, 17; in 19:10; 20:4, it may be an objective genitive). This is supported by the present verse.

The single name Jesus identifies the heavenly revelator with the Jesus who had been known historically by his disciples. But Jesus is not only a man who lived and died in Palestine; he is the Davidic Messiah, **the root and the offspring of David.** He is the shoot that grows out of the stump of Jesse (Isa. 11:1; see Isa. 53:2), the great Son of David (Matt. 1:1; 9:27; 15:22; 21:9; Rom. 1:3; II Tim. 2:8; Rev. 5:5). He is also **the bright morning star.** This reminds us of the old prophecy "a star shall come forth out of Jacob" (Num. 24:17).

Verse 17. Again, without warning, the narrative changes, and John is now himself the speaker. **The Spirit and the Bride say, "Come." And let him who hears say, "Come." And let him who is thirsty come, let him who desires take the water of life without price.** This invitation is susceptible of two very different interpretations. The *Spirit* is the Holy Spirit who speaks through the prophets (Rev. 19:10); the Bride is the church, the wife of the Lamb (19:7). It is possible that the first half of the verse is a call to Jesus to come and reward his people. This makes good sense and fits the context (22:12, 20). However, in this case, the second half of the sentence involves an unreasonably abrupt shift in viewpoint, for the second invitation is addressed to the world — to all who are thirsty, to come and quench their spiritual thirst by drinking of the water of life. Therefore it is better to interpret the first half of the verse by the second half and understand the entire invitation to be addressed to the world. When the Lord comes, it will be too late; there will come a time when repentance is impossible. But that hour has not yet come; and until that day, the Spirit issues the invitation through the prophets for men everywhere to come; the church re-echoes the invitation saying, *Come.* Those who hear and heed the invitation add their voices saying, *Come;* and in conclusion John adds his own words inviting all who read his prophecy to come and drink of the water of life.

Verse 18. John now adds a solemn warning against any who might be offended by the message contained in his prophecy and therefore try to distort or misrepresent its teaching. Some have felt that this warning was addressed to future scribes who might copy his book, demanding faithful transmission of the text. It is true that in a Jewish writing known as the letter of *Aristeas,* which tells the story of the translation of the Old Testament from Hebrew into Greek, such an exhortation is to be found (*Aristeas* 311). However, John's warning is addressed to **every one who hears the words of the prophecy of this book.** The Apocalypse was sent to seven churches in Asia where John expected it to be read aloud in public worship (see on 1:3). John now addresses these hearers, warning them to accept the divine authority of his prophecy and not distort his message.

The form of the warning is derived from Deut. 4:2 where God admonishes Israel, "You shall not add to the word which I command you, nor take from it; that you may keep the commandments of the Lord your God." Sometimes, these words have been interpreted with strict literalness, applied to the whole Bible, and used to authenticate a literalistic hermeneutic which rejects any kind of critical study of the Bible. However, this is John's vivid way of authenticating the message of his prophecy. He is not concerned about possible mechanical errors in transmission or mistakes of judgment in interpreting his message, but in deliberate distortions and perversions of it.

Verse 19. The second half of the warning, taken literally, seems to be a warning to believers who have access to the tree of life and the holy city that they will lose their salvation if they tamper with the wording of John's prophecy. However, such a warning is not designed to teach theology but to emphasize the seriousness of tampering with the truth of God's

Word. God's Word is neither a human discovery nor a human invention; it is divinely disclosed truth. It requires all the intellectual and scholarly skill the student of Scripture can muster to determine what a given passage or book means, for the Word of God has been given to us in the words of men in non-English languages and in ancient historical situations. But when the message of Scripture has been understood, then the believer no longer sits in judgment upon its truth but lets its truth judge and control his life and thinking. John assumes that all who have access to the tree of life and the holy city will treat his prophecy in this way.

Verse 20. The final affirmation in the Revelation is a word of the Lord who gave the witness of the consummation to the churches (see 1:2; 22:16) reassuring the prophet as to the central fact of the consummation: **Surely I am coming soon** (see notes on 1:1; 3:11; 22:7, 12). John responds with the familiar Hebrew affirmation, **Amen,** meaning "So be it." He adds his own prayer, **Come, Lord Jesus!** This prayer for the coming of the Lord is deeply rooted in the most primitive Christian liturgy. The same prayer appears as a fixed liturgical phrase in Aramaic in I Cor. 16:22: *marana tha.* That this phrase appears in Aramaic form in a letter to a Greek-speaking church proves that it comes from the earliest Jewish-Christian community. The longing for the Lord's coming stands at the heart of the Christian faith; apart from Christ's return, his redemptive work remains forever incomplete. His return is the only sure hope for the future of the world.

Verse 21. John concludes with the typical Christian salutation: **The grace of our Lord Jesus Christ be with all the saints. Amen.**

SELECTED BIBLIOGRAPHY

Alford, Henry. "The Revelation" in *The Greek Testament.* New York: 1872.
A classic and still valuable interpretation from the historical point of view.

Barclay, William. *The Revelation of John (The Daily Study Bible Series).* Philadelphia: Westminster, 1959. 2 vols.
A very readable but scholarly exposition.

Beasley-Murray, G. R. "The Revelation" in *The New Bible Commentary,* F. Davidson, ed.; Grand Rapids: Eerdmans, 1953; third rev. ed., 1970.
A conservative scholar who combines the preterist and the futurist viewpoints.

Beckwith, Isbon T. *The Apocalypse of John.* New York: Macmillan, 1919; reprinted, Grand Rapids: Baker, 1967.
One of the best commentaries in English. Contains outstanding introductory studies on the history of apocalyptic literature, interpretation of the Revelation, etc.

Bietenhard, Hans. *Das tausendjährige Reich.* Zürich: Zwingli Verlag, 1955.
A careful interpretation of Rev. 19^{11}-20^{10}.

Caird, G. B. *The Revelation of St. John The Divine (Harper's New Testament Commentaries).* New York: Harper, 1966.
Caird understands much of the symbolism in the Revelation to represent imminent historical rather than eschatological events. A very readable commentary.

Charles, R. H. *A Critical and Exegetical Commentary on The Revelation of St. John (International Critical Commentary).* New York: Scribners, 1920. 2 vols.
A mine of grammatical and historical information by the great master of Jewish apocalyptic literature.

_____. *Studies in The Apocalypse*. Edinburgh: Clark, 1913.

Important for the history of interpretation.

Elliott, E. B. *Horae Apocalypticae*. London: 1826. 4 vols.

The classic commentary embodying the historical interpretation. In addition to the commentary, this work contains a wealth of material on the history of interpretation.

Hendriksen, W. *More Than Conquerors*. Grand Rapids: Baker, 1940.

Hendriksen makes radical use of the recapitulation method in the interests of the symbolical interpretation.

Lilje, Hanns. *The Last Book of the Bible. The Meaning of the Revelation of St. John*. Philadelphia: Muhlenberg, 1955.

An interpretation which views the Revelation essentially as a prophecy of the eschatological consummation.

Milligan, William. *The Book of Revelation (The Expositor's Bible)*. London: Hodder and Stoughton, 1909.

A classic interpretation from the symbolical point of view.

Minear, Paul S. *I Saw a New Earth. An Introduction to the Visions of the Apocalypse*. Washington: Corpus Books, 1969.

Minear interprets the Revelation in terms of God's judgment on a faithless church. Comprehensive bibliography.

Moffatt, James. "Revelation of St. John The Divine" in *The Expositor's Greek Testament*, vol. V. Grand Rapids: Eerdmans, n.d.

Commentary on the Greek text with special interest in problems of comparative religions.

Morris, Leon. *Revelation (Tyndale New Testament Commentaries)*. Grand Rapids: Eerdmans, 1970.

An outstanding conservative scholar who combines the preterist and futurist views.

Pieters, Albertus. *Studies in the Revelation of St. John*. Grand Rapids: Eerdmans, 1954.

A conservative scholar who interprets the Revelation from the preterist viewpoint.

Ramsay, W. M. *The Letters to the Seven Churches of Asia*. New York: Armstrong, 1905.

The classic historical-archaeological study of the seven churches.

Rissi, Mathias. *Time and History*. Richmond: John Knox, 1966.

An essay on the meaning of time and history in the Revelation.

Simcox, William Henry. *The Revelation of S. John The Divine (Cambridge Greek Testament)*. Cambridge: University Press, 1893.
Brief but helpful exposition of the Greek text.

Stauffer, Ethelbert. *Christ and the Caesars*. Philadelphia: Westminster, 1955.
Historical sketches on the emperors, including their attitude toward the church.

Summers, Ray. *Worthy is the Lamb*. Nashville: Broadman, 1951.
A conservative scholar who interprets chapters 1:1 — 20:10 from the preterist viewpoint and only 20:11 — 22:5 as eschatology.

Swete, Henry Barclay. *The Apocalypse of St. John*. London: Macmillan, 1917.
One of the classic commentaries on the Greek text. Eclectic in viewpoint.

Walvoord, John F. *The Revelation of Jesus Christ*. Chicago: Moody, 1966.
A dispensational interpretation by the professor of theology at Dallas Theological Seminary.

Zahn, Theodor. *Die Offenbarung des Johannes*. Leipzig: Deichert, 1924. 2 vols.
One of the classic commentaries by Germany's great conservative scholar.

INDEX OF SCRIPTURE

OLD TESTAMENT